NASCAR, STURGIS, AND THE NEW ECONOMY OF SPECTACLE

Studies in Critical Social Sciences Book Series

Haymarket Books is proud to be working with Brill Academic Publishers (www.brill.nl) to republish the *Studies in Critical Social Sciences* book series in paperback editions. This peer-reviewed book series offers insights into our current reality by exploring the content and consequences of power relationships under capitalism, and by considering the spaces of opposition and resistance to these changes that have been defining our new age. Our full catalog of *SCSS* volumes can be viewed at https://www.haymarketbooks.org/series_collections/4-studies-in-critical-social-sciences.

NASCAR, STURGIS, AND THE NEW ECONOMY OF SPECTACLE

DANIEL KRIER
WILLIAM J. SWART

Haymarket
Books
Chicago, IL

First published in 2016 by Brill Academic Publishers, The Netherlands.
© 2017 Koninklijke Brill NV, Leiden, The Netherlands

Published in paperback in 2018 by
Haymarket Books
P.O. Box 180165
Chicago, IL 60618
773-583-7884
www.haymarketbooks.org

ISBN: 978-1-60846-835-5

Trade distribution:
In the U.S. through Consortium Book Sales, www.cbsd.com
In the UK, Turnaround Publisher Services, www.turnaround-uk.com
In Canada, Publishers Group Canada, www.pgcbooks.ca
All other countries, Ingram Publisher Services International, ips_intlsales@
ingramcontent.com

Cover design by Jamie Kerry of Belle Étoile Studios and Ragina Johnson.

This book was published with the generous support of Lannan Foundation
and the Wallace Action Fund.

Library of Congress Cataloging-in-Publication Data is available.

Contents

Preface

Globalization had a particularly negative impact upon the industrial economy of the United States, and many states—especially those in the West and Midwest—looked to entertainment, tourism and other non-industrial sectors as fertile ground for economic development. Central to these non-industrial regions of the economy were spectacular events: races, rallies, concerts, sporting matches, expos, and various forms of shoppertainment. While social scientists have long studied the cultural dynamics of spectacle, this study maps the unique political and economic structure of spectacle that differentiated such ventures from manufacturing and other traditional industries.

The enclosure and commercialization of public spectacles has a long history, but deindustrialization and capital flight in the age of neoliberalism caused significant changes to these enclosures and to the economic engine that drives them. On the one hand, widespread fear of capital flight and concomitant job loss increased the attractiveness of spectacular events as mechanisms for economic development. On the other, the forces of neoliberalism spawned new financial instruments and new structures of governance at the federal, state, and local level that enabled publicly financed free gifts to capital on an unprecedented scale.[1] Economic development tools such as Tax Increment Financing (TIF), Sales Tax Revenue Bonds (STAR), and Payment in Lieu of Taxes (PILOT) programs forced the public to assume risk for investments that served private sector profit yet provided dubious long-term public benefit. The diffused political bodies that arranged these deals (chambers of commerce, convention and visitors bureaus, and a veritable alphabet soup of local yet fragmented economic development corporations) lacked transparency and political accountability. Thus, what was "new" in the new economy of spectacle was the growing taste for spectacle as a legitimate economic substitute for lost manufacturing jobs coupled with the growth of new, neoliberal funding mechanisms and

---

1   The role of public finance in private industry is hardly new; indeed, this process was theorized by some of the earliest analysts of modern capitalism. Adam Smith, for example, used the concept of original accumulation to reference savings and frugality as the precursor to capital investment (Smith, 1999 [1776]; Harvey, 2005). Karl Marx translated Smith's concept as primary or primitive accumulation and refocused it on the expropriation of public property as a necessary precursor to capitalist accumulation (Marx 2010 [1867]). Similarly, scholars of new urbanism or new urban sociology often foreground the use of tax credits, abatement programs, and other forms of public funding to promote economic development and business relocation (Gotham, 2005, 2007; Gottdiener and Dickens, 1999), but do not closely analyze the institutional mechanisms that make these processes possible.

speculative financial tools designed to shelter private interests behind public risk and financial investment.

This book maps this new economic structure of spectacular entertainment and tourism events through a detailed case study of American motorsports. American motorsports spectatorship and commercialization grew dramatically in recent decades. The National Association of Stock Car Racing (NASCAR) was the fastest growing spectator sport in the U.S. during the 1990s and early 2000s, and saw a dramatic geographic expansion from the backcountry South into the West and Midwest during this time. Concurrently, American motorcycling culture reached similar levels of economic and geographic expansion, an explosion of motorcycle enthusiasts, rally events, and marketing across the country. During the time of our study American motorsport spectacles reached a point of total commodification, including the complete integration of commercial, political and religious themes. The arena of American motorsport thus represents a unique and important microcosm in which to anchor the study of the new economy of spectacle.

The concepts deployed in this book were refined during the course of a multi-year comparative case study of the economic structure of NASCAR and Sturgis, two leading American motorsports spectacles. Our case materials included field observations from motorsports spectacles in six U.S. States (Florida, Iowa Virginia, Kansas, South Dakota, and Wisconsin), the documents collected from a variety of governmental, electronic, archival and print sources, and informal interviews with city officials, rally organizers, motorsports customer experience professionals, local business leaders, motorsport event attendees and local residents. We also consulted comparative motorsports events (Grand Prix racing, dirt-track racing, sport motorcycle events, etc.) in order to confirm and delimit the generalizability of the concepts we deploy. As in all Weberian studies, our research concerns itself with the development of theoretical concepts or 'ideal types' that inform historically significant cases. As such, our primary interest is not to uncover novel empirical findings in these historical cases so much as to develop and refine ideal type concepts that have general applicability for interpreting and explaining specific 'historical individuals' (Krier, 2005, pp. 20–27; Weber, 1949, p. 47). Our goal is to advance useful concepts that illuminate the developmental dynamics of economies of spectatorship broadly defined, including those outside motorsports events.

The book begins with a historical sociology of spectacle across three epochs: the pre-modern, modern, and postmodern. Drawing upon the work of Mikhail Bakhtin, Chapter 1 explores the pivotal role of *carnival* in the traditional societies of medieval Europe. We present a sociological theory of carnival that is critical to understanding the dynamics of pre-modern social life and provides a foundation for analyzing spectacles in the modern and postmodern West. Extrapolating from this starting point, we explore how the dynamics of industrial and postindustrial capitalism transformed the modalities of medieval carnival into modern and postmodern spectacles. The result was a fundamental transformation: from the carnivalesque as a dialogic support system of traditional societies to the carnivalesque as a dialectical negation of modern and postmodern social life.

Chapter 2 grounds our study of motorsports in a tale of two cities: Newton, Iowa, site of the most recently developed National Association of Stock Car Auto Racing (NASCAR) track, and Sturgis, SD, home to the longest running large displacement motorcycle rally in the United States. Dating back to 1937, the Sturgis Motorcycle Rally is an enduring event that enables us to trace the emergence of the new economy of spectacle. Newton, Iowa is a more recent case; a rural community that quite literally "bet the farm" on NASCAR during the hey-day of American stock car racing in response to the loss of some 4000 industrial jobs. Our analysis locates these economies of spectacle within the context of neoliberalism and micro-primitive accumulation, the widespread use of public funds to promote private development.

Economies of spectacle emerged as public social activities were privatized and rendered inaccessible to all but those who paid to see. These enclosures fostered the development of three interrelated markets: spectator markets (markets for those paying to see), sponsorship markets (markets for those paying to be seen) and trophy markets (markets for evidence that valorizes spectatorship). These markets intersected with three forms of spectacular production: in-venue, broadcast, and digital/virtually augmented spectatorship. Chapter 3 dissects the anatomy of spectacular economies, highlighting the role of these three markets and three modes of spectatorship in NASCAR's enclosure of Southern back-country automobile racing.

Chapter 4 explores economies of spectatorship in the Sturgis Motorcycle Rally. Economies of spectatorship emerged when public legends were privatized as a spectacular diegesis and sold as commodities to spectators and sponsors. The pursuit of profit within this structure led to the dialectical process of progressive decontextualization. In order to advance profitability, diegeses were cross-marketed with discrepant products and services to reach new customers. Progressive decontextualization led to diegetic incoherence: the broadening array of brands marketed within the diegesis that blurred the diegetic focus, negating its central theme and destabilizing its profitability. As an economy of spectatorship, the Sturgis Motorcycle Rally produced an outlaw biker themed diegesis replete with vicarious action and consumable character gambles. The profitability of the Rally exploded as increasing numbers of attendees and sponsors "paid to see" themselves within this outlaw diegesis, situating themselves within a setting themed with danger, action, and character-gambling situations. As the Rally grew, profit streams were maximized by cross-marketing the outlaw diegesis with establishment corporate, religious and political themes. This progressive decontextualization and the resulting diegetic incoherence threatened profits and required the Rally's producers to make significant investments in order to stabilize the flow of spectators and sponsors necessary to sustain profit. Economies of spectatorship were thus inherently negating systems; the very process by which profit expanded negated the coherence of the diegesis and threatened profit. This dialectical process was critical to understanding the economy of spectacle in mature capitalism.

Capital in the post-industrial economy increasingly assumed the form of intangible assets, especially trademarked corporate brands. Brands within economies of spectatorship were typically farmed by commodifying iconic cultural images and legendary narratives in a spectacular diegesis. This process constituted a "second enclosure movement" (Boyle, 2008); the routinized privatization of the cultural commons and its integration within capitalist circuits of accumulation. Chapter 5 examines sponsorship markets in economies of spectatorship, specifically the role sponsorship, brand development and brand management played in enclosing the cultural commons. After its enclosure, the outlaw biker diegesis became central to the sponsorship markets of the Sturgis Rally. Corporate sponsors made significant financial investments "paying to be seen"—associating their products and services with the outlaw biker diegesis. In order to ensure brand security, the outlaw biker legend was managed by Cross Marketing Licensing Networks (CMLN); coalitions of corporate and state actors, each holding a piece of the legendary pie. The Sturgis CMLN was organized into two political divisions, rally-profiteers and civic leaders, with overlapping but differentiated interests and approaches to the management of the Sturgis legend. The CMLN intervened in the cultural commons to overcome a variety of legendary degradations (banality, incoherence, undesirability) caused by progressive decontextualization. This *legend work* was central to economies of spectacle. CMLN's captured value by enclosing the public domain, and then managed the brand value of the diegesis through the ongoing manipulation and coordination of unpaid, immaterial labor of working consumers.

A third circuit in the economy of spectacle centers in the production and marketing of special economic objects that we theorize as trophies of surplus enjoyment. Attendees at spectacular events such as Sturgis and NASCAR focused much of their activity upon trophy markets, trophy hunting and anticipated trophy display rather than the spontaneous enjoyment of the event. Chapter 6 incorporates Veblen's theory of trophies as invidious objects and insights from Goffman, Lacan and Žižek to explain what makes "paying to be seen enjoying" more important to spectators than "paying to enjoy." We argue that trophies function as distorting mirrors; reflective surfaces in which viewers misrecognize the trophy owner's apparent experience of legendary pleasures as their own dispossessed surplus enjoyment. Spectacles and their trophy markets produce and sustain envy inducing legends. They ritually load trophies with three forms of potential envy: status trophies are loaded with the envy of symbolic prowess, action trophies are loaded with the envy of imaginary risk taking, and trophies of jouissance are loaded with envious yet repressed desire for libidinal pleasure. Our analysis shows that while spectacles may not directly pleasure their attendees, spectacles provide attendees with opportunities to obtain the trophies required to derive indirect pleasure by disturbing and disrupting the pleasure of others. Markets for trophies of surplus enjoyment are thus a critical component of economies of spectatorship.

The diegeses of both NASCAR and the Sturgis Motorcycle Rally were unequivocally conservative. Both centered on right-wing social, economic, and political themes that mirrored dimensions of authoritarianism. Chapter 7 examines the use of an authoritarian diegesis and forms of social organization in the economic enclosure of American motorcycling. Pre-War motorcycling exhibited orthodox authoritarian tendencies that stressed submission and conventionality, while the rebel authoritarianism of post-War motorcycle culture promoted aggressive and anti-establishment behaviors. Both forms were crucial to the economic enclosure of American motorcycling. National organizations and the motorcycle industry exploited orthodox authoritarianism to build early motorcycle markets and promote a positive public image of motorcycling. When these markets were challenged by post-War motorcycle outlaws, the media, film and motorcycle industries enclosed rebel authoritarianism into an outlaw biker diegesis that became central to its marketing and promotion. We conceptualize *dark spectacle* as the result of this aestheticization of economics. Dark spectacle, in which spectators immerse themselves in a commodified environment themed with the authoritarian elements of the outlaw biker diegesis, was central to the economy of American motorsports. Both NASCAR and large displacement motorcycle rallies centered their economies of spectacle squarely within conservative political and authoritarian diegetic tenets.

We conclude with a discussion of virtually augmented spectatorship as the contemporary response to the negating forces in economies of spectatorship. Situated within the growth of virtual and augmented reality, the virtually augmented spectacle became a new, postmodern genre of spectacle with newly emerging dynamics for spectators, sponsors, and trophy markets. In the wake of virtual augmentation, spectatorship was stripped of its social quality and spectators became atomized and interpassive, tantalized by the scopophilia of impossible camera angles, multiple subjectivities and individually controlled views that rendered them god-like in their omnivoyance.

As Midwestern states continue to shed manufacturing jobs under the pressure of globalization, understanding the structure and dynamics of an economy rooted in spectacles is important. Few analysts predict a resurgence of U.S. manufacturing, at least not in a form that will replicate the mass factory employment of mid-century. Instead, the U.S. economy will likely continue its move towards service sector employment with economic development focused upon entertainment, tourism and retail consumption. Prevailing academic models of the economy are grounded in industrial production and in economies organized and structured by manufacturing. Our work is important because development bets continue to be placed on entertainment/tourism as local officials seek to hit the jackpot in the economy of spectacle. Our goal in this book is to conceptually map and empirically explore the structure and dynamism of such an economy.

Acknowledgements

The authors thank David Fasenfest, Series Editor of Studies in Critical Social Sciences, for his ongoing support and guidance in the preparation of this book. We are grateful for the insightful comments, criticisms, and suggestions of David Aday, Daniel Ainsely, Kevin Amidon, Bob Antonio, Larry Beckhouse, Chet Britt, Mark Carstensen, Graham Cassano, Harry Dahms, Geoffrey Dipple, Tony Feldmann, Giles Fowler, Kevin Gotham, Jason Harris, Patrick Hicks, Andy Hochsteter, Satoshi Ito, Russ Hoffmann, Richard Krier, Paul Lasley, Christian Lotz, George Lundskow, Jere Maddux, Douglas Marshall, Ken Moore, Patrick Murray, David O'Hara, Dan Otto, Steve Peihl, Sue Schrader, Tony Smith, Jeanne Schuler, David N. Smith, Daniel Swart, Michael Thompson, Mark P. Worrell, and Alan Young. We especially acknowledge Lauren Langmann for encouraging our work and for providing a critical audience at so many conferences. We thank the editors and publishers of *Critical Sociology, Current Perspectives in Social Theory,* Routledge Press and Brill Publishing for allowing us to incorporate our earlier work into this book. We acknowledge Iowa State University and Augustana University for awarding faculty development assignments and the financial support of the Augustana University Artist and Research Fund (ARAF). Above all, we thank our families—Judy, Adele and Johanna Krier and Dawn, Liam and Kieran Swart—for their ongoing support and encouragement throughout the life of this project.

List of Figures and Tables

Figures

Tables

A Historical Sociology of Spectacle: Economics and the Changing Modalities of the Carnivalesque

Mikhail Bakhtin's literary analysis of French author François Rabelais is often considered a paradigm shift in medieval literary theory. A Russian historian, literary scholar and cultural theorist, Bakhtin's *Rabelais and his World* recovered Rabelais writings from obscurity by interpreting them in the context of medieval carnival—those Saturnalian folk festivals that celebrated the inversion of the normative standards and social hierarchies of everyday medieval life. As a result, Bakhtin not only rescued Rabelais from the misunderstanding of literary critics, but also provided an extremely cogent analysis of the carnivalesque and its central importance to medieval social life.

In the process of resituating the work of Rabelais, Bakhtin custom-built his own conceptual vocabulary of medieval social life. This conceptualization, although widely incorporated into cultural studies, drew very little from historically-parallel sociological theories of medieval life and has had only a limited impact on the field of sociology. Interestingly, many of Bakhtin's most important concepts, such as "general and reduced laughter," or "first and second life," align very closely with sociological theories of traditional society, especially the classic works of Emile Durkheim: *Division of Labor in Society* (1984[1893]) and *Elementary Forms of Religious Life* (1915). We find that Bakhtin's concepts powerfully integrate with sociological theories. This integration simultaneously strengthens both Bakhtin's analysis of medieval carnival and sociological analyses of traditional society. It also provides a theoretical foundation from which to trace the transformation of the carnivalesque into modernity and post modernity.

Our analysis is divided into two parts (see Table 1). We begin with an overview of the modalities of medieval carnival as put forward in Bakhtin's writings on Rabelais (Bakhtin, 1965) and Dostoyevsky (Bakhtin, 1973). According to Bakhtin, the overriding principle or modality of the carnivalesque "second life" during the medieval period is *travesty*, the content of which is an inverted *mirror* of everyday "first life" culture and social structure. The relationship between the first and second life is *dialogic*, a term that has been recognized as Bakhtin's most enduring theoretical contribution to cultural studies, referring to mutually supporting alterations between these mirror-image phases of culture.

Our sociological reading of Bakhtin emphasizes that the carnivalesque occurred within a medieval economy without modern market relations. This world, still unified by a collective consciousness and without a thoroughgoing division of labor, was capable of active, universal *participation* in the carnivalesque, which Bakhtin conceptualizes as *general laughter*. Incorporating the work of Emile Durkheim, we move toward a sociological theory of the dialogic. While under-theorized by Durkheim, we argue that the carnivalesque mode of the collective consciousness was a crucial dialogical mechanism for the development and maintenance of mechanical solidarity in pre-modern cultural systems.

The second part of this chapter extrapolates from Bakhtin to explore how changes in the first life—specifically the rise of industrial and postindustrial capitalism—reconstructed the carnivalesque second life with new organizing principles and cultural forms. Moving into modernity, the carnivalesque transforms from travesty into *spectacle*. The content of the spectacular second life no longer fully mirrors everyday-first life experience, but shrinks into a *distraction* from it. As it does, the relationship between first and second life experience loses its dialogic quality. While the medieval carnivalesque was a crucial mechanism supporting the reproduction of an unchanging, coherent culture, the modern spectacle *dialectically* negates a modern culture that is

TABLE 1   *The modalities of the carnivalesque*

Medieval	Modern	Post-Modern
Travesty	Spectacle	Simulation
Mirror	Distraction	Projection
Dialogic: Travesty	Dialectic: Spectacle	Delusion: Simulation
Supports Social Life	Negates Social Life	Projects the Illusion of Social Life
Premodern Market: Barter/Trade	Industrial Capitalism: Class/Gender Distinctions	Global/Speculative Capitalism: Total Commodification of Everyday Life
General Laughter: Universal Consciousness/Culture	Reduced Laughter: Subcultural Specialization in Consciousness/Culture	Hyper-Reality: Simulation of shared consciousness/Culture where none exists
Mechanical Solidarity	Organic Solidarity	Collective Interpassivity

itself contradictory and incoherent. The spectacular second life occurs within *modern economic relationships*, whose complex division of labor, class antagonism and gender divisions, erodes both collective consciousness and its universal, carnivalesque mode, general laughter. Just as Durkheim theorized the emergence of organic solidarity to characterize modernity's sub-cultural specialization, Bakhtin's concept of *reduced laughter* designates the differentiated, specialized consciousness and social relations of the modern first life. While the medieval carnivalesque featured universal, active participation with the spirit of generalized laughter, the modern spectacle features specialized performances before passive, spectator-audiences with the spirit of reduced laughter.

The postmodern era marks another radical shift in the central modality of the carnivalesque: from spectacle to simulation. While the modern spectacle was a distraction from alienated first life, the postmodern second life is a simulated *projection* of a first life that no longer exists. Much like Baudrillard argues that Disneyland masks the postmodern reality that all life experiences mirror an amusement park, the postmodern carnival exists as a mechanism to *mask* both the erosion of the authentic first life and the fact that both first and second life are carnivalesque. The features of the *postmodern economy*, especially its global scale, speculative nature, and total commodification of everyday life, simultaneously disintegrates real social bonds in actually-existing human communities and replaces them with illusory, commodified mechanisms for social solidarity (Facebook "friends" or the "community" of Harley-Davidson enthusiasts). These "hyper-real" (Baudrillard 1983a) social connections and cultural forms create a user's delusion that social relationships and communities exist, effectively replacing social interaction with *collective interpassivity* (Žižek 2007).

Thus the journey of the carnivalesque from its origins in travesty that mirrors all-too-real traditional social relations, through spectacles that distract from alienated modern society, arrives in the bleak, socially-impoverished postmodern world as simulation that projects to atomized individuals an illusion that shared heritage, culture, and meaning exist at all.

The Medieval Carnival: Mechanical Solidarity and Universal Spirit

Carnival is not a spectacle seen by the people; they live in it, and everyone participates because its very idea embraces all the people. While carnival lasts, there is no other life outside it. During carnival time life is subject only to its laws, that is, the laws of its own freedom. It has a *universal spirit*; it is a special condition of the entire world, of the world's revival and renewal, in which all take part. Such is the essence of carnival, vividly felt by all its participants

BAKHTIN 1968, p. 7

In our reading of primary and secondary sources on Bakhtin, it is clear that Bakhtin's foray into social theory was subordinated to and directed by his central project of literary criticism. Bakhtin did not intend to analyze carnival and the carnivalesque as a "dependent variable" but rather as an "independent variable" that would help him explain what he really cared about, the literary productions of Rabelais and Dostoevsky.

Bakhtin's citations of social theory are few.[1] It seems likely that Bakhtin was familiar with leading social theorists[2] but found that their conceptual categories and theoretical framings failed to appreciate the *dialogic* quality of medieval social life. While Durkheim and other sober social theorists had developed an appreciation for ritual, their models posited a unipolar collective consciousness with a single focal totem at the center of mechanical solidarity. Rabelais' obscene, grotesque imagery and transgressive prose could not be meaningfully located within this one-dimensional model of the collective consciousness. To Bakhtin, collective consciousness of traditional societies dynamically moved through unending, rotary phase-shifts between serious/official life and unserious/carnival life. Bakhtin positioned Rabelais' writings in the lower arc of the bi-polar phase shift that constituted medieval culture. In explaining Rabelais' writings, Bakhtin rediscovered the lost significance of the medieval cultural underlife: the carnivalesque in all of its forms. In this sense, Bakhtin wrote a ground-breaking piece of social theory almost by accident, as a detour along the main road of literary criticism.

Bakhtin and the Carnivalesque

Carnival is a pageant without a stage and without division into performers and spectators. In the carnival everyone is an active participant,

---

1　Bakhtin cites Marx at five points in the Rabelais study and Georg Simmel once in the study of Dostoevsky. There are numerous references in both volumes to literary critics immersed in social theory, however.

2　Bakhtin's studies of Rabelais and Dostoevsky incorporate ideas and conceptual framings from social theory even when he does not cite specific authors. His studies of Freud and Marx display broad reading in social thought and sociological theory.

everyone communes in the carnival act. Carnival is not contemplated, it is, strictly speaking, not even played out; its participants live in it, they live according to its laws, as long as those laws are in force, i.e. they live a carnivalistic life. The carnivalistic life is life drawn out of its usual rut, it is to a degree "life turned inside out," "life the wrong way 'round'"

BAKHTIN, 1973, pp. 100–101

Bakhtin (1973) unified a diverse complex of traits under the concept of carnival: crowning/discrowning of carnival kings, the widespread use of disguise, masks and costumes that were either sexually charged or grotesquely distorted, an emphasis upon lower-body organs and drives, the staging of "bloodless carnival wars," verbal abuse contests, cursing matches and potlatch-style gift exchanges (1973, p. 103). In the section that follows, we briefly outline Bakhtin's most central, anchoring characteristics of medieval carnival as depicted in Table 2.

For Bakhtin, a key characteristic of the medieval carnival was its inversion of the normative standards and social hierarchies of everyday life. This "wrong way 'round'" inversion of the official, ecclesiastical strictures of medieval life produced a "second world" or "second life" (Bakhtin, 1968, pp. 5–6). Key to this inversion was the notion of *travesty*; literally a burlesque (ludicrous or ridiculous) imitation of social life. Bakhtin was careful to distinguish carnivalesque travesty from one-sided insults, put-downs or mockery that was directed by one group within society against another. Instead, travesty was an inversion or laughing mirror-image of the culture and social structure taken as

TABLE 2   *The modality of medieval carnival*

Travesty	First life inverted and made ridiculous; a burlesque translation or imitation; grotesquely incongruous in style.
Mirror	Carnival as a travestied second life that inverts yet supports official life
Dialogic	Phase shifting between first and second life without negation or synthetic resolution
Premodern Market	"Language of the Marketplace is the language of Carnivalesque" = Billingsgate and market culture
"General Laughter"	Universal Consciousness/Culture
Mechanical Solidarity	Carnivalesque as expression of Durkheimian Collective Consciousness

a whole: no group or individual was abused personally, but holistically as the entire society was upended in burlesque.

Travesty was characterized by high levels of *profanation*: "carnivalistic blasphemies, a whole carnivalistic system of lowering of status and bringing down to earth ... carnivalistic obscenities connected with the reproductive power of the earth and the body" (Bakhtin, 1973, p. 101). Carnival provided a travestied mirroring of social life by inverting social hierarchies (kings became peasants; peasants became kings), unleashing restrained sexual conduct and mocking the seriousness of everyday life. Key to profanation in the carnivalesque was the notion of "debasement"—literally an association with the lower stratum of the body (Bakhtin, 1968, p. 21). Carnival emphasized debased "grotesque realism," whose imagery fluidly integrated the anatomy and activity of reproduction and excretion. These debasing images were not viewed with abhorrence in medieval life, but rather perceived with ambivalence (in the sense of being creatively destructive.)

> ...such debasing gestures and expressions are ambivalent, since the lower stratum is not only a bodily grave but also the area of the genital organs, the fertilizing and generating stratum. Therefore, in the images of urine and excrement is preserved the essential link with birth, fertility, renewal, and welfare. This positive element was still fully alive and clearly realized in the time of Rabelais.
>
> BAKHTIN, 1968, p. 148

Debasement as a linguistic form was widely understood and accepted in medieval society, and to Bakhtin, the very source of the medieval acceptance of grotesque realism was the dialogic association between destruction and regeneration of the debased region.[3]

Travestied conduct also involved high levels of *eccentricity*, interaction styles that were out-of-joint or out-of-character with the roles and habits of first-world life. This conduct was liberating to individuals, in that it permitted "the latent sides of human nature to be revealed and developed in a concretely sensuous form" (Bakhtin, 1973, p. 101). Freud's influence upon Bakhtin was obvious here, as lower body desires, emotional release and frivolity that were denied expression in everyday life were precisely those desires, emotions and frivolities that were characteristic of the carnivalesque. However,

---

3 Bakhtin's reading of carnival as rooted in the ambiguity of double-images such as death/ rebirth, decay/growth is very similar to Frazer's emphasis upon the death and burial of the king of carnival (Frazer, 1900, p. 98).

unlike Freud, these regions of life were not repressed into the unconscious but were consciously and culturally accommodated in the space and time of carnival.

Another of Bakhtin's anchoring concepts was *general laughter*, carnival's universal spirit encouraging participation across all everyday social boundaries. Carnival was experienced by everyone regardless of their positions in economic, political, age, or gender stratification systems. Medieval carnival "does not know footlights" (Bakhtin, 1968, p. 6); footlights would turn carnival into a theatrical performance by a limited cast of active players performing before a larger, passive audience. Carnival had no spectators: "all were considered equal during carnival...a special form of free and familiar contact reigned among people who were usually divided by the barriers of caste, property, profession, and age" (Bakhtin, 1968, p. 10).

The universality of carnival was symbolized by its geographic fluidity and its domination of public spaces. The carnival square or town square was the central scene of carnival, a public space of generalized milling and social mixing. While carnival often spilled into private domains and spaces, "carnival belongs to the whole people, it is universal, everyone must take part in its familiar contact" (Bakhtin, 1973, 105–106). Bakhtin defined the active, generalized mixing in carnival as a "pageant without a stage" that eliminated the boundaries separating audiences from performers. This is in strong contrast to modern spectacles that decisively redivided participants into spectators and audience (see below).

The universal spirit of carnival was evident in Peter Paul Rubens 1690 painting *Village Fête* (see Figure 1). The artist's representation of a Flemish farm fair clearly depicted universal participation in carnivalesque activity. Mothers nursed children alongside drinking and bantering men and amorous dancing couples. There were no spectators; while forms of participation may differ, Rubens depicted no "alienation from interaction" (Goffman, 1961, 1974), no removal from the prevailing frame of action. The range of activities depicted was quite diverse: participants were seen breastfeeding, engaging in sexual play, dancing, frolicking, drinking or conversing. These actions represented diffuse involvements within the single, unitary, celebratory occasion rather than separate activity systems psychologically or physically-bounded from the carnivalesque spirit. Rubens' image depicted more than narrowly-sexual coupling behavior, but broad polymorphous perversity that was full-bodied, full-blooded and multi-sensual (not just pleasures of the flesh, but also music, food, wine). This image was consistent with Bakhtin's portrait of carnival participant's total involvement in the flowing events, their consciousness completely responsive to the open-ended second life.

FIGURE 1   *Peter Paul Rubens* Village Fête (*1690*)
            SOURCE: FUCHS *SITTENGESCHICHTE* 1909.

As Ruben's image illustrated, carnival paradoxically constrained individuals into mandatory, but freely-directed participation in liberatory festivities. Medieval carnival bound all social categories and classes with a universal spirit and a formal posture of equality. Goffmanesque social division into performance teams and audience was prohibited as Durkheimian joint-participation in ritual experience reigned. Bakhtin used several concepts to capture this quality of carnival. One concept, *familiarity*, referred to the suspension of "distance between people" under the reign of "free, familiar contact among people." (Bakhtin, 1973, p. 101).

The universal character of medieval carnival is further developed through Bakhtin's use of the concept *mesalliance*—literally an unsuitable marriage to someone of lower social status. Carnival mesalliance sliced medieval society to the bone, cutting across social statuses and dissimilarities while providing the opportunity for an "unfettered familiar attitude" to emerge between differing social ranks. "All the things that were closed off, isolated and separated from one another by the non-carnivalistic hierarchical attitude entered into carnivalistic contacts and combinations" (Bakhtin, 1973, p. 101). Rubens depicted infants alongside the elderly, aristocrats alongside peasants; a polymorphous group freed from normal repressions and controlled, first-life segregation and co-experiencing unfettered, embodied pleasure.

A third concept from Bakhtin, *heteroglossia*, referred to the polyphony of voices and subject positions that were co-present, separated, yet united within carnival. Discourse and symbolic exchange within the carnival assumed the form of heteroglossia: many voices, language styles, interaction modes and meanings co-existed without higher unification or synthesis. The diversity within carnival " brings together, unites, weds and combines [even] the sacred with the profane" (Bakhtin, 1973, p. 101).

Bakhtin's analysis of carnival stresses that the laughing, travestied second life *mirrored* the serious, first life. Many of the features of the carnivalesque, especially its unifying spirit that meaningfully enveloped the entire community, was predicated upon the existence of a cohesive and meaningfully-ordered first life. In Durkheimian terms, the mechanical solidarity and robust collective consciousness that characterized the carnivalesque was a mirror-image, albeit a distorted one, of the solidarity and consciousness of everyday life. These two phases of life, the serious and the un-serious, were in fact doubles, intimately related to each other, while remaining distinctive and separate. In this sense:

> ... the medieval man lived, as it were, two lives, one, the official, mono-lithically serious and gloomy life, subject to a strict hierarchical order, filled with fear, dogmatism, reverence and piety, and the other, the life of the carnival square, free, full of ambivalent laughter, blasphemy, the profanation of all that was holy, disparagement and obscenity, and famil-iar contact with everyone and everything. Both of these lives were legal and legitimate, but were divided by strict temporal limits.
>
> BAKHTIN, 1973, pp. 106–107

It is important to bear in mind that the mirror-image produced by travestied carnival did not negate or synthetically merge with everyday life but stood for-ever apart from it. As Bakhtin (1968) noted, "bare negation is alien to folk cul-ture" (1968, p. 11). The "laws, prohibitions and restrictions ... [as well as] forms of fear, awe, piety, etiquette" that were associated with normal hierarchical life were temporarily *suspended* during carnival, they were not permanently over-come or cancelled (Bakhtin, 1973, p. 101).

Bakhtin characterized the mutually-supporting alterations between the first and second life as a *dialogic* (dialogue-like) process.[4] The dynamism of traditional societies was structured by this cyclical, bi-polar, phase-shift be-tween mirror-image modes of culture. The upper-phase of late Medieval Eu-ropean culture was the mode of serious, stratified, sober, gloomy everyday life

---

4 Bakhtin's later work, *The Dialogical Imagination* (1981) shifts his focus from historical analysis to literary theory. Building from the sociological overtones in his previous work on Dosto-evsky and Rabelais, Bakhtin uses *The Dialogical Imagination* to connect the novel as a spe-cific literary form to the diversity and heteroglossia of modern culture.

while the lower-phase was the mode of travestied, laughing carnival. Bakhtin's dialogic, bi-polar theory of medieval culture enabled him to properly situate Rabelais' archetypal carnivalesque writings in this travestied lower-arc.

In explaining Rabelais's writings, Bakhtin rediscovered the lost significance of the medieval cultural underlife, the carnivalesque in all of its forms. Carnival replenished the first world by providing a revitalizing release from the "social rut" and the repressive controls of everyday social life (Bakhtin, 1973, p. 106). The second life was not a mere unproductive respite from productive first-life routines, but was itself profoundly *re*-productive, in part because it allowed all-too-human needs and desires (sexualized, liminal, libidinized) that were out-of-sync with first-life culture to be expressed and realized, thus enabling the ongoing viability of the entire social order. The *dialogic* phase-shifting between the first and second life was structurally necessary to the ongoing viability of medieval society. Carnival replenished society through these cycles of birth and death: "to bury, to sow, and to kill simultaneously, in order to bring forth something more and better" (Bakhtin, 1968, p. 21).

Toward a Sociological Theory of Dialogic

Bakhtin's terms *carnivalesque* and *dialogic* have found their way from cultural studies into sociology but have not been thoroughly integrated with sociological theory. Bakhtin himself, even in the two major studies that made his reputation, did not write as a sociologist; Weberian ideal types and Durkheimian structural models were beyond the scope of Bakhtin's project. As such, the diverse concepts that Bakhtin deployed in his descriptions of the carnivalesque were *asserted* rather than precisely theorized. At the same time, Bakhtin's work identified characteristics of premodern life that were left undertheorized by established sociological theorists, especially Emile Durkheim. In what follows, we specify a *sociological* theory of carnival. Doing so fills a gap in both the Bakhtin literature and Durkheimian sociological theory, and, more importantly, allows us to effectively trace the transformations of the medieval carnivalesque into modern spectacle and postmodern simulation.

The resonance of Bakhtin's ideas, even without close sociological specificity, have led them to be adopted by scholars studying surprisingly diverse topics. However, these diverse appropriations have often been mutually incompatible. Some scholars use Bakhtin's work to support the argument that carnivalesque activity allowed lower orders to engage in oppositional struggle and dissident challenges to the status quo (known as the *subversion* thesis; see Justice, 1994; Eco, 1984), while others use Bakhtin's work to support the notion that the carnivalesque was a profoundly powerful source of elite social control (known as the *safety-valve or containment* thesis; see Humphrey, 2001; Camille, 1992; Brandist & Tihanov, 2000). We ultimately locate Bakhtin's dialogic theory of the carnivalesque closest to the safety valve thesis, where scholars like Camille claim that carnival was "licensed" by first-life authorities so that:

> ...inversion, cross-dressing, riotous drinking and parodic performance at carnival time ... was a carefully controlled valve for letting off steam.... what looks at first like unfettered freedom of expression often served to legitimate the status quo, chastising the weaker groups in the social order.... We have to face up to carnival's complicity with the official order, played out in the supposed subversion of it.
>
> CAMILLE, 1992, p. 143

The "carnival as safety valve" focus, while not incompatible with Bakhtin, is too narrow and precludes a multi-dimensional, sociological specification of the dialogical relationship between the first and second life. Carnival was a necessary regenerative process in the cycle of medieval life. To Bakhtin (1968), "the characteristic trait of laughter was precisely the recognition of its positive, regenerating, creative meaning" (1968, p. 71). General laughter, as a universally experienced travesty of the first life, provided a dialogic support system that replenished the first life. Thus, carnival did not merely provide relief from the rigid strictures of medieval life; moments of carnival restored social energies, dialogically regenerating the possibility for the first life to continue forward. Eco (1986), following Freud, further developed this point when he argued that carnival represented a case of *contradictio in adjecto* or "happy double binding—capable of curing instead of producing psychosis" (1986, p. 6).

Evidence for the regenerative nature of the carnivalesque can be seen in its general ubiquity in medieval social life. The medieval calendar was punctuated with widespread carnivals, festivals and feasts that together constituted a significant percentage of medieval cultural life. European cities in the late Middle Ages "lived a full carnival life for three months of the year (and sometimes more)" (Bakhtin, 1973, pp. 106–107). A carnivalesque atmosphere pervaded not only official carnivals, but also sporadic fairs and public gatherings, such as the sixty days of festivities surrounding the four annual fairs in Lyon (Bakhtin, 1968, p. 154). Other scholars have highlighted the immense amount of time that late medieval workers spent in second life activities. E.P. Thompson (1967), for instance, found that late medieval workweeks featured long weekends that began on Saturdays, consumed Sundays, spilled over into riotous Saint's Mondays and culminated in unproductive, hung-over Tuesdays. Work in the first life was largely confined to Wednesdays through Saturdays, with escalating intensity before the return of another long weekend (Thompson, E.P., 1967). The pervasiveness of the carnivalesque in medieval social life is a further indication of the important role it played in supporting first life activities.

But while the two sides of medieval life remained distinct, they did not cancel each other out or combine into a blended synthesis. Instead, they were in dialogue with each other, co-existing side by side while taking alternating turns animating the action of medieval society (Holquist, 1990, p. 20). While carnival lived, its forms—travesty, general laughter, mesalliances and the rest—abounded, only to disappear entirely upon the first chill rays of sober dawn marking the return of official, workaday life. Other medieval scholars have also noted this peculiar, but nearly absolute separation of official seriousness and carnivalesque travesty. Camille (1992), for example, found that Medieval sacred texts were often illuminated with profoundly subversive, travestied and comedic images (fornicating couples, bird-headed Christs, Madonna's suckling monkeys, bowling games with feces, nuns picking penises from trees), but carnivalesque images did not intermix with serious ones. They were relegated to the margins where they remained segregated from the sacred words and images in the center of the page.

To Bakhtin, the full truth of medieval society could only be understood as a *dialogue* between official and carnival life. Like someone overhearing only one side of a telephone conversation, a scholar who studies only the serious, official world will misunderstand much of medieval society. As carnival disintegrated in Europe after the Renaissance, scholars increasingly lost the carnivalesque ear needed to hear its laughter in medieval culture. As a result, they lost the ability to appreciate Rabelais writings, whose debasing imagery and billingsgate language became ever-more-mystifying as the years passed. Rabelais' laughing travesty struck Voltaire as the incoherent work of a drunken buffoon: "we are annoyed that a man who had so much wit should have made such wretched use of it" (Bakhtin, 1968, p. 117). John Calvin rebukes Rabelais in a 1555 Sermon, translated into Elizabethan English in 1583:

> [Rabelais] casteth forth lewd scoffes against the holy scripture, as doeth that divelish fellowe which is called Pantagruell, and all his filthie and ribauldly writings: and this sort of men pretende not to set up any newe Religion, as thought they were deluded by their owne follish imaginations: but like madde dogges they belke out their filthinesse against the majestie of God, and their meaning is to overthrowe all religion: and should such be spared?.
>
> QUOTED IN PRESCOTT, 1998, p. 81

Calvin's followers strictly suppressed carnivalesque feasting and frivolity. New England Puritans condemned all feast days and holy days, including the celebration of Easter and Christmas (Fischer, 1989). The Puritan Cromwellian

Parliament in England similarly banned Christmas observances in 1644 (Catholic Encyclopedia, 1917).[5] The Roman Church during and after the austere Counter-Reformation joined in the suppression of carnival. For example, in 1748 Pope Benedict XIV instituted an ascetic "Forty Hours' Devotion" during the last days of lent to block carnivalesque frivolities. Early modern capitalists, seeking to increase production through intensified, routinized labor, implemented strict time-discipline over workers and eliminated carnivalesque feasts and festivals (Thompson, E.P., 1967). In Eco's (1986) terms, once carnival ceased to be an authorized transgression, it ceased to function as a unified second life.

Classical sociologists also lacked an ear for the carnivalesque, including Durkheim, whose theory of nonmodern society was rooted in a case study of the Australian Arunta, a tribe that appears to lack carnivalesque forms. The texts that form the basis of Durkheim (and Freud's) analysis of primitive peoples were written by people with nineteenth and twentieth century British sensibilities—who very likely also lacked an "ear" for the carnivalesque. Scholars of carnival have noted the muted quality of the carnivalesque in the British Isles; the carnivalesque traditions so embedded in medieval European societies were not as prominent in Britain. Humphrey (2001) notes that scholars of British folk life tend to avoid the terms carnival or carnivalesque, using "festive misrule" to refer to folk merry-making and rebellion. Whether the Arunta lacked a carnivalesque second life or the British anthropologists failed to detect it, Durkheim's primary sources were devoid of carnivalesque forms.

Using a framework that was silent on the dialogic carnivalesque, Durkheim did not make the connection between the carnivalesque and the regeneration of collective consciousness over time. This may also explain his enigmatic treatment of fatalism in his study of suicide (1951). In this study, two opposing pairs of consciousness: egoism and anomie existed as modern psychic opposites, representing extremes of social isolation and social disorganization. Altruism and fatalism existed as premodern psychic opposites, representing extremes of social integration and social organization. Durkheim's theoretical

---

5 Modern people have lost even very basic knowledge of the significance of carnivalesque forms in medieval life. Christmas celebrations were highly carnivalesque—Rabelaisian "mumming" (parading in masquerade) was widespread, Christmas Eve was known as Modranicht (Mother's Night) whose festivities included the eating of cake in honor of Mary's "afterbirth" and much drinking and feasting. At Easter, priests would participate with congregations in "Easter Laughter" encouraged by sermons that travestied Jesus life and works. Reversals of authority were common on and about Easter: for example, women gained the right to clout husbands, servants to scold masters.

model compelled him to recognize that fatalism and fatalistic suicide should have been widespread in the deterministic systems of non-modern societies. Yet he left this form of consciousness theoretically undeveloped. Durkheim devoted entire chapters to egoism, anomie and altruism, but brushed off fatalism with one obscure footnote. Fatalism, says Durkheim,

> ... has so little contemporary importance and examples are so hard to find ... that it seems useless to dwell upon it. However it might be said to have historical interest. Do not the suicide of slaves, said to be frequent under certain conditions,... belong to this type, or all suicides attributable to excessive physical or moral despotism?
>
> DURKHEIM, 1951, p. 276[fn]

Why were the rigid strictures of mechanical solidarity not a more overtly destructive force in traditional society? Durkheim's description of fatalistic consciousness amidst "excessive regulation," "oppressive discipline," and "inflexible rules" (Durkheim, 1951, p. 276[fn]) seems very close to Bakhtin's description of consciousness in the social rut of serious first life. Fatalism and fatalistic suicide should have been widespread, yet Durkheim provides little explanation for why it was not. Bakhtin helps clarify this unresolved dilemma in Durkheim's theory. To Bakhtin, fatalistic suicide was suppressed by carnival, which provided an *antidote* to fatalism.

Both Durkheim and Bakhtin recognized that traditional societies were characterized by rotary motion (Žižek, 1997); a cyclical reproduction of relatively stable culture over time. Bakhtin, more than Durkheim, problematized the source of energy necessary for cultural reproduction within mechanically-bonded, traditional societies. Without carnival, medieval people would have lived in a society "monolithically serious and gloomy ... [with] strict hierarchical order [and] filled with fear, dogmatism, reverence and piety" (Bakhtin, 1973, p. 106–107). Under this "excessive regulation," their psychic energies would soon be depleted by the sheer weight of fatalism as Durkheim suggests. Overcoming fatalism with rejuvenating carnival was crucial to cultural reproduction: carnival was "free, full of ambivalent laughter, blasphemy, the profanation of all that was holy, disparagement and obscenity, and familiar contact with everyone and everything" (Bakhtin, 1973, p. 107); a total release from excessive regulation. Traditional society's ability to reproduce was dependent upon periodic, dialogic carnivalesque release. Carnival was crucial time out of oppressive first life. More than a Sabbath-like day of rest, carnival was an alternate phase of mechanical solidarity that regenerated social energy.

Bakhtin's emphasis on the dialogic phase-shift between official and carnival culture captures something important about the way that traditional societies regenerated themselves over time. Bakhtin argues that the dialogic movement into and out of carnival generated social energy. Just as alternating current is generated by the movement of a coil through the two distinct polarities of a magnetic field, traditional societies reproduced their energy by moving through two distinct phases of collective consciousness. Bakhtin recognized that carnival displaced and desecrated the official collective consciousness and installed a carnivalesque collective consciousness in its place. For the duration of the carnivalesque cultural phase, mechanical solidarity was sustained by this travesty of first-life collective consciousness.

Durkheim's unipolar theory of collective consciousness missed the significance of this dialogic carnivalesque phase to the ongoing maintenance of mechanical solidarity. It is the periodic phase-shifting between the two worlds that is crucial to the regeneration of the carnivalesque. Eco (1986) correctly argued that a permanent carnival would be at least as stifling and oppressive as permanent official life. The liberation from fatalism and the generation of reproductive energy occurs during these "moments" of transition between the two worlds. Durkheim leaves untheorized this alternating phase shift in and out of everyday life and the carnivalesque, and instead posits unipolar totemic collective consciousness as the mainstay of traditional social life.

Durkheimian fatalism was profoundly overcome through the frequent, lived experience of shifting into and out of carnivalesque phases of the collective consciousness. Carnival's phase-shift in the collective consciousness released and replenished emotional energy through the lived experience or "pathos of vicissitudes and changes, of death and renewal" (Bakhtin, 1973, p. 102). Carnival was a "festival of all-destroying and all-renewing time" that allowed participants to experience "jolly relativity of every system and order, every authority" (Bakhtin, 1973, p. 102). The future of a person in a carnival culture was not "pitilessly blocked" nor were their "passions violently choked" (Durkheim, 1951, p. 276). Because of the second life, the first life, no matter how excessively regulated or oppressive, was never fated to become a Weberian iron cage of unceasing disciplinary power and behavioral regulation. Fatalism was reduced by carnival laughter, which degraded and mocked the highest earthly and spiritual authority, thereby renewing them (Bakhtin, 1973, p. 104).

> ... the ambivalent laughter of carnival possessed enormous creative, genre-forming power. This laughter could seize both poles of evolution within a phenomenon in their continuous, creative, renewing changeability: death is foreseen in birth and birth in death, defeat in victory and

victory in defeat, discrowning in coronation, etc. Carnival laughter does
not allow any one of these elements of change to be absolutized or grow
stiff and cold in one-sided seriousness.

BAKHTIN, 1973, p. 137

Another strong contrast between Durkheim and Bakhtin was found in their
divergent view of *markets*. For Durkheim, markets *disrupted* collective consciousness and destroyed mechanical solidarity; for Bakhtin, markets *incubat-
ed* carnivalesque forms of collective consciousness and *generated* mechanical
solidarity. In Durkheim, mechanical solidarity and collective consciousness
were rooted in traditional production of goods for local use rather than for
market exchange and distant trade. Markets eroded mechanical solidarity
because they generated occupational specialization (division of labor): they
did not bring people together but divided them up. Bakhtin took the opposite
view, especially in his book on Rabelais: the language of the carnivalesque is
the "language of the marketplace" (Bakhtin, 1968, pp. 145–195). Though little
discussed in the secondary literature on Bakhtin, markets were identified by
him as a crucial source of late medieval carnivalesque imagery and language.
Bakhtin used a now-archaic phrase, *billingsgate abuse*, to connote ribald,
profane, and invective forms of speech and behavior. Billingsgate Market in
London was the location of a medieval wharf and fish exchange notorious for
particularly obscene and abusive discursive forms used by fish-mongers and
market traders. Marketplaces like Billingsgate were a perpetual carnivalesque
space of travesty in which official, first-world morality, especially displays of
deference, demeanor, courtesy and civility, were suspended. Billingsgate abuse
functions as an equalizer of social status to facilitate exchange by degrading
high status people and bringing them down to the common ground of market haggling, banter and bargaining. Markets brought hierarchically-separated
people together and billingsgate abuse placed them on the common footing
of trade (Bakhtin, 1968, pp. 15–17). Markets were also the first-life refuge of carnivalesque forms, a kind of warehouse for the carnivalesque during the reign
of official life. Thus, in contrast to Durkheim, markets did not erode collective consciousness, but were fundamentally and permanently infused with the
carnivalesque phase of collective consciousness. They served as the official
world's incubator and storage facility for carnivalesque forms.

Durkheim attributed the disintegration of mechanical solidarity to the
spread of markets, but Bakhtin attributed the disintegration of medieval carnival to capitalism's traumatic fragmentation and modernization of culture.
His works avoided direct sociological analysis of this process, but nevertheless traced the inflection of this process in the increasingly critical reception

of Rabelais. Bakhtin charted the historical shrinkage of carnival's warm, full-blooded "general laughter" (a lived mirth that engulfed an entire mechanically-bonded society) into cold and biting "reduced laughter" (specialized, sarcastic, satirical, scapegoating). Calculating modern culture was no longer capable of dialogue with carnival forms and could not meaningfully live in carnivalesque travesty. Moderns seemed especially repulsed by carnivalesque imagery of the grotesque body. Rabelais' writings, which featured breasts, buttocks, genitalia, sexual acts and defecation on almost every page, were criticized as unabashedly vulgar, obscene, filthy and valueless. Bakhtin described leading bourgeois thinkers, protestant reformers and early-modern moralists as *agelast:* "not laughing," humorless, or mirthless. Rabelais' critics' shrunken capacity to laugh at carnivalesque forms signaled their inability to comprehend the mechanically-bonded traditional society that it helped sustain.

To summarize our integration of Durkheim and Bakhtin, the carnivalesque is an important, yet often unrecognized phase of the premodern collective consciousness. Mechanical solidarity was sustained and even intensified by the general laughter, universal participation, and mesalliances that predominated during carnival. We argue that carnival provided a crucial antidote to the fatalistic tendencies of tightly-bonded mechanical societies, providing liberatory release from the workaday cares, feudal hierarchies, and moral rigors of everyday medieval life. Like an electrical generator, the alternating movement of the entire society into and out of travestied phases of collective consciousness produced social energy. As such, the carnivalesque was far more than a subversion of feudal authority structures or a safety valve to the rigors of everyday medieval life. Instead, it was a regenerative cycle that allowed the very foundations of traditional social life to reproduce through history.

Carnivalesque Modalities in Modern and post-Modern Society

The problem of carnival (in the sense of the totality of all the various festivals, rituals and forms of a carnival type), its essence, its roots deep in the primordial order and the primordial thinking of man, its development under the conditions of class society, its extraordinary vitality and undying fascination is one of the most complex and interesting problems of cultural history.

BAKHTIN, 1973, p. 100

Our sociologically-thickened reading of Bakhtin distilled the central modality of carnival in traditional society. Carnival was a travestied second life that mirrored the mechanically-bonded first life. The two phases of the collective consciousness (the official and the carnivalesque) were in dialogue with each other, remaining distinct while mutually supporting and regenerating the energies of traditional social life. The carnivalesque occurred within a medieval economic system infused with billingsgate markets that were themselves embedded in traditional economic production supportive of mechanical bonding. Mechanical solidarity was produced through cyclical shifts within the two-in-one collective consciousness of the first and second life. Universal participation and general laughter in the carnivalesque phase provided the necessary social energies for the stability and maintenance of traditional social life.

In this section, we trace alterations in the modalities of carnival that occurred as the late medieval European world of the Renaissance was dissolved by advancing industrial capitalism. Our sociological reading of Bakhtin allows us to discern how changes in the first, official life caused the cultural reconstruction of the carnivalesque second life. We begin with the *modern* capitalist economy and the transformation of the carnivalesque second life into the consumption of products and leisure time in the society of the *spectacle* (Debord, 1967). We then examine how the *postmodern* economy (neoliberal, global, post-Fordist) reconstructs the spectacle into *simulations* of carnivalesque forms and experience (Baudrillard, 1983a, 1988).

Modern Carnival: From Travesty to Spectacle

Bakhtin analyzed the successive breakdown of carnival from its Renaissance peak (Bakhtin, 1973, p. 107). Bakhtin's explanation for this decline, especially in his book on Dostoevsky, followed arguments made by historical-materialist literary critics in the early 20th century, who viewed Dostoevsky's writings as "a pure and genuine expression of the 'spirit of capitalism'" (Bakhtin, 1973, p. 15). By shattering the social vacuums isolating traditional societies from one another and from encroaching modernity, capitalism eliminated the mechanical solidarity and collective consciousness necessary for carnival. Capitalism's rapid urbanization and cultural diversity contributed to the impossibility of carnival in modern society. As traditional status hierarchies were flattened, differences between bourgeoisie and proletariat were too fluid and unstable to be inverted in the carnivalesque travesty (Bakhtin, 1973, p. 137). Further, the detailed division of labor and occupational specialization required for production in the capitalist economy generated a fragmented first-life that was too fractured to be mirrored in carnival forms.

This loss of mechanical solidarity made traditional carnival impossible. Capitalism's smashing of communities and collective bonds left behind a "disorganized dust of individuals" (Fromm, 1955) fragmented by class hierarchies and isolated by religious schism. Carnival's dialogic and rejuvenating "pregnant death" was nowhere to be found in capitalism. Instead, a new form of dialectical creative destruction (Schumpeter, 1975) emerged with features more akin to carnivalesque spectacle (Debord, 1967) than traditional carnival.

We find that Guy Debord's concept of the spectacle best captures the shifting modality of the carnivalesque from traditional to modern societies (see Table 3). Best and Kellner (1997) argue that Debord's concept of spectacle is difficult to pin down, but generally

> refers to a media and consumer society, organized around the consumption of images, commodities ...[as well as] the vast institutional and technical apparatus of contemporary capitalism... which subject individuals to societal manipulation, while obscuring the nature and effects of capitalism and its deprivations (1997, p. 84).

TABLE 3   *From medieval carnival to modern spectacle*

Travesty → Spectacle	Carnival has no stable/universal culture to mirror: replaced by diverse, specialized spectacle
Mirror → Distraction	Carnivalesque incapable of second life mirroring of fragmented modernity and becomes a split-off escape
Dialogic → Dialectic	Carnivalesque becomes spectacle under specializing heterogeneous forces of modernity: dialectical movement
Pre-Modern Market → Industrial Capitalism	Carnivalesque spectacle suspends market culture, industrial production; reflects class and gender stratification.
General Laughter → Reduced Laughter	Fragmentation of "universal spirit" into heteroglossia of incommensurate, simultaneous specialized spirits
Mechanical → Organic Solidarity	Rise of division of labor/personal difference/social heterogeneity, Durkheim's "dust of individuals" Subcultural Specialization in Consciousness/Culture

In this sense, spectacle is not life, not even a second-life, but a flickering series of representations that distract people from life. Unlike Bakhtin, who equated carnival with travesty, Debord viewed spectacle as the opposite, even the antithesis, of travesty. Debord's spectacle did not overturn the official order, even temporarily; instead, it referenced the permanent, perpetual cultural forms that become the official world's strongest ideological and cultural support. Modern people do not vibrantly live in spectacle as a second life, but are momentarily stupefied by spectacular consumption.

According to Eco (1984), travesty can only occur when the everyday rules that are suspended and upended in carnival are embedded deep within the collective consciousness of a community. Social rules, hierarchical orders, authority relationships all must be "presupposed and taken for granted" in order for their transgression to produce general laughter (Eco, 1984, p. 6). The deep embeddedness of the collective consciousness was precisely what capitalism destroyed. Modern people were profoundly alienated from each other in a society grown too large, fragmented, and fluid to authentically connect. Because the official first life was no longer sufficiently consistent and integrated to be travestied, the carnivalesque second life became impossible.

Within this anomic world of Durkheimian organic solidarity, isolated individuals came to increasingly rely on spectacle to create "a social relation among people, mediated by [projected] images" (Debord, 1967, #4). As work and other sober first-life activities ceased to integrate society, the projected images of spectacle provided substitute forms of communication and indirect relationships through leisure and consumption. Thus, "as information or propaganda, as advertisement or direct entertainment," the spectacle emerged as the "model of socially dominant life" (Debord, 1967, #6). Since carnival could no longer travesty first life experiences that had been fragmented by the forces of industrial capitalism, travesty was replaced by spectacle, which provided the illusion of a unified first life while deepening social fragmentation and isolation.

The erosion of collective consciousness, community and participatory living in the society of the spectacle replaced travestied mirroring with spectacular distraction. Medieval carnival had served an inverted version of a meaningful society back to its members. The spectacle, on the other hand, transported the consciousness of spectators away from their first world entirely. Television, advertising, conspicuous consumption and leisure could not mirror the first-life of work and production, but blocked spectator's conscious acknowledgement of the empty hole at the center of their social world. Once begun, spectacle recreated is own preconditions. The more people became immersed in the society of the spectacle, the less time was available for genuine, participatory living. As individuals cathected strongly with their cars, homes, clothing, entertainments and other regions of consumption, they progressively disconnected from one another (Debord, 1967, #28).

> In societies where modern conditions of production prevail, all of life presents itself as an immense accumulation of spectacles. Everything that was directly lived has moved away into a representation.
>
> DEBORD, 1967, #1

While the essence of carnival was active living, the essence of spectacle was passivity. The enthusiastic, uproarious living of medieval carnival rejuvenated participants while regenerating the world. The spectacle, on the other hand, depended upon and simultaneously produced a kind of extreme social and psychological isolation of individuals. It provided an illusion of social life while in fact enforcing deep estrangement of self from other.

Whereas carnival regenerated the first world, the spectacle exhausted it. The carnivalesque spectacle could not maintain the dialogic, phase-shifting relationship between the first and second lives that was so crucial to the regeneration of medieval social life in Bakhtin's theory. Official life and carnival were in dialogue but remained bounded, so that the lived experience of each life did not blend or intermix with the other. As time-out-of-life (what Debord calls "pseudo-cyclical time"), the carnivalesque spectacle was a *visible negation of life*" (Debord, 1967, #10). The two lives of modern society, the productive and the spectacular, did not cycle through bounded, separate cultural phases, but rather co-existed alongside and inside of each other in a dialectical, negating relationship.

When the tide of medieval carnival crested and the king of carnival was dethroned, the carnivalesque spirit receded to the fringe of official first life: the medieval market. Like a storage battery, the pre-modern market kept the energy of carnival alive during the ordinary time of the first life. But under industrial capitalism, markets move from the fringe to the center of modern economic life. As the critical location where value was realized in economic exchange, modern markets lost their carnivalesque second-life character: they no longer served as the incubator of carnival forms but became the archetype of modern, serious, and calculating first-life. The modern spectacle, like medieval carnival, continued to stimualte trade and consumption. The carnivalesque was purged from increasingly serious haggling, but became attached to spectacles of branding, advertising, consumer marketing, entertainment, tourism and other leisure activities. Debord refers to these spectacles as "vulgarized pseudo-festivals" whose primary function is to "incite a surplus of economic expenditure" (Debord, 1967, p. 154). The modern market no longer sustains the spirit of carnival, but warehouses and displays the depleted husks of carnivalesque forms to stimulate consumer spending.

Bakhtin refers to the remnants of the carnivalesque forms that survive the death of carnival as reduced laughter. He characterized reduced laughter as laughter "muted down to a minimum: it is as if we see laughter's footprints in the structure of represented reality, but do not hear laughter itself" (Bakhtin, 1973, p. 137). Carnivalesque spectacles evidence reduced laughter in at least two ways. First, the erosion of mechanical solidarity meant that carnivalesque laughter could only be partial, limited to certain strata or subgroups. In medieval carnival, participants laughed *with* each other in universal spirit. In carnivalesque spectacles, women might laugh *at* men (or vice versa), elites *at* the poor (or vice versa), city dwellers at their country cousins (or vice versa) but no one laughs together. Second, as the capitalist division of labor eroded the unified culture of traditional societies, carnivalesque spectacles could only project anomic, fragmented and contradictory imagery split-off from the totality of human experience.

By the end of the nineteenth century, carnival had become a spectacle performed by specialists who paraded before passive spectators consuming leisure. This distinction between spectators and performers is clearly evident in Figure 2, which depicts carnival in Vienna circa 1899.[6] Here, a woman attired in a revealing carnival costume dances with abandon before what appears to be an entire gallery of transfixed men, who are not only immobile but also fully dressed in "first-life" dinner jackets, ties and top-hats. The differentiation between active carnival performers and passive spectators is even more pronounced in Figure 3, an image depicting Viennese Carnival in 1881. The men in this image, again immobile and clad in military uniforms or formal dinner attire, do not just ogle the carnivalesque woman, they minutely survey her with opera glasses. The reduced laughter observed in these images is representative of most late 19th and early 20th century illustrations of European carnival that we have located.

One important dimension of reduced laughter that was highly visible in images of modern spectacular carnival was gender. Women were consistently portrayed as active participants, performing ritualized displays that travestied *fin-de-siècle* bourgeois gender roles. Often depicted in the throes of enjoyment, women were still capable of living in carnival with dialogic laughter. Men on

---

6   We have compiled a data base of roughly 300 images of carnival from a variety of late nineteenth century publications. This specific image is taken from the #4 1899 edition of the Austrian newspaper *Die Bombe.*

FIGURE 2   *Carnival, Vienna circa 1899*
SOURCE: *DIE BOMBE* 22 JANUARY 1899.

the other hand, appear to have lost the capacity to live a second life. They maintained the dress, demeanor and subjectivities from their official first-life. While women burlesque the constrictions of their everyday sphere, displaying their unbuttoned carnival-selves with abandon, men seem confined to passivity as voyeuristic spectators. Men maintain their structured positions and sober identities, often without allowing a single button to slip. Bakhtin's analysis of reduced laughter does not focus on gender, but these images are consistent

FIGURE 3   *Carnival, Vienna circa 1881*
SOURCE: *WIENER CARICATUREN* 17 FEBRUARY 1881.

with his theory (and with Durkheim's). Through most of modernity, bourgeois men's lives modernized with a division of labor, occupational specialization and individualized subjectivity earlier than bourgeois women's lives, which were restricted to the confining sphere of domesticity, marriage and mother-hood. Such women could live in carnival far later than men because carnival was capable of laughing travestying of women's not-yet-modern first lives. Men had dropped out of the capability of full enjoyment and participation in general laughter: carnival was reduced to a spectator sport.

Gender contributed to reduced laughter in another way: men were not only spectators to women's activity but also became the target of carnival mockery and forms of billingsgate abuse. Many images of modern spectacular carnival depict women laughing *at* men but not *with* them. Figure 4 is one example in which four energetic young women surround a sleeping older man to taunt and humiliate him. One young woman delicately balances upon a sofa while dancing a jig, toasting champagne and removing the man's top hat with her stiletto-like shoe. Far from eliminating status differences in universal familiar-ity, the abundance of such mildly sado-masochistic imagery signals that the modern spectacular carnival reinforced the social distance and hierarchical distinctions that medieval carnival (temporarily) suspended.

FIGURE 4   *Carnival, Vienna circa 1881*
SOURCE: *WIENER CARICATUREN* 11 JANUARY 1891.

Another important, if less visible, dimension of reduced laughter was social class. The mesalliances between high and low strata, so much a feature of medieval carnival, had disappeared by the late nineteenth century. The social distance separating upper and lower classes in the first-life was maintained in carnivalesque spectacles: each class had a carnival of its own. Receding from the public square, spectacular carnival flowed into privatized, class stratified spaces. This was one reason why social class, unlike gender, was conspicuous by its absence from carnival representations. Most of the images depicted exclusive gatherings of homogenous, primarily bourgeois, people who related to each other with a degree of carnival familiarity as privileged equals. Spectacular carnival took place within refined and fashionable venues: ballrooms, opera house foyers, exclusive clubs and banquet halls. The expense and exclusivity of these elegant lifestyle enclaves removed carnival from the public square, restricting participation to those with financial means and personal connections.

Figure 5 is set in Berlin during the 1920's, entitled "Under the Sign of the Herring Barrel" and captioned with the phrase "my pet ... couldn't you have left your pearls behind in the coat room? Then we would really have freedom to dance." Here, men and women co-participate in festivities more or less equally (spectator men are absent) in a surface appearance of general laughter. Men frolic in festive costume, women frolic even more in the festive *absence* of costume. However, the eight piece orchestra, high-ceilinged ornate ballroom, staffed coat room, obviously-expensive costuming, and pearls upon every woman whose bodies remain unmarked by the rigors and calories of working class life clearly depict reduced laughter and the erosion of mesalliance in the carnivalesque spectacle. Like a movie comedian clad only in a barrel, the activities of these participants in the modern carnivalesque spectacle are covered by the "herring barrel" of a festooned hall that guarantees social class exclusivity. The precondition of the depicted activity, full of such overt transgressive body display, high levels of sensuality, and *universal* enjoyment, was the *exclusion of the other*. The frame surrounding these refined partiers, defining the specific rules of their mutual transgression, would collapse should the crasser sort of partier mix in with them. This risqué carnivalesque spectacle with such exclusive participants would have been impossible in the public square that was the normal venue for traditional carnival.

Nineteenth century bourgeois carnival was an exclusive, class-stratified, and stylized ritual segregated from working classes. By barring lower orders at the door of the ballroom, the upper orders excluded the possibility that their official position and high-status lifestyles would be mocked or travestied by the riff-raff below. Mesalliances made medieval carnival's general laughter safe

FIGURE 5   *Carnival, Berlin circa 1926*
SOURCE: *ULK* 1926.

(and mandatory) for elite participation in travesty. Class segregation made carnivalesque spectacle's reduced laughter safe (and comfortable) for elite participation in risqué transgression. Class segregation also made carnivalesque
spectacle possible for the lower orders as well. Degradation of an excluded
"other" appears in images of working class people who mock the manners
and parody the appearance of elites. Since these elites have first-life authority
over them, reduced laughter cannot be generated without their exclusion from
working-class carnivalesque spectacles.

In medieval carnival, the volume of general laughter was turned up to its highest settings; In the carnivalesque spectacle, the volume of reduced laughter is muted. The correspondence between Bakhtin's muted, reduced laughter and Debord's distracting but forgettable spectacle is obvious. In both theories, modern carnivalesque spectacles lack the strong and concentrated emotional energy that flowed through the collective consciousness of unified traditional society. The transformation from mechanical to organic solidarity dissipated passions and encouraged calculating reason. Modernity's distribution of people into diverse social locations, specialized occupations and mutually-incompatible subjectivities disrupted the emotional energy needed to produce the high volume of authentic carnival.

Durkheim's theory of capitalism's reconstruction of consciousness and Weber's theory of the development of the sober, calculating spirit of capitalism align with Bakhtin's writings in interesting and as yet unexplored ways. Bakhtin's work (especially his book on Dostoevsky) draws our attention to the need to augment the sociological story of the loss of mechanical solidarity, collective consciousness, traditional economic ethics, and cultural enchantment with an account of the *war on carnival* that occurred contemporaneously with these other movements (Bakhtin,1973). Bakhtin reveals just how central carnivalesque activity and subjectivity were to European peoples on the cusp of industrialization. Bakhtin's writings suggest that carnivalesque culture declined not only because of structural change, but also because of suppression on multiple fronts. Political, religious, and economic elites each had a stake in the suppression, reduction or redirection of the carnivalesque.

In conclusion, modernity's alienated production, detailed division of labor and deep egoism could no longer be a source of solidarity, collective consciousness, or the travestied mirroring of social life so prevalent in premodern societies. As capitalism reconstructed European society, traditional culture's periodic, dialogic oscillation out of official life and into carnival ceased. Capitalism's emerging one-dimensional culture—serious, sober, production-oriented—preserved fragments of old carnivalesque forms, not as an organized, separate, unserious phase of life but rather as a dialectical aspect of serious life itself. Following Debord (1967), we contrast traditional carnival's active participation to capitalism's *carnivalesque spectacle* that demands behavioral passivity and spectatorship. Central to leisure and consumer culture, carnivalesque spectacles did not generate or reinforce social solidarity and authentic collective consciousness. Instead, they distracted already-alienated workers from conscious awareness while further isolating them from each other as spectators. The carnivalesque spectacle dialectically promoted high-levels of consumption and profit, but cut spectators off from participation in the rejuvenating energies of authentic, (re)productive carnival life. Alienated at work and at leisure, denied carnival's refreshing sea change, spectators treaded water in the perpetual pool of capitalism.

The post-Modern Turn: From Spectacle to Simulation

In the same way that Marx & Engel's *Communist Manifesto* was forever linked to the 1848 revolutions, Debord's (1967) *Society of the Spectacle* was strongly linked to the May 1968 revolutionary moment in France. Debord's Situationist International had promoted carnivalesque activity as revolutionary practice. These practices included travesty-like *detournement* of popular culture against itself, drifting through urban spaces and public squares, the creation of situations that disrupted official life, generated mesalliances and allowed for the emergence of playful moments of community. Crucially, the general strike and mass revolts of May 1968 prominently featured just such Bakhtinian carnivalesque activities: the travesty of official life, especially the discrowning of De Gaulle, the mesalliance of workers and students, billingsgate abuse as revolutionary rhetoric, sexual license, public milling and merry-making. Prior to the May 1968 revolts, scholars and activists tended to view revolution and resistance as serious, violent forms of collective action. May 1968 demonstrated how genuine protest activity could connect laughing crowds with revolutionary resistance in carnivalesque activity and community. This carnivalesque activity is widely held in the popular discourse of contemporary anti-globalization and anti-consumerist social movements (see, for example Klein, 2000, the Situationist International website www.notbored.org, or culture-jamming as practiced in the chic, detournement journals and website Adbusters).

The revolutionary moment of 1968 passed quickly. In the intervening forty years, capitalist official life, including the pacifying, alienating spectacle, grew geographically to incorporate the entire globe and intensified to colonize every last region of human life, from food preparation to sexual intimacy. Debord's early writings celebrated the potential for carnivalesque travesty of corporate culture as a mechanism of effective resistance and revolution. But over time, he was forced to recognize that capitalism had learned to negate the negation by hijacking the carnivalesque (Debord, 1988). This new integrated spectacle, witnessed in the mainstreaming of anti-capitalist hip-hop culture or in the retooling of revolution to sell conservative political philosophies, or pickup trucks, negated counter-cultural social movements by reducing them to profit motive.

Debord's later writings anticipate the pessimistic and dystopian insights of his contemporary Jean Baudrillard, whose writings recognized that the proliferation of advertising, media, and other virtual realities had altered the sign system of late capitalism and rendered all social life a *simulation* (Baudrillard, 1983a). Distinct and discernible difference between the authentic and the counterfeit, between originals and copies, collapsed as the integrated spectacle absorbed authentic social life. In this ubiquitous "carnivalization of the world," (Langman, 2005) the modality of the carnivalesque shifted from spectacle to simulation (see Table 4). We view the explosion of carnival forms in recent years as something that can only be understood as capitalist-powered simulations of an authentic life that no longer exists. Music festivals, Mardi Gras, Burning Man, motorcycle rallies, stock car racing, and other mass events no longer function merely as spectacular forms of leisure and consumption but as *carnivalesque simulations* that create the appearance of authentic social life.[7]

From this perspective, the carnivalesque simulation no longer provides spectacular distraction from the alienation and anomie of social life but rather projects the appearance of a first life that has now totally disappeared.

TABLE 4   *From modern spectacle to post-modern simulation*

Spectacle → Simulation	Carnivalesque becomes simulated travesty of a universal culture that no longer exists
Distraction → Projection	Simulation projects the illusion of second life that masks the absence of the social
Dialectic → Delusion	Carnivalesque simulations camouflage the anomie of late modernity with the illusion that community and shared experience are still possible
Industrial Capitalism → Global/ Speculative Capitalism	Intensive commodification of everyday life and pervasive alienation
Reduced Laughter → Hyper-Reality	Simulation of shared consciousness/ culture where none exists
Organic Solidarity → Collective Interpassivity	Collective spectatorship generates simulation of community, freedom, equality and abundance

---

7   Though Best and Kellner (2001) have fittingly proposed that these massive, multi-dimensional and semi-participatory forms constitute a new type of mega-spectacle (See also Best & Kellner 1997), we find greater utility in analyzing these events through the lens provided by Baudrillard, and thus refer to them as postmodern *carnivalesque simulations*.

Baudrillard (1983a) points to the characteristics of *carnivalesque simulations* in his discussion of Disneyland and Watergate. Just as Watergate was a simulation designed to convince Americans that politics as usual operate within the law; or Disneyland is a simulation that masks the fantasy of ordinary social life, the postmodern carnivalesque prop up modern life by camouflaging the simulated nature of everyday life. While carnivalesque simulations go beyond spectatorship to involve the participants in some limited way, their action serves as a user's illusion where atomized individuals without any shared heritage, culture, meaning, or ties simulate a shared experience that masks the ongoing erosion of the social in the postmodern experience.

Central to the theories of both Bakhtin and Debord was an emphasis on the division of society into two separate spheres. To Bakhtin, carnival dialogically supported official life; to Debord, consumer spectacles dialectically negated productive work life. In contrast, Baudrillard's writings emphasized the erosion or breakdown of all boundaries separating different social spheres. In postmodern society, carnivalesque simulations cannot be distinguished in any meaningful way from authentic first life. Unlike the traditional and modern modes of the carnivalesque that were temporally separated from the rest of life, the postmodern carnivalesque is perpetual. One no longer rotates in and out of the carnivalesque sphere but permanently dwells within it. The perpetual carnivalistic simulations of postmodern society approximate Eco's (1986, p. 6) "diabolic world" Everlasting carnival sustains the delusion that an obdurate, authentic, and non-carnivalesque realm of social life exists while promoting equally repressive and authoritarian social experiences as the first world they supposedly replace.

We see a similar shift in the economic characteristics of carnivalesque simulations. Whereas Bakhtin equated traditional carnivalesque forms with the premodern market and Debord equated spectacle with modern marketing and consumption of leisure, we draw from Baudrillard (1983a; 1983b) and Jameson (1991) to argue that all of postmodern society, including carnivalesque simulations, are thoroughly penetrated with the language and logic of capitalist markets. The omnipresence of advertising, branding and marketing, the rise of the entertainment and tourism industries, the centrality of consumer services, and the global mobility of industrial production has broken down the distinction between production and consumption in late capitalism. Whereas Bakhtin argued that official life was fully separated from carnival and Debord argued that productive work life was separated from leisure and consumer spectacles, no region of postmodern life escapes the dynamics of speculative capitalism. The logic of the marketplace is never absent from carnivalesque simulations, even though these simulations often suppress or submerge crass concerns over money, payment, price, haggling and the rest. Carnivalesque simulations, such as amusement parks and all-inclusive vacation resorts, the advanced purchase of holidays or the deferred payment of restaurant and hotel bills, simulates the suspension of the rules of the market. This creates the false illusion that there is any difference between carnivalesque simulation and the equally carnivalesque world of postmodern consumption.

In addition, carnivalesque simulations unrelentingly infuse every television commercial, shopping mall and sales pitch. Postmodern people constantly encounter carnivalesque imagery and language, not only in their leisure life but also in and through their work. Unlike their modern Fordist counterparts, postmodern workers produce simulations of carnival rather than durable goods. The post-modern economy is not only composed of workers "cooking each other hamburgers" as Robert Reich once wrote, but more to the point, of workers producing and selling carnivalesque simulations to each other. An excellent illustration of this is provided by the recent transformation of the historic Old Billingsgate Market in London, the source of Bakhtin's concept of billingsgate abuse, into an elite, themed event center and exhibit hall. Branded with the patina of down-market fish-mongering and abusive haggling, Billingsgate has been transformed into a postmodern simulation of itself, a venue marketed to marketers as a stage for marketing: "from cars to computers, fashion to financial services... ITunes to Xelibri, a world *stage* for world class products" (Finn, 2014).

Finally, the postmodern economy has become increasingly dominated by trading on speculative financial markets (Krier, 2005). Stock trading, security speculation, currency swapping, real estate flipping: all of these speculative activities shade off into gambling, which Bakhtin identifies as the *modern* economy's most carnivalesque realm (Bakhtin, 1973, p. 143–144). As speculation penetrates all facets of capitalist activity in *postmodern* society, simulated staging's of casino excitement proliferate (games shows, HGTV programming, state lotteries, sales incentive events).

To Bakhtin, medieval carnival was a world of general laughter that temporarily suspended social distinctions and promoted a ubiquitous collective consciousness. But as European society modernized, social fragmentation atomized the collective conscience and eroded general laughter into a reduced laughter that restricted the possibility for shared social experiences. The carnivalesque simulation marks the death of laughter altogether. The postmodern loss of cohesive relations and shared meanings buries "the social beneath a simulation of the social" (Baudrillard, 1983b, p. 67), effectively silencing even the possibility of reduced laughter. Unable to discern reality from illusion or authentic experiences from commodified images, shared consciousness is increasingly replaced by hyper-reality (Baudrillard 1988): a simulation of shared consciousness and culture where none authentically exists.

Our discussion of the modern spectacle described how modernity's division of labor, social density and cultural fragmentation eroded the Durkheimian mechanical solidarity necessary for medieval carnival. Modern carnivalesque spectacles did not promote organic solidarity (defined as recognition of inter-dependency and the sacredness of individuality), but deepened the alienation of already-alienated workers. In our view, postmodern carnivalesque simula-tions do not build either organic or mechanical solidarity but promote *inter-passivity* (Žižek, 2007).

Interpassivity manifests itself along two fronts. First, while carnivalesque simulations appear to promote higher levels of participation than modern spectacles, it is a pseudo participation that is shallow, stylized and profoundly self-referential. Whether earning beads at Mardi Gras or selecting Miss Buffalo Chip at the Sturgis Rally, participants in these events are often alone-together while a simulated staging of carnival plays out around them. This points to the second manifestation of interpassivity that mirrors Žižek's (2007) claims about prayer wheels, video recorders and laugh tracks, all of which complete important tasks automatically, without active participation. The omnipres-ence of pre-packaged, simulated carnivalesque forms enables postmoderns' to experience carnival without emotional or psychic involvement. No matter what else we are doing, carnivalesque simulations *enjoy for us*. We participate while remaining disengaged as the carnivalesque forms simulate our general laughter, like the laugh tracks on a sitcom.

As a consequence, collective interpassivity in postmodern simulations can-not rejuvenate social energies. In medieval culture, the creative experience of joint participation in authentic carnival was an inwardly sufficient end in it-self. Carnival was not staged for or dependent upon the appreciative gaze of an audience but was the expression of an exuberant universal spirit. Postmodern carnivalesque simulations, by contrast, are not ends-in-themselves. Like jazz music on a CD, they are not lived but played, and serve primarily as a means to enhance profitability.

Conclusion and Implications

While there is a growing literature on the importance of the carnivalesque in traditional, modern, and postmodern societies, a fully theorized sociology of carnival remains largely undeveloped in the field of sociology. Our sociologi-cal reading of Bakhtin attempts to contribute to this vacancy. With Bakhtin, we affirm carnival as an integral component of medieval social life. Building on Bakhtin, we have developed a sociological theory of the dialogic that more specifically theorizes the importance of the carnivalesque to mechanical solidarity and traditional society. Extrapolating from Bakhtin, we have explored the transformation of carnival modalities into the modern and postmodern eras.

Interwoven with the dynamics of capitalism, modern spectacles and postmodern simulations represent severe ruptures in the rejuvenating social power of the traditional carnivals of medieval society. Contemporary carnivalesque simulations offer participants and virtual observers a shallow and momentary experience of solidarity, a surface appearance of shared collective consciousness and an illusory travesty of official power. In reality, the collective interpassivity of carnivalesque simulations does not approach the radical transgression of social boundaries characteristic of medieval mesalliances. The solidly middle class "Burners" in the Black Rock Desert, "Dale Junior" fans at Talladega, or "Hells Angels Wannabes" at Sturgis only play at mesalliance: they safely slum with others of their own class. With the working and lower classes excluded from participation and virtual spectatorship, deep travesty of official power and authority becomes impossible. As Debord's (1988) concept of the integrated spectacle made plain, postmodern carnivalesque simulations cannot travesty political and economic power; they can only legitimate it (even with mild satire and mockery).

Authentic carnival activity was anti-official, and therefore, potentially threatening to modern and postmodern power (Eco, 1986, p. 6). Yet the family resemblance between carnivalesque forms and subversive resistance to power, already suspect at the time of Debord, has become even more problematic in these postmodern times. Though carnivalesque forms have been associated historically with revolutionary and resistance movements (the popular mobs of the French Revolution, for instance), contemporary carnivals, fairs and festivals are much more likely to resemble capitalist billboards than revolutionary placards. Ironically, when carnivalesque forms appear in 21st century protest activity, they are organized around power itself rather than opposed to it.

Carnivalesque simulations of protest have been widespread in recent times. For example, the Tea Party was recognized early in the Obama Presidency for its aggressive disruption of "town hall meetings." These meetings were themselves simulations of authentic New England town hall meetings (admission was controlled, questions were pre-screened, answers were pre-scripted). Hijacked by people loosely affiliated with the Tea Party movement, protesters directed billingsgate abuse at lawmakers, travestied the current administration, scorned potential beneficiaries of the law, and claimed mesalliance across a broad spectrum of the population. These actions simulated the appearance of authentic, spontaneous and expressive grass-roots collective action, yet were actually simulated astro-turf protests, pre-scripted, organized and coordinated by political operatives. The festive yet disruptive actions surrounding the recount of the disputed 2000 Florida election, where protesters held signs that mocked the stupidity of voters and paraded a joker-like character dubbed "Hanging Chad," are a similar case. Neither of these carnivalesque protests travestied or discrowned official power. Instead, they travestied the idea of protest against official power. In this travesty of travesty, carnivalesque forms were inverted in an effort to uphold power and put down those who would challenge it.

Carnivalesque forms, which began as a rejuvenating phase of medieval life, transformed under the pressures of industrial capitalism into spectacles that distracted alienated workers from the full consciousness of their degraded life. These pressures grew within postmodern political economy, flattening carnival forms into mere simulations incapable of producing social solidarity or liberatory experience. Bakhtin's carnival was a wholly-other life that revitalized individual and social energies depleted in the grinding cycle of serious workaday production. In contrast, carnivalesque simulations are coextensive with the rest of inauthentic, postmodern existence. Medieval carnival lifted the human spirit temporarily out of the rut of official life, something contemporary carnivalesque simulations cannot do, precisely because postmodern society lacks both a stable, well-trodden rut to be lifted out of and a genuine carnival plane to be lifted onto. Without clean separation between first and second life, the very atmosphere of postmodern society is decentralized, yet ubiquitous carnivalesque simulation.

CHAPTER 2

Economies of Spectacle and Micro-primitive Accumulation: A Tale of Two Cities

Newton and Iowa Speedway

For more than a century, Newton, Iowa was home to Maytag Corporation, a leading manufacturer of washing machines, dryers and other durable home appliances. Through the end of the 20th century, Newton was a quintessential company town, with more than 4,000 of Newton's 15,000 citizens employed by Maytag. Many worked in high-paying, unionized jobs in the local appliance factory while others staffed offices in Maytag's downtown corporate headquarters. During the 1980s and 1990s, Maytag and Newton seemed immune from the troubles plaguing most U.S. manufacturers, inoculated by highly productive workers, a brand with a reputation for quality and consistent profitability. Newton's fortunes began to decline when Maytag's stock price fell sharply in the early 2000s, triggering a series of layoffs, restructurings and persistent rumors of a corporate takeover (Krier, 2009b). Although Newton's factory remained profitable, by 2005 Maytag's demise appeared imminent, and with little hope of attracting new manufacturing jobs to compensate for those lost, city and state officials struck a deal to build a privately-owned motorsports complex in a nearby cornfield (see Figure 6).

Promoters in Iowa had been laying the groundwork such a deal for several years, hoping to bring to the state a racing facility capable of hosting National Association of Stock Car Auto Racing (NASCAR) and Indy Racing League (IRL) events. The early 2000s were boom years for NASCAR with rapid growth in viewership, track attendance and sponsorship revenue. Beginning in the 1990s, NASCAR found success by geographically expanding from its Southern, Eastern and backcountry roots into the American Midwest and West. In 2001, major racing facilities opened near Joliet, Illinois (Chicagoland Speedway) and Kansas City, KS (Kansas Speedway) to sell-out crowds and, in the case of Kansas City, KS, brought a surprising amount of retail trade and commercial investment. Iowa had long been home to the Knoxville Nationals, the title event for the smaller-scale dirt-track motorsport of sprint cars, but with two recently opened NASCAR tracks within a few hours drive, central Iowa seemed a risky location to build another motorsports facility. In the years leading up to Iowa Speedway's deal in Newton, the catchphrase from the 1989 film, *Field of*

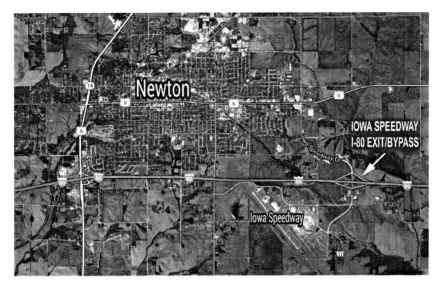

FIGURE 6   *Map of Newton and Iowa Speedway*
             SOURCE: GOOGLE MAPS.

Dreams, in which Kevin Costner constructed a baseball diamond in the middle of an Iowa cornfield to attract the ghosts of baseball-past (and paying spectators), became linked to the racetrack: "If you build it, they will come." ("If you build it they will come," 2003, n.p.). Citing Kansas Speedway's Faust-like transformation of local real estate values, commercial activity and entertainment development, Iowa Speedway promised to deliver a new hope to the residents of Newton, a company town about to lose its company.[1]

Maytag Corporation was, as expected, acquired by Whirlpool in 2005. By 2007, all Maytag-related jobs in Newton had vanished and parts of the factory were bulldozed. Given this dark news, public officials touted the Iowa Speedway deal as a $70 million dollar "genie granting Newton's economic wish," a "shot in the arm" that would attract "thousands of tourists" while generating enough jobs to keep young people from leaving the state for greener pastures. "This is a great day for Newton, Jasper County and the State of Iowa," noted one local politician, likening the racetrack to "winning the lottery in Newton" (Karr and Hussmann, 2005, n.p.). Racetrack officials stoked resident's dreams,

---

1   By Faust-like development, we reference the end of Goethe's Faust, where the protagonist devotes his demonic powers to a massive land reclamation and real estate development scheme that Berman (1983) uses as a metaphor for high modern transformative development projects such as Robert Moses' reconstruction of New York.

specifying how the racetrack would "put Newton on the map," not only for racing, but for "company meetings, car testing, driving schools, concerts, farm machinery shows, swap meets or whatever you can draw up" (Karr, 2005, n.p.). "This community is on its way to realizing a huge amount of economic growth in the years to come. Boogity, boogity, boogity!" said another (Hansen, 2005, n.p.). With their industrial economy gone, Newton residents replaced Maytag insignia on their town square with Iowa Speedway-themed checkered flags, investing their hopes, their tax dollars and their community's resources in a new economy of spectacle.

Neoliberalism, Economic Development Corporations and Micro-primitive Accumulation

Newton's financial support for Iowa Speedway was not atypical for communities in the late 20th and early 21st centuries when neoliberalism (the Washington consensus) reigned in the U.S. as the dominant political philosophy. Neoliberalism valorized private enterprise while denouncing government involvement in the economy. Ironically, though deregulation, fiscal discipline, private entrepreneurship and free markets figured prominently in discourse, in actual practice, neoliberalism often expanded the economic role of government, especially at the local and regional level (Johnson & Man, 2001; Peters & Fisher, 2004, Girardi, 2013). Deregulated capital was *mobile*, which meant that industries like Maytag Corporation were free to leave communities like Newton. To forefend capital flight, community officials bent low in servility, competing against each other to assemble the most attractive package of publicly-funded economic incentives, tax rebates, development funds and other free gifts that would retain existing industries or attract new ones. New forms of semi-transparent, quasi-government agencies, known as *economic development corporations*, emerged during these years to assist elected officials in the extraction of resources and concessions from an often unwitting public, packaging them in forms suitable for legal gifting to private capital. Economic development corporations, unlike city officials and other members of local growth coalitions, need not reveal their activities, including deal-making, to the public. Their deals tend to avoid general obligation bonds that require voter approval on bond issues, preferring revenue bonds, direct grants, tax-increment financing schemes and tax rebates that commit public funds without public vote.

Industries under neoliberalism grew dependent upon government and quasi-government for initial and periodic infusions of capital, infrastructure and other resources taken from the public (the commons). Such practices parallel capitalism's secret, original sin analyzed by Karl Marx as "so-called primitive accumulation." The historical emergence of capitalism as a self-expanding system of accumulation depended upon a prior, militarized seizure-by-force of other people's land, gold, natural resources and bodies; the clearing of the land and the enclosure of the commons (Marx, [1867]1977, pp. 873–895; see also Hardt & Negri 2009, pp. 86–95). In neoliberalism, economic development corporations perform similar dirty work, albeit on a routinized small-scale, expropriating public resources (tax revenues, land, infrastructure, public indebtedness) and turning them into private property. We identify this process as *micro-primitive accumulation*. Though lacking the military brutality and historical bravado of enclosure and colonization, micro-primitive accumulation represents new mechanisms to supply appropriated public capital to businesses as a precondition for and supplement to industrial production and commercial activity.

In the case of Iowa Speedway, micro-primitive accumulation, the extraction of public resources for gifting to private capital, was coordinated through the Newton Development Corporation. Though a precise accounting is difficult, a partial tally of city resources provided to Iowa Speedway developers includes: direct gift of the land upon which the speedway was to be built; $3.7 million development grant (financed through a municipal revenue bond); $9.7 million infrastructure improvements (financed through an infrastructure bond), and an $8.8 million tax abatement. At the state level, micro-primitive accumulation was provided to speedway in the form of a $6.8 million Revitalizing Iowa's Strong Economy (RISE) grant that redirected state-collected fuel tax revenues for private development, a $12.5 million state sales tax rebate, and state-sponsored promotion and advertising of racing events through Iowa's Tourism Office. Over and above local and state gifts, the U.S. federal government allowed motorsport facilities associated with NASCAR to dramatically reduce their income taxes by accelerating infrastructure depreciation so that expenditures could be written off over seven years. Even after the speedway was built, the financial condition of the speedway was periodically stabilized with infusions of public resources, including additional local tax abatements, ongoing infrastructure work, extensions of state tax rebates ($9 million granted in 2014), dramatic slashing of assessed property values (from $40 million to $20 million), restructuring tax payment plans and extensions of preferential tax treatment at the federal level. Despite these gifts, in 2015, after a decade of speedway operation under three different owners, the City of Newton was still struggling to make interest payments on its $17 million of speedway-related indebtedness.

Iowa Speedway: NASCAR's Growth and Newton's Dream

By the 2000s, spectator infrastructures in most major sports were routinely funded through micro-primitive accumulation, not only in NASCAR, but also professional baseball, football, basketball, soccer, Olympics, and multi-purpose municipal event centers (Delaney and Eckstein, 2007). Though local publics financed and absorbed the risk of these facilities, under cover of promises of prosperity that rarely materialized, profits from the spectator events staged within them remained in the hands of private owners. Most NASCAR tracks are owned by either International Speedway Corporation (ISC), a holding company directly controlled by NASCAR's ruling family, the France's of Daytona Beach, Florida, or by Speedway Motorsports, Inc. (SMI), another holding company directly controlled by long-time North Carolina NASCAR promoter Bruton Smith (see Table 5).

NASCAR, wholly-owned by the France family (among the top 150 wealthiest U.S. families according to Forbes), was founded in 1948. The stock-car racing that NASCAR enclosed, produced and promoted had legendary origins in whiskey-running, bootlegging "duels" between southern, backcountry delivery drivers, such as Junior Johnson in Tom Wolfe's *Last American Hero*. The outlaw drivers of early stock cars honed their skills outrunning revenue agents and badass sheriff deputies while hauling large loads of moonshine from woodland stills to urban markets. Primal honor was central to southern backcountry masculinity, compelling bootleggers to compete against each other in street racing and county fairgrounds. NASCAR routinized these races into a circuit and promoted them as spectator events that charged admission (the primary source of revenue). NASCAR races were occasionally broadcast, but most races remained local, small-scale affairs. This changed in 1972, when the R.J. Reynold's tobacco company, banned from directly advertising its cigarettes on television, purchased indirect advertising by signing as the official sponsor of NASCAR's most elite series, which carried a cigarette brand name for three decades: the Winston Cup. This triggered a dialectic of development: national television broadcasting attracted more prominent national brands as racing sponsors, which attracted more television exposure, which attracted more sponsorship dollars.

During this time, the outlaw origins of the NASCAR spectacle, including much of its rough and tumble, "rubbin' is racin'," fighting and cursing sideshow, was suppressed: the diegesis produced by NASCAR became more corporate, professional and to please sponsors like Tide, Coca-Cola, M&M's, and McDonald's, suitable as family entertainment. In the 1990s, NASCAR negotiated circuit-wide revenue sharing of a broadcast rights contract to televise the

TABLE 5   *NASCAR Affiliated Racetracks in the United States (selected)*

Track Name	Owner	Location	Year of First Race
Richmond International Raceway	International Speedway Corp.	Richmond, VA	1946
Martinsville Speedway	International Speedway Corp.	Ridgeway, VA	1947
Watkins Glen International	International Speedway Corp.	Watkins Glen, NY	1948
Darlington Raceway	International Speedway Corp.	Darlington, SC	1950
Daytona International Speedway	International Speedway Corp.	Daytona Beach, FL	1959
Atlanta Motor Speedway	Speedway Motorsports, Inc.	Hampton, GA	1960
Charlotte Motor Speedway	Speedway Motorsports, Inc.	Concord, NC	1960
Bristol Motor Speedway	Speedway Motorsports, Inc.	Bristol, TN	1961
Phoenix International Raceway	International Speedway Corp.	Avondale, AZ	1964
Michigan International Speedway	International Speedway Corp.	Brooklyn, MI	1968
Sonoma Raceway	Speedway Motorsports, Inc.	Sonoma, CA	1968
Talladega Superspeedway	International Speedway Corp.	Talladega, AL	1969
New Hampshire Motor Speedway	Speedway Motorsports, Inc.	Loudon, NH	1990
Homestead-Miami Speedway	International Speedway Corp.	Homestead, FL	1995
Las Vegas Motor Speedway	Speedway Motorsports, Inc.	Las Vegas, NV	1996
Texas Motor Speedway	Speedway Motorsports, Inc.	Fort Worth, TX	1996
Auto Club Speedway	International Speedway Corp.	Fontana, CA	1997
Kentucky Speedway	Speedway Motorsports, Inc.	Sparta, KY	2000
Chicagoland Speedway	International Speedway Corp.	Joliet, IL	2001
Kansas Speedway	International Speedway Corp.	Kansas City, KS	2001
Iowa Speedway	NASCAR (France Family)	Newton, IA	2006

entire 36 week series on national broadcast television. The national television exposure led NASCAR to geographically expand its racetrack circuit to include Midwest and Western states to better capture profit from spectators and sponsors from these regions. NASCAR-affiliates built tracks and promoted races in Mexico, Canada, Texas, Nevada, California, Illinois, and Kentucky: Iowa

Speedway was the last track added to the NASCAR circuit. By the time Iowa Speedway was constructed, NASCAR was big-business and thoroughly corporate: drivers earned millions in salaries, they wore livery branded with the logos of sponsors and their hand-crafted, multi-million dollar simulated "stock" cars had the uncanny appearance of corporate billboards roaring in circles at 200 m.p.h.

Iowa Speedway was majority-owned from 2005–2011 by members of the Manatt family (who also owned the construction company that built the track). "NASCAR Legend" Rusty Wallace, a retired stock car driver whose persona retained traces of the backcountry style central to NASCAR lore, was given a minority-ownership stake in the speedway to secure his star power in negotiations, public relations and supposedly, in racetrack design. The speedway, promoted as a $70 million facility when it was built, was sold for an estimated $40 million in 2011 to members of the Clement family, before being sold again in 2013 directly to NASCAR. NASCAR's purchase price was not disclosed officially, but tax filings indicated that the purchase price was as low as $10 million and the City of Newton, at the request of NASCAR, lowered the assessed value of the track to $20 million. Hence, the citizens of Newton, Iowa, after a decade of sustained high unemployment rates in the wake of losing their major employer, found that they owed $17 million of debt on a racetrack that now belonged to one of America's wealthiest and most politically connected families. When the speedway was built, public discourse stressed the need to invest public resources to replace Maytag's lost payroll: "no guts, no glory ... it takes money to make money" in the words of one city official (Karr, 2005b, n.p.). But the promised jobs and economic growth failed to materialize. In the years following the speedway deal, 1,600 of Newton's 15,000 residents left the city while average worker pay dropped from 106% of the state average to 87% (Swenson, 2010). For their $20 million gift to Iowa Speedway, Newton had created a mere 22 full time jobs and additional part-time jobs on event weekends that aggregated to 58 full-time equivalents (Swenson, 2010, p. 11). If the city had confiscated the entire Speedway payroll, it would barely have covered its interest payments on speedway debt.

The economic shortcomings of Iowa Speedway were not due to a lack of audience for races. Like the cinematic Field of Dreams, once the facility was built, spectators did indeed come, lining up at 4 a.m. to purchase season tickets, selling out (or nearly selling out) race events. Ticket sales at Iowa Speedway remained brisk during its first years of operation, posting annual gains in attendance through 2010. Most NASCAR tracks experienced sharp declines in ticket sales during this period (see Figure 7) and many tracks began removing excess seating (see Figure 8).

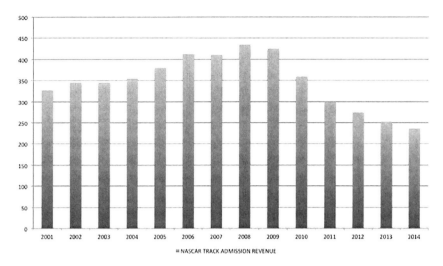

FIGURE 7   *Admissions Revenue at NASCAR Racetracks owned by Speedway Motorsports, Inc. and International Speedway Corporation*
SOURCE: SMI AND ISC ANNUAL REPORTS.

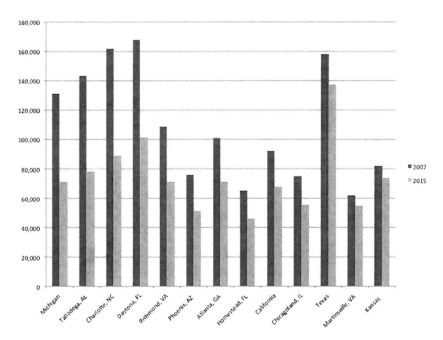

FIGURE 8   *Reductions in Seating Capacity at Selected NASCAR Racetracks*
SOURCE: SMI AND ISC ANNUAL REPORTS.

Iowa Speedway's solid attendance encouraged "NASCAR Legend" Rusty Wallace and other track promoters in 2013 to seek (unsuccessfully) $8 million of state appropriations from the legislature. From NASCAR's standpoint, Iowa Speedway performed better than most of its motorsports venues. The central problem was that city negotiations with Iowa Speedway were framed by the false premise that the primary source of revenue for the track was admission tickets purchased by in-venue spectators. In fact, the bulk of revenues for the track owner came from "intangible" sources—broadcast rights, sponsorships, and the like—that were not revealed to or shared with the city that funded the track. Our analysis of the financial statements of ISC and SMI reveal that broadcast rights generated between two and three times as much revenue as admissions tickets and catering to on-site spectators (see Figure 9).

Iowa Speedway and Newton officials maintained an illusion of public-private partnership, but their interests were not aligned. Newton's local growth coalition depended entirely upon physically-present spectators as retail customers while Iowa Speedway received the bulk of its revenues from broadcast rights, sponsorships and other intangibles. Iowa Speedway's debt, like that of most micro-primitive accumulation schemes, was to be serviced and eventually paid off, at least in part, with repurposed sales and property tax payments and through surcharges paid by spectators at the gate, $1 per ticket originally, later raised to $4 and then lowered to $3. No provision was made to pay interest or to service debt using funds from the major revenue source of the track, its broadcast rights contract.

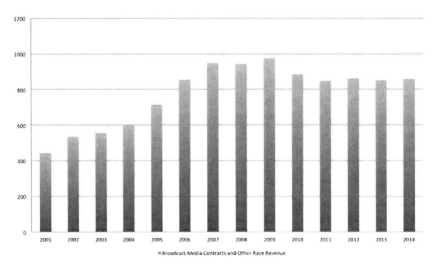

FIGURE 9   *Non-Admission Related Revenue at NASCAR Racetracks owned by Speedway Motor-sports, Inc. and International Speedway Corporation*
SOURCE: SMI AND ISC ANNUAL REPORTS.

Speedways, Peripheral Development and the Prosperity that Bypassed Newton

While it is unlikely that Newton's city officials fully understood that the speedway owner's economic interests were not aligned with theirs, it is likely that officials expected that the major economic payoff of the Speedway would not come from the Speedway itself, but from the peripheral development catalyzed by it. Kansas Speedway, NASCAR's most often cited economic success story, generated rapid and significant peripheral development in its locale of Kansas City, KS.

As the Iowa Speedway deal was finalized, city officials and economic development corporation staff from Newton travelled to Kansas City for a site visit. Prior to speedway construction, the area around the speedway was the downmarket western edge of Kansas City, KS, a city that had lost 30,00 residents and many jobs in the decades before the track was built, and lagged behind its suburban neighbors in commercial development, industrial employment and property values. The peripheral development surrounding Kansas Speedway in the fifteen years since the construction of the speedway is indeed impressive and continues to expand as this book goes to press (Nalbandian, 2005). While the speedway proper created just 40 full time jobs, peripheral development generated 3,000 mostly retail jobs by 2006, a number that has continued to grow to 10,000 in 2015 (Morris, 2015, n.p.). As described by the editor of Newton's newspaper, Kansas City, KS was once a "sleepy burg" that was "viewed as a poor country cousin" but "now boasts some pretty fancy threads and is the envy of many surrounding communities unwilling to take the initial risk" (Hussmann, 11 March 2005, n.p.).

Seeing the development surrounding Kansas Speedway "was enough to rock my boat" said one council member, noting that the racetrack functioned as a "tax-generating cash cow." Other promoters called the racetrack" "a status symbol," a "miracle story," a "catalyst" that put Kansas City, KS "on the fast track to a development bonanza." City officials noted that the racetrack soon attracted a Cabela's and Nebraska Furniture Mart, and "with those plum retail pieces in place ... the development snowballed into an avalanche.... The peripheral development is the sweetest part of landing the speedway" (Karr, 2005, 17 May, n.p.). Like Iowa Speedway, the economic development corporations and growth coalition surrounding Kansas Speedway deployed a full array of micro-primitive accumulation to fertilize growth, including multiple tax-increment financing districts and ongoing public gifting of infrastructure. One difference: whereas 15,000 citizens of Newton financed the bulk of the public giveaway to Iowa Speedway, Kansas Speedway was financed with State Tax Revenue (STAR) bonds backed by the nearly 3,000,000 residents of Kansas.

Newton's gamble was much larger: approximately $1,500 for every man, woman and child in town.

Within months of Iowa Speedway construction, the Newton Development Corporation announced that an out of state corporation would build a $65 million, 300 room hotel, waterpark, and conference center near Iowa Speedway in the "Prairie Fire" tax increment financing (TIF) district. The development would include "a national retailer" and "15 to 20 outlets" for "national franchised restaurants." The Speedway seemed to be working as a catalyst for travel and tourist development: "Newton grows as a destination location... This also moves Newton one step closer to having a diversified economy" (Jennings, 2006). Doubts seemed to evaporate from skeptics, as one columnist in Newton's local paper commented:

> A gentleman...told me that in two years you wouldn't be able to recognize this area with all the development that will follow the track. I believe it. If they can raise a $70 million racing complex from a field of soybeans in little more than a year, than anything's possible. I look out beyond the illuminated speedway onto the darkened roadways behind them and I step into the future. There's a huge Cabella's store with a Starbucks and an Outback in its parking lot. Across the way is a BP gas station and a Holiday Inn, which sit next to a little strip mall with a handful of specialty stores.
>
> KARR, 2006, n.p.

Of course, these subsidiary developments never quite materialized (as often happens with such Faustian development projects). A hotel was indeed built on the site, but it sat empty for several years, weeds growing in its parking lot. NASCAR, faced with declining broadcast ratings (see Figure 10), severe recession, and bankruptcy of the automakers who were core sponsors of the sport, reduced the number of annual race event weekends at the track from five to three. This new speedway, designed, partially-owned and highly-praised by "NASCAR legend" Rusty Wallace, was occupied by major circuit racing spectators for a few short hours on three weekends a year. The gleaming publicly-financed stands, parking lots, signage, even "Rusty Wallace Drive" itself, were empty and all but unused for the remaining 350+ days. Rather than capital development, the speedway became anti-capital: a massive black hole on the outskirts of Newton, emitting little value, but taking hundreds of acres of land out of productive use (Worrell 2009). Since the City of Newton had used up much of its bonding capacity to finance the speedway, the speedway effectively foreclosed other development opportunities (see Figure 11).

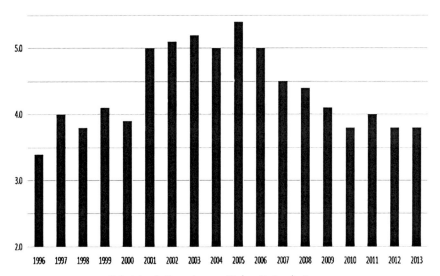

FIGURE 10   *NASCAR Television Ratings, Average Nielsen Rating by Season*
              SOURCE: JAYSKI.COM.

FIGURE 11   *Map of Iowa Speedway Development Area*
              SOURCE: GOOGLE MAPS.

Newton's dream of a thriving economy of spectacle foundered on a common shoal: the entire scheme depended upon attracting paying guests to the city, guests who would come for the race and stay for the food, hospitality, shopping and other amenities. The speedway attracted too few spectators (permanent seating capacity is 25,000) on too few weekends (three). Even more significantly, as visible in Figure 11, the spectators that did come to the speedway had little reason to visit Newton itself, since the city's development funds were used to construct a convenient Iowa Speedway exit from Interstate 80 two miles east so that *racing spectators could bypass Newton altogether.* Further, even if peripheral development around the speedway were to occur, especially in the Prairie Fire TIF district near the interstate exit, it would merely forestall (in the technical market sense) visitors, who would be routed away from Newton's existing commercial core into new businesses created with public gifts.

Sturgis, SD and the Sturgis Motorcycle Rally

Motorcycle clubs and events have a long history in American automobility (Urry, 2004). Between 1903 and the beginning of World War II, nearly 300 motorcycle and scooter manufacturers went into business in the United States (Nichols, 2007, pp. 104–115). Coupled with the development of a market for subsidiary products (accessories, parts, tools, apparel, etc.) their competition fueled the need to expand consumption and solidify a consumer base. In 1903 the American Federation of Motorcyclists emerged as a spinoff of the New York Motorcycle club, its goal to encourage the use of motorcycles, facilitate touring, defend the rights of motorcyclists and regulate motorcycle races and other events (The History of the AMA, 2013). The FAM and its successors (the Motorcycle and Allied Trades Association (1916) and American Motorcycle Association (1919)) worked to build clubs, membership networks, and publications that would connect the motorcycle enthusiasts of the day to the industry. By 1924, the AMA had set a goal to register at least 50,000 riders by hosting membership contests and developing trade publications that would promote its message to the wider population.

The Black Hills Motorcycle Classic, precursor to the Sturgis Motorcycle Rally, emerged within this context. In 1936 Clarence "Pappy" Hoel and his wife Pearl purchased an Indian Motorcycle dealership in Sturgis, South Dakota and founded the "Jackpine Gypsies" motorcycle club. These were difficult times for the motorcycle industry. The depression economy of the 1930s slowed motorcycle sales across the country, and the relatively rural location of Sturgis (Rapid City, population 13,800 in 1940, was the closest population center for 350 miles) offered a very limited motorcycle market. Hoel sponsored the first Black Hills

Motorcycle Classic as a "gypsy" tour and weekend racing event in 1938. His motivation was as much economic as cultural. While the Classic was certainly an opportunity for social interaction among motorcycle enthusiasts, Hoel created the Classic to bolster the market for Indian motorcycles and used the rally and races to expand his relatively limited market base. The AMA had been publishing information about using gypsy tours and motorcycle events to build motorcycle markets as early as 1917 (Swart & Krier, 2016). The Jackpine Gypsies chartered with the AMA in 1938, at least in part to attract rising star racer Johnny Spiegelhoff to the Black Hill's Motorcycle Classic races. Spiegelhoff refused to participate in events void of AMA regulation (Woodruff, 2015); AMA sanctioning gave the Black Hills Motorcycle Classic the national publicity, reputability, and access to a slate of professional riders necessary to overcome the locational disadvantages to enclosing this emerging arena of public life for private profit.

The post-War era saw an important change in cultural leitmotif of American motorcycling. Increasing numbers of veterans, attracted to the libertarian possibilities of the motorcycle and its emphasis on freedom, adventure, and risk flooded motorcycle culture. They formed clubs outside the official sanctioning of the AMA (the origin of the outlaw motorcycle club) and added the tenor of rebellion to the culture of American motorcycling. Virtually every analyst points out that rebellion among post-war motorcycle enthusiasts was exaggerated by sensationalist media attention (Austin, Gagne & Orend 2010; Nichols 2007; Reynolds 2000; Thompson 1967; Wood 2003; Yates 1999). Nevertheless, the public panic generated from rallies in Hollister, Riverside and Porterville, CA and Weirs Beach, NH, led rally cities and the industry itself to avoid tying their brands to the trope of the outlaw biker. Harley Davidson Corporation, whose contemporary marketing embraces outlaw themes, actually shunned the outlaw biker during this time by refusing to honor warranties or service motorcycles that had been chopped or modified from stock (Yates, 1999). Between 1954 and 1983 Harley Davidson pursued a marketing strategy that condemned outlaw riders; a strategy that contributed to the company losing nearly 40% of its market share during this period.

Apprehension over the new breed of bikers made many of the residents and city officials in Sturgis cool to the idea of expanding the rally for economic development. Like Harley Davidson, the Black Hills Classic remained relatively undeveloped through the early 1980s. As we detail in Chapter 4, attendance remained below 1000 spectators until 1963, and although the event was extended from 2 to 5 days in 1965, reached a mere 18,000 by 1975. The city didn't begin granting vendor licenses until 1979: only 9 licenses were granted the first year and numbers remained small until the mid-1980s. Overall, the event produced gross revenue less than $150,000 by 1967; factoring in the expenses of additional law enforcement and city personnel, net revenue was modest until the early 1980s. Most importantly, the city developed little of the infrastructure needed to expand the rally during the two decades following World War II. Beyond the races, the vast majority of rally activity was centered in the Sturgis city park. Attendees gathered in the park to party and camp, and the park gradually replaced the races as the epicenter of the rally. In the mid-1970s, public nudity, drinking and violence in the city park, coupled with the high cost of additional law enforcement, prompted concerned residents to petition the city council to end the rally. By 1982, the park had become the site of impromptu drag-racing, debauchery, and public violence. In response, the city instituted control measures, including limiting the number of campers and visitors in the park, forcing campers to register, increasing fees, and policing racing and alcohol consumption. During the 1982 Classic, restrictions and regulation led to riot conditions in the park; bikers tore out traffic gates and speed bumps, burned outhouses and motorcycles, and threw rocks at vehicles and city employees. Several incidents of gunfire were reported in the park, and at one point, a camper detonated a stick of dynamite. In response, the city voted to close the park to camping in November 1982 (Holland, 2015, May 12).

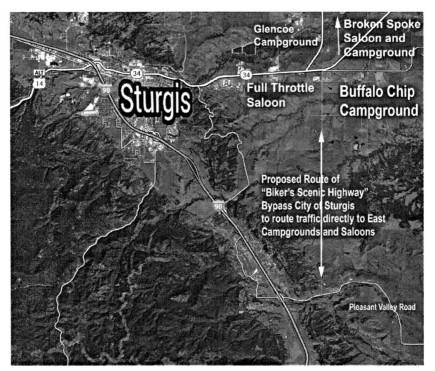

FIGURE 12   *Map of Sturgis, SD, East Campgrounds and Biker Scenic Byway*
SOURCE: GOOGLE MAPS

While the city park closure eased public concern over the tenor of the rally, it also decentered the rally outside the city limits. Local developers responded with the creation of several Rally venues east of the city—most notably the Buffalo Chip Campground (1981), the Glencoe campground (1983), and the Full Throttle Saloon (1999). These venues attracted increasing numbers of riders, forestalling the city as the epicenter of the rally and threatening its economic impact for the city (see Figure 12).

The 1980s also saw deleterious changes to the U.S. economic climate. As globalization, recession, deindustrialization and capital flight threatened the economic stability of American communities, civic leaders began looking beyond the traditional industrial base—including the entertainment, tourism, and service sectors, to diversify revenue. Motorcycle events became a growing part of this trend. Literally hundreds of new rallies sprung up across the country. The Republic of Texas Rally (Austin, TX), Rolling Thunder (Washington, DC), Bikes, Blues and BBQ (Fayetteville, AK), Biketoberfest (Daytona Beach, FL), Leesburg BikeFest (Leesburg, FL), Lone Star Bike Week (Galveston, TX), Delmarva Bike Week (Ocean City, MD), Ohio Bike Week (Sandusky, OH) are just a few of the myriad large displacement motorcycle events founded in the U.S. after 1985.

Public versus Private: Revenue Growth and Micro-primitive Accumulation in the Sturgis Motorcycle Rally

The massive growth of the Sturgis rally is located within this context. In 1992 the City of Sturgis replaced the not-for-profit local Chamber of Commerce and Black Hills Motorcycle Classic Board with "Sturgis Rally and Races, Inc.," a private, for-profit promotional company charged with more effectively managing the growth and promotion of the event. SRRI changed the name of the event from the Black Hills Motor Classic to the Sturgis Rally and Races in 1992 in order to more fully promote the City and its legacy cache as one of the oldest motorcycle events in the country. Professional promotion is at least partly responsible for the massive increases in revenue after 1990. The number of vendor licenses grew by over 400% between 1990 and 2000. Similarly, rally revenues increased to $3 million in 1990 and to $14.3 million by 2000 (Sturgis Motorcycle Rally Statistics, 2015).

Yet despite these significant revenue increases, the Rally actually provided limited revenue to the City of Sturgis through 2011. The Rally was a net loss to the city every year through 2005, and by 2010 Rally revenue remained below $400,000 (Sponsorship Open House, 2015). The City of Sturgis began to improve these outcomes between 2012–2014 by significantly revising vendor license fees and launching a concerted effort to police sales tax remission. Prior to 2012, city vendor fees were charged a modest flat fee; in 2013 the fee was increased by $50, and in 2014 the fee restructured to a per-square footage charge that more than doubled the revenues from some large-space vendors. Similarly, the city had little authority in policing vendor taxes prior to 2012. According to South Dakota State law, failure to remit taxes is a misdemeanor, and only becomes a felony offence if the vendor fails to remit more than once during a twelve month period. Since most Rally vendors are itinerant and travel the rally circuit from state to state throughout the year, they have little incentive to accurately report their sales and remit their taxes. According to Sturgis City Planner Dan Ainslie, limited tax reporting, coupled with community fears that vendors would intentionally avoid what they considered a "punitive tax environment," kept City officials from effectively policing vendor taxes until very recently (D. Ainslie, personal communication, 10 September 2012). In 2013, the City of Sturgis, in conjunction with the Sturgis police department, stepped up efforts to enforce sales tax reporting. In 2015 the Sturgis City Council enacted an ordinance requiring all vendors to provide point of sale receipts and maintain physical receipts for auditing purposes (2015 Rally Reports, 2015). Both measures appear to have had the greatest impact on improving city revenues, which increased from $474,000 to $1.6 M between 2011 and 2015 (Sponsorship Open House, 2015).

Most recently, however, micro-primitive accumulation has threatened Sturgis' progress toward accessing and controlling Rally revenue. In an attempt to better capture Rally revenue the City of Sturgis turned over control of important Rally trademarks, including the name of the city itself. In 2011, Sturgis Motorcycle Rally, Inc, a private corporation, acquired trademark ownership over the name Sturgis for any use associated with the Rally (it also acquired trademark control over the names Sturgis Motorcycle Rally, Sturgis Bike Week, Take the Ride to Sturgis, Sturgis Rally & Races, and Black Hills.) The Sturgis Chamber of Commerce spent several years and thousands of dollars trying to clarify trademark control, arguing that the name "Sturgis" (among others) were geographic references and thus could not be copywritten. In 2013, the City abandoned the legal search for copyright clarification and chose to ink a 5 year contract with SMRi, agreeing to forfeit 10% of its sponsorship revenue (roughly $25,000 annually) for the right to use its own name (Holland, 2013, 30 July). The role of SMRi provides an interesting example of micro-primitive accumulation. SMRi has no owners or shareholders. It is run by a volunteer board with positions that interlock with the Sturgis Area Chamber of Commerce, City of Sturgis, Sturgis Area Commercial Property Owners, and rally- and non-rally oriented businesses. The contract with SMRi forced the city to give up control over its name to a collection of community interests with relatively little public transparency. While it is certainly true that, as a non-profit, SMRi distributes its revenue to dozens of local charities and projects, the City has less influence over the direction and use these contributions. Instead, the stewarding of the Rally's intellectual property remains detached from the community from which the trademark itself takes its name.

As discussed earlier, the development of Rally venues east of the City after 1982 threatened to shift the epicenter of Rally and forestall City revenue (see Figure 12). This competition became even more pronounced as the City of Sturgis struggled to extract greater revenue from the Rally. For example, when the City raised license fees for vendors within the city limits in 2013, the Meade County Commission responded by reducing its fees on vendors outside the city limits. While advocates praised the policy as a "pro-business decision" that fought local and state governments' tendency to "raise fees and put more restrictions on vendors every year." (Meade Country lowers vendor fees, 2013), we suggest that County government extended financial benefits to private industries at the expense of its own tax paying residents.

An even more bizarre example of micro-primitive accumulation occurred when one of the largest east campgrounds, the Legendary Buffalo Chip, filed for municipal status with the Meade County Commission. Founded the year before the City of Sturgis closed the city part to public camping, the Buffalo Chip has since developed the infrastructure (electricity, water, sewer, and high-speed internet) to accommodate hundreds of RVs, campers, and tents on its 600 acre grounds. The campgrounds owner, Rod Woodruff, along with 43 people who held permanent addresses (though largely absentee residence) at the campground filed for municipal status in early 2015, their rationale squarely positioned in the neoliberal agenda of protecting business interests from a perceived deteriorating political and economic climate:

> ...we needed the security of being able to control our own destiny and becoming a municipality by bikers for bikers that has that dedication and that devotion to individual freedom and for basic promotion of American free enterprise allows us to be able to tell these businesses what they can expect in the future if they make an investment here.
>
> HUNTINGTON, 2015

Citing a list of concerns, including the need to add infrastructure for firefighting and wastewater management (at Sturgis residence tax expense), fear over the new municipality annexing nearby lands for increase its tax base, barriers to Sturgis growth eastward, and competition with Sturgis for Federal grants, the City of Sturgis and local residents spent much of early 2015 fighting the incorporation in South Dakota State court (Holland, 2015, 20 February). When arguments countering the residency status of campground occupants and attempts to annex property that would put the campground illegally close to the Sturgis City limits failed (Holland, 2015, 3 May), the Meade County Commission approved the municipality vote, which the campground residents passed 43–0 on May 13, 2015. At the time of publication, several interest groups, including the City of Sturgis, local landowners, and the South Dakota Municipal League have challenged the incorporation, saying that the Meade County Commission wrongfully approved the incorporation based upon a misreading of the statutory powers of the campground's fictitious residents (Holland, 2016).

Throughout the fight, East Campground officials maintained that incorporation of the Buffalo Chip would not adversely affect Sturgis Rally business, stating that "it should benefit them quite a bit, because if we're able to attract businesses here and more people they should be able to develop more retail" (Wooster, 2015). But in this odd case of micro-primitive accumulation, where the private becomes public in order to fuel private enterprise and the boundaries between state and corporate completely overlap, incorporation provides a number of important economic advantages to the Buffalo Chip Campground that would not otherwise be available. As a municipality, Buffalo Chip can control its own zoning, licensing and regulation; Buffalo Chip can sell up to 3 liquor licenses, which the newly elected town council met to discuss within a week of incorporation. Buffalo Chip announced it would begin levying a 2 percent sales tax in 2016 (Buffalo Chip to begin collecting taxes, 2015). Incorporation allows Buffalo Chip to issue tax free municipal bonds (Huntington, 2015) and compete with the City of Sturgis for State and Federal grants, development funds and other public free gifts, but the overlapping boundaries between Buffalo Chip and the Buffalo Chip Campground make suspect the level at which these sources of public funding will serve private corporate interests.

Finally, for some time the east Sturgis Rally venues and the bikers who patronize them have wanted a more direct route between themselves and the interstate (Stemp, 2015; Sturgis Biker's Scenic Byway, 2015). Currently, the two most direct routes between Interstate 90 and venues east of the city are Old Stone Road and the I-90, Hwy. 34 exit (See Figure 12). The former is a twisting, mostly gravel road that runs northeast along Fort Meade Recreation Park before joining Hwy. 34 on the edge of the city; the latter directs traffic, most importantly air-cooled Harley Davidson motorcycles, through the Sturgis city center, which is reduced to a 100+ degree stop-and-go, bumper-to-bumper traffic jam during the early weeks of August. In early 2014, the Meade County Commission proposed a Tax-Increment Financing (TIF) district that would include a paved road directly linking Pleasant Valley Road at I-90 exit 37 with County Highway 34/79 immediately west of the Buffalo Chip Campground entrance (see Figure 12). Citing the need to provide a secondary emergency access to the Fort Meade Veterans Administration Hospital, the Commission proposed the $3.5–$8.5 million project amidst a massive TIF district: over 600 square miles including a portion of the proposed Keystone Pipeline and one of Keystone's major pumping stations. When it became clear that the TIF would divert revenues from the Sturgis School district, school board officials and members of the Meade County Taxpayers for Responsible Government launched a campaign against the District (Heidelberger, 2014), which was defeated in a public referendum in spring 2015 (VanOstrand, 2015).

Despite public criticism, the Meade County Commission moved forward with an alternate plan to develop a less expensive unpaved road along the same route. Earlier in the year, the owner of the Buffalo Chip campground pledged $1 million of his private funds to support the road and alleviate the public tax burden. The contract was written to release the owner from this financial obligation should the bids come in lower than expected (below $1.6 million). In November 2015, Meade County Commissioners awarded a $1.3 million contract to a Rapid City contractor to begin construction, absolving the campground owner from the financial agreement and ensuring the road would be predominantly financed by public funds (Matthews, 2015).

Public funding for Fort Meade Way, or the "Biker's Scenic Byway" as it has come to be called, is another example of the role of public free gifts in economies of spectatorship. The Byway clearly serves the economic interest of private Rally enterprises east of the Sturgis city limits. Like the Interstate 80 Iowa Speedway bypass, the Biker's Scenic Byway, paid for with predominantly public funds, will re-route traffic around the city of Sturgis, effectively forestalling the city and funneling spectators and their dollars directly into privately owned venues. According to the Meade County Geographic Information System, several owners of prominent Rally venues east of the city also own property directly on the proposed Byway route. Meade County Taxpayers for Responsible Government have voiced concerns that, while the Byway is being referred to as a "section line road," the route actually runs through the middle of sections, giving these property owners complete control over economic development on both sides of the Byway's frontage and ensuring future private gain paid for by public dollars (Meade County Taxpayers for Responsible Government, 2015).

In sum, while the economic benefit of the Rally to the City of Sturgis has grown significantly over the past half-decade, the context of neoliberalism and the forces of micro-primitive accumulation have become game changers in this new economy of spectacle. Intellectual property management, competition over vendor license fees, the incorporation of Buffalo Chip, and the Biker's Scenic Byway threaten the economic advantages of the Rally to the public and, more importantly, increasingly divert public dollars into private corporate growth. Micro-primitive accumulation was central to the development of the economies of spectacle at Iowa Speedway and the Sturgis Motorcycle Rally. In both cases, public funds channeled into the infrastructure of spectacle became free gifts to private capital. Neoliberalism did not free capital from government: capitalists were less interested in getting government off their back than getting government on their bandwagon. Capital and the state were increasingly intertwined under neoliberalism, blurring interstices between public and private, eroding transparency and masking the flow of public dollars to the private sector.

The Structure of Economies of Spectacle

The previous chapter highlighted difficulties encountered by residents of New-ton, Iowa and Sturgis, South Dakota as they attempted to make a living with motorsports spectacles. In this chapter, we model the structure of economies of spectacle. Our model evolved significantly as our study progressed, initially framed in terms of Debord's spectacle (1967; 1988), culture industry (Adorno, 1991), immaterial production (Hardt & Negri, 2005), digital labour and audi-ence commodity (Fuchs, 2014), working consumers (Cova & Dali, 2009), pro-sumption (Ritzer & Jurgensen, 2010; Ritzer, 2014), and consumer culture theory (Arnould & Thompson, 2005). We have borrowed insights from other authors, but the model, framing and conceptualization constructed to organize our case material are unique to this study. This model was tuned to our primary cases (NASCAR and large-displacement motorcycle rallies like Sturgis) and refined through sustained comparison and contrast against other economic spectacles, including European Grand Prix racing (Formula 1), rally racing, bi-cycle racing, sailboat racing, professional sports and collegiate athletics. The model we present here is a Weberian ideal type, a heuristic to render meaning-ful interpretation of our cases, but is general enough for meaningful interpre-tation of other spectacular economies. We begin with a summary of the basic parts and overall structure of our model (see Figure 13):

> An economy of spectacle develops upon *enclosure* of fascinating social forms circulating within the cultural commons. These enclosed cultural forms must radiate social energy (Durkheimian *collective effervescence* or Benjaminian *aura*), shine with *legend* (imaginary narratives that are widely-shared, ritually-honored, culturally-valorized) and manifest *action* (chanciness, risk, danger, uncertainty, fatefulness). Enclosures privatize the cultural commons, transforming collective life into private intellectual property that functions as immaterial capital. Enclosures are legal but also physical, controlling access to a *spectacular diegesis*. Enclo-sures enables three intertwined economic markets to develop: *spectator markets* (payments to see the privatized spectacle), *sponsorship markets* (payments to be seen within the privatized spectacle) and *trophy markets* (payments to obtain valorizing proof of attendance). *Broadcast* and *digital* modes of spectatorship frequently augment *in-venue* profit streams. The dynamics of economies of spectacle result from dialectical interactions between these three markets and three modes of spectatorship.

FIGURE 13   *The Structure of Economies of Spectacles*
SOURCE: PHOTOGRAPH BY AUTHORS.

The structure of the NASCAR economy of spectacle is outlined in Table 6. Along the top of the table are the three markets that formed around the enclosed racing diegesis: spectator markets (paying to see), sponsorship markets (paying to be seen), and trophy markets (paying to be seen enjoying). Along the vertical axis are three modes of NASCAR spectatorship: in-venue, broadcast, and digital. We flesh out this structure with a discussion of enclosures and spectator infrastructures that generate in-venue spectator markets. The assembled spectators, having paid to view the diegesis, find their eyes and attention packaged and sold as an "audience commodity" (Smythe, 1981) to sponsors and advertisers. This second sponsorship market is particularly developed and specialized within NASCAR and accounts for the tremendous value of NASCAR's broadcast rights. Trophy markets, of special centrality to both NASCAR and the Sturgis Motorcycle Rally, are treated next. We conclude the chapter by considering dynamics in spectacular economies generated by these different components.

Paying to See: Cultural Commons, Enclosures and Spectator Markets

The social forms that were enclosed as the NASCAR diegesis had long and varied roots: racing being one of the oldest sporting activities in human history. Foot racing, horse racing, chariot racing, yacht racing, even bicycle racing were all precursors to motor racing as a social form. The specific legendary content of NASCAR differed from other auto racing series due to a strong infusion of

TABLE 6   *Structure of economic spectacles: Modes of spectatorship and triple markets*

Mode of diegetic delivery	Spectator market: Paying to see the diegesis	Sponsorship market: Paying to be seen in the diegesis	Trophy market: Paying to be seen enjoying
In-Venue Spectatorship: Admissions: 20% of NASCAR Track Revenue Vending: 7% of NASCAR Track Revenue	– Admissions and Spectator Enhancements: – Event Tickets – Premium VIP – Luxury Suites – Fan Walk/Garage Access/Pit Access – Parking – Food – Beverage	Sponsorships: – Corporate – Government – Cause/NFP Entitlement/Naming – NASCAR official sponsors – Event Sponsors – Car Sponsors – Subsidiary naming and entitlement sponsorships	Merchandise Vendors – Collectibles – T-Shirts – Caps – Other merchandise Photographs and Images
Broadcast Spectatorship: Broadcast rights: 47% of NASCAR Track Revenue	– Network Broadcast Consolidated 5 year Broadcast Contract – Cable Television Subscriptions to Speed Channel or FoxSports1	Sponsorships: – Corporate – Governement – Cause/NFP – Event Sponsor – Car Sponsor – NASCAR official sponsor – Sponsored on-screen features – Advertising buys	– Water-Cooler Status
Virtually-Enhanced Spectatorship: Various Digital Revenues	– Fanvision – Raceview Simulation – Iracing/Gaming – Racebuddy – Digital Dash App – Revenue/ – Spectator – Subscriptions	– Iracing Entitle-ment Rights and Sponsorships – Digital Double of In-Venue sponsors	– Social Media postings – Gaming Scores – Retweets and Likes

backcountry, outlaw culture characteristic of the Southern hill-country that coalesced during prohibition in the early decades of the twentieth century. While other motor racing spectacles emphasized technology and purpose-built racing machines that bore little resemblance to cars and motorcycles actually used as transportation, stock car racing featured showroom models that were modified for racing. Modifications focused upon increasing the power of the engines and beefing up the chassis, the same tricks used by outlaw whiskey-runners in the wilds of the cultural commons. Early motor racing, including contests for primal honor between bootleggers, tended to be point-to-point races run on public roads, like bicycling's *Tour de France* or contemporary rally racing. It was not feasible to keep spectators away from such races, spread out over many miles of road: crowds assembled spontaneously, drawn by the legendary action, heroism and drama on display (Figure 14).

Spectators sometimes attempted to get a piece of the action by positioning themselves very close to the racecourse, even touching competitor's cars as they passed. It was not uncommon for spectators to be injured or killed, and stories circulate in contemporary rallying of competitors finishing a race to find the torn-off finger of an action-seeking spectator stuck in a side mirror.

FIGURE 14   *Spectators at Non-Enclosed Point-to-Point Race, circa 1920*
            SOURCE: LIBRARY OF CONGRESS.

The popularity of motor racing led promoters to begin enclosing the action, charging spectators an admission fee while blocking the view, sometimes crudely, of those unwilling or unable to pay (see Figure 15). More successful and typical of contemporary NASCAR racing were purpose-built enclosures: oval racetracks, originally with wood plank surfaces, surrounded by privacy fencing to thoroughly privatize the diegesis and grandstands for spectators who paid admission (Figure 16 and 17).

Frequently, the banked corners that increased racing speeds at tracks doubled as infrastructure to block non-paying eyes from viewing the spectacle (Figure 18). This reified culture of motor racing, promoted by track owners as a commodity for sale to spectators, encouraged several generations of mostly Southern, backcountry, working-class, white men, many with family or community ties to bootlegging, to enter the competition within the enclosed arena of stock car racing. With rudimentary safety equipment, crashes, injuries and death were frequent and became central to the auratic legend of stock car racing. Attending races at regional tracks often required overnight lodging or camping, with drinking, fighting and other carnivalesque activity. Hence, stock car racing, both before enclosure and afterward, was interwoven with

FIGURE 15   *Spectators Peeking through Enclosures in Early Motor Racing, circa 1920*
SOURCE: LIBRARY OF CONGRESS.

FIGURE 16   *Spectator Infrastructure near Washington, D.C., circa 1922*
SOURCE: LIBRARY OF CONGRESS.

FIGURE 17   *Enclosed Speedway with Racing Action and Spectators, circa 1922*
SOURCE: LIBRARY OF CONGRESS.

FIGURE 18   *Workers Constructing Banked Curve on Motor Speedway, circa 1910*
SOURCE: LIBRARY OF CONGRESS.

vacations, community celebrations, fairs, festivals and the like. Stock car racing radiated social energy, shined with *legend* and manifested *action*.

Racetracks and other spectator infrastructures served the dual purpose of concealment and facilitation, preventing unpaid spectatorship while providing ticket holders with effective and comfortable views. As we saw in the previous chapter, NASCAR racetracks were highly specialized and expensive facilities, requiring millions of dollars of expenditures. In actual practice, spectator infrastructures became the property of NASCAR and other sporting capitalists through micro-primitive accumulation facilitated by local communities, states and the U.S. government. Large spectator facilities required enormous blocks of land: Kansas Speedway occupied 1,200 acres, Iowa Speedway occupied 600 acres, Richmond Speedway occupied 1000 acres, Daytona Speedway occupied 480 and Talladega Speedway consumed a whopping 3,000 acres. Despite the enormous scale of these publicly-financed infrastructures, in-venue spectatorship was insufficiently profitable to support an ongoing economy of spectatorship. Revenues from physically-present spectators were supplemented by revenues derived by "doubling" the spectacle in broadcast and digital modes. In a travelling circuit like NASCAR, each venue was relatively unimportant: unlike stick and ball sports, home teams did not exist in motorsports. Each venue was entirely dependent upon NASCAR (the legal entity at the center of the entire web of contracts that constituted the sport) for economic survival.

In NASCAR, speedways were filled with spectators just a few days annually: the rest of the year they were anti-capital whose massive inert presence produced no value while foreclosing other, more temporally continuous usage. At the local level, the growth coalitions and economic development corporations who funded these spectator infrastructures hoped that their investment would trigger Faustian-level peripheral development at the rim of the infrastructure's event horizon.

Spectator markets (attendance tickets) were the primal economic transaction of economies of spectacle: in NASCAR revenues from sales of admissions to spectators at its various speedway aggregated to $332 million in 2014, or 20.3% of the revenues collected by the duopoly track owners, Speedway Motorsports, Inc. (SMI) and International Speedway Corporation (ISC). In addition to basic ticket charges, NASCAR tracks also upsold spectators premium parking, premium seating, luxury suites, special events and VIP access to drivers and teams, scanners and Fanvision devices (see digital spectatorship below), "Fan Walks" in which spectators paid stroll on the track surface before a race, and special access to team garages. In addition there were sales of basic creature comforts, such as food, beverages, raingear, cushions and backrests, all of which were notoriously expensive: though food and beverages were a small portion of overall revenue for NASCAR tracks, their profit margins were high.

Beyond In-venue Spectatorship: Broadcast Revenues and NASCAR's Profits

For NASCAR, broadcasting revenues increased sharply after 1972, when a U.S. government ban on tobacco advertising led cigarette companies to search for other ways to reach their customers. They settled upon sponsorship: rather than purchasing ads on television, R.J. Reynolds became sponsors of NASCAR's elite racing series: the Winston Cup. In exchange for payments to NASCAR, R.J. Reynold's brand name, logos and products were visible everywhere within the NASCAR diegesis. The spectators assembled to view the race became "working consumers" whose regard of logos, brand names and icons generated brand awareness that was spread whenever they interacted with NASCAR or with other fans (Smythe, 1981; see also Cova & Dalli, 2009; Ritzer, 2014). NASCAR steadily increased the number of races broadcast nationally until 2001 when all 36 Winston Cup Series races were telecast to national audiences in their entirety. The broadcast spectacle dwarfed the in-venue spectacle in terms of audience size: in 2014, in-venue attendance at races rarely exceeded 100,000 while 5 million tuned in for the average televised broadcast. By 2014, revenues from the sale of NASCAR broadcasting rights far exceeded revenues from in-venue admissions sales ($820 million per year versus $332 million) and broadcast revenues accounted for just under half of total revenue.

Paying to be seen: Sponsorship Markets and Reified Culture

There was a clear affinity between sponsorship markets and broadcast spectatorship. Large, nationwide television audiences drew in different NASCAR sponsors than in-venue races held in backcountry speedways: the plumbing distributors, muffler shops and hardware stores that had sponsored NASCAR races for decades were displaced by national consumer brands and corporate sponsors. NASCAR developed one of the largest and most profitable cross-marketing licensing networks (CMLN) ever constructed. NASCAR became, at core, a law firm that managed contracts for sponsorships, intellectual property and cross-marketing licensing agreements. NASCAR owned little tangible property. Apart from Iowa Speedway, NASCAR owned no actual racing facilities (owned by SMI and ISC), nor racing teams (owned by separate businesses), nor broadcast facilities (owned by the holders of the broadcasting rights). NASCAR was the ultimate asset-light, post-Fordist corporation. Rather than a traditional organization or production facility, NASCAR was essentially a nest of legal contracts, a spidery web of immaterial capital spun from the pen of its dealmakers and attorneys.

NASCAR Official Sponsorships

An astonishing variety of sponsors co-existed within the NASCAR "family of brands," spanning across the full terrain of contemporary capitalism. To get some sense of the size of NASCAR's web of contracts, examine the following list of forty-one corporations that purchased a marketing license from NASCAR in 2014 and gave them the right to advertise as one of NASCAR's "official sponsors." In the list that follows, the sponsorship title that was purchased for the year is in parentheses. The list includes: 3 M (Official Partner: Automotive Appearance Products), 5.11 Tactical (Official Tactical Apparel & Gear), ACORE (An Official NASCAR Green Partner: Renewable Energy), Affinity Road & Travel LLC-Good Sam (Official Partner: Roadside Assistance), Bank of America (Official Bank), Camping World (Official Outdoor and RV Retail Partner), Canadian Tire (Official Automotive Retailer), Chevrolet (Official: Automobiles), Coca-Cola (Official Non-Alcoholic Beverage, Official Soft Drink, Official Sport Drink, Official Energy Drink), Coors Light (Official Beer), DRIVE4COPD (Official Health Initiative), Exide (Official Auto Batteries), FDP Friction Science

(Official Brakes), Featherlite Coaches (Official Trailer), Featherlite Trailers (Official Trailer), Ford (Official Partner: Automobiles), Freescale (Official Automotive Semiconductors), Freightliner (Official Big Rig, Official Hauler), Goodyear (Official Tire), Green Earth Technologies (An Official NASCAR Green Partner), Growth Energy (Official Partner: American Corn-Based Ethanol), Hewlett-Packard (An Official Technology Partner), K&N (Official Partner: NASCAR K&N Pro Series), Mars (Official Chocolate, Official Chocolate Bar), McLaren Electronics Systems (Official Engine Control Unit Supplier), Mobil 1 (Official Partner: Lubricant, Motor Oil, Gear Lube, Automotive Grease), Mondelez [Kraft] (Official Cookies and Crackers), National Corn Growers Association (Official Partner: Promoting the Interest of Corn Growers), Nationwide Insurance (Official Auto, Home and Life Insurance), New Holland (Official Partner: Agricultural Equipment), Prevost (Official Luxury Motorcoach), Safety-Kleen (Official Supplier: Automotive Waste Removal), Sherwin Williams (Official Paint of NASCAR), SIRIUS XM Radio (Official Satellite Radio Partner), Sprint (Official Series Sponsor: Telecommunications), Sunoco (Official Fuel and Official Convenience Store), Toyota (Official Partner: Automobiles), UPS (Official Delivery Service), UTI (Official Partner: Automotive Education), Visa (Official Card), Whelen (Official Partner: Series Sponsor, Safety Lighting) (NASCAR official sponsors, 2015, n.p.). This long list of almost comical sponsorships mirrors those at the Sturgis Motorcycle Rally (see Figure 19).

FIGURE 19   *Official Sponsorships at Sturgis Motorcycle Rally: South Dakota Pork Producers*
SOURCE: PHOTOGRAPH BY AUTHORS.

Racetrack Sponsorships

Racetracks also signed cross-marketing licensing agreements, usually including NASCAR as a partner, with sponsors seeking entitlement rights to racetracks ("Lowe's Motor Speedway," "Autoclub Speedway," "Infineon Speedway"), events ("Spongebob Squarepants 400," "Duck Commander 500," "Coca-Cola 600"), or subsidiary entitlements within race venues. At Iowa Speedway, for example, entitlement rights were available to "put your name on highly visible facilities on the track" that included "Annual Naming Rights" for "Speedway, Newton Club, Pizza Ranch Victory Lane, Party Decks, General Campground, Reserved Campground, Casey's Fan Walk, Hospitality Village, Garage, Suite Tower, Mediacom Media Center, MidAmericanTech Building. Fan Tram, Scoring Pylon" (Naming Rights, 2015, n.p.). In addition to these sponsorships, racetracks sold vendor space that was often occupied by NASCAR official sponsors, track sponsors, event sponsors or race team sponsors as seen in Figure 20 and Figure 21.

Race Team/Car Sponsorships

Race teams also sold sponsorships for individual racecars that were subdivided on a variety of ways. Primary sponsors received a larger space on the car for their logo than did associate sponsors, who received as little as a square foot of space on the rear quarter panel of the car, which was often difficult to read at 200 m.p.h. Sponsorships also varied by the number of races covered by the sponsorship agreement (ranging from a single race to an entire season), during which time the racecar and its driver were contracted to wear branded livery (Figure 22). Hendrick Motorsports. a premiere owner of race teams, lists seventeen primary sponsors (3 M, Axalta, Diet Mountain Dew, Farmers Insurance, Drive to End Hunger, Great Clips, to name a few) and nineteen associate sponsors (Mac Tools, Miller Welders, Lord Ask Us How) for four race teams (Partners, 2015, n.p.). With forty-three cars entered in each race, hundreds of corporate sponsorships are activated each week, all covered by a cross-marketing licensing agreement. The brands that have festooned NASCAR driver's firesuits have included traditional consumer brands (Coca-Cola, Tide, Target, Viagra), less well-known brands (Boudreaux's Butt Paste, RedneckJunk.com, Depend Undergarments), military and governmental units (Army, Navy, Airforce, Marines, Coast Guard, National Guard, U.S. Border Patrol), political campaigns (Rick Santorum, Rick Perry, Bob Graham) and less frequently, religious organizations ("Racing with Jesus").

Broadcast Sponsorships

The broadcast spectacle creates opportunities for additional sponsorships. The broadcast diegesis is distinct from that in-venue (different announcers,

FIGURE 20   *Sponsors and Vending at NASCAR, circa 2003*
SOURCE: PHOTOGRAPH BY AUTHORS.

full array of dynamic camera angles, replays, advertising). Brands that purchase prominent "in-venue" sponsorships will generally get some exposure
on the broadcast spectacle: cars and drivers are in livery, advertising panels
are installed on raceway walls, branded logos are etched upon tarps that cover
unused stands and these will be picked up by cameras and broadcast to television audience (Figure 23). Event sponsors and "official sponsors" purchase
airtime to run commercials that infuses their brand with the aura, legend

FIGURE 21   *Sponsor and Vending at NASCAR: Cabot Cheese and the 1,500 pound Cheddar Cheese*
            #5 Chevrolet, circa 2003
            SOURCE: PHOTOGRAPH BY AUTHORS.

FIGURE 22   *Sponsors and Livery on Racecars and Teams, circa 2010*
            SOURCE: LIBRARY OF CONGRESS.

FIGURE 23   *Sponsorships, Low Attendance and Tarp "Pastie" Covering Empty Stands, circa 2011*
SOURCE: CREATIVE COMMONS, FLICKR.COM.

or collective effervescence of NASCAR. Many commercials feature NASCAR drivers in branded livery directly hawking the virtues of sponsor's products.

The outsized value of NASCAR's broadcast rights contract was accounted for by the attention that working consumers devoted to sponsors, brands and commercials during race broadcasts. In 2015, NASCAR Sprint Cup contract holders (Fox/Fx1 and NBC) televised a total of 108 hours and 9 minutes of racing-related content that was intercut with 4,537 traditional television commercials lasting 29 hours and 50 minutes. In addition, NASCAR race telecasts were shrunk to half-screen to air an additional 529 split-screen commercials lasting 4 hours and 8 minutes. Further, NASCAR races carried 2,963 brief sponsor promotions that floated across the broadcast diegesis. In addition, the average NASCAR sponsor received 2 hours, 47 minutes and 28 seconds of on-air exposure within the broadcast racing diegesis over the course of the 2015 NASCAR season (Walker, 2016). Given an audience of 5 million for the average Sprint Cup series telecast, more than 550 million hours were worked by consumers attending to traditional commercials and perhaps another 200 million hours attending to split-screen ads and brief promos. However, because NASCAR's broadcast diegesis was so thoroughly penetrated by brands, logos and advertising, even if viewers used a DVR to skip commercials, they were always already working while watching the race. While the size of the audience commodity and the total working-consumer labor-time for broadcasts from Iowa Speedway were somewhat lower—Indy Racing League, NASCAR Nationwide Series and NASCAR Camping World Truck Series Races drew smaller broadcast audiences—broadcast revenues nevertheless exceeded in-venue admissions. We could not find another economic spectacle that developed broadcast sponsorship markets more completely and profitably than NASCAR. Sponsors not only bought large volumes of consumer attention, but also transferred the social energy of outlaw legend, driver charisma and the aura of dangerous action directly onto their brands and into their commodities.

Paying to be seen Enjoying: Trophy Markets and the Trophy Logic of Spectacle

As spectatorship grows in scale, vendors in and around speedways expand the scope of their offerings from immediate consumables for creature comfort (food, beverage) to wearable and totable merchandise. These products form the base of the third market to form around a spectacular diegesis: trophy markets. Themed apparel and licensed products function as trophies that display proof of participation in a scene of legendary enjoyment. Trophy markets are remarkably prominent in motorsports venues like NASCAR and Sturgis: admission to a speedway or motorcycle rally requires spectators to navigate a maze of merchandise vendors, hawking themed apparel and licensed collectibles. Branded and cross-marketed t-shirts constituted the largest segment of the trophy market at motorsports spectacles. These t-shirts typically depicted the purchaser's favorite driver. Displays of affiliation with a particular driver were frequently wearing jackets and caps that mimicked the firesuit livery worn by drivers and crew, including again, prominent displays of sponsor's brand images. At major NASCAR races, and at the Sturgis Motorcycle Rally, the most sought-after wearable trophies were those that commemorated the event: 2012 Daytona 500 t-shirts, for example, or the ubiquitous date-stamped, officially licensed Sturgis Motorcycle Rally t-shirts (see Figure 24). These t-shirts, when worn back home in the spectator's workaday life, were insignia of participation in the event, evidence that the wearer was present at the scene of action, proof of enjoyment. Photo opportunities, especially selfies that place the image of the spectator squarely within the diegesis, were particularly powerful trophies

FIGURE 24   *Trophy Market and Vending at Sturgis Motorcycle Rally, circa 2012*
              SOURCE: PHOTOGRAPH BY AUTHORS.

that were pursued with single-minded purpose by trophy-hunting spectators. Motorsports venues met the demand for such photo opportunities by
organizing meet-and-greet sessions with drivers or providing tableau scenes
fully kitted out with legendary imagery and themed props as a convenient
backdrop for photographs. Digital technology and social media dramatically
transformed trophy markets in recent years: digital trophies in the form
ofreal-time, in-venue postings to social media have displaced wearable and
displayable merchandise as preferred trophies. This has prompted NASCAR
to outsource its licensed merchandising business while investing heavily in
digital media. NASCAR's 2016 Daytona Rising project, a $400 million (partially
publicly funded) makeover of Daytona Speedway, features vastly upgraded
wifi and cellular capabilities to enable in-venue spectators to post digital trophies in real-time. NASCAR's investment in digital spectatorship seems driven
by the belief that social media will increase the pool of people who are "white
hot" about NASCAR events, thereby increasing demand for in-venue attendance while increasing the magnitude of envy charging their trophies. Trophy
markets, trophy hunting and trophy display are the focus of Chapter 6.

Broadcast Spectatorship, the Sponsorship Market and the Thickened Diegesis

Enclosure, technological reproduction and broadcast lead to a thickening of the diegesis: new content, streams of images, music, and information that were not originally part of the spectacular legend, were layered upon the in-venue diegesis. For example, NASCAR speedways were remarkably devoid of technical data because the noise of race engines drowned out announcers, no replays of moments of action were possible, and the only numerical data available was a pole that displayed running order of the cars. NASCAR broadcasts "thickened" the diegesis by overlaying data streams: telecasts included leaderboards, lap-times, pit sequencing, vehicle speeds and dynamic cameras that replayed moments of action from every conceivable angle. After 2007, NASCAR developed multiple platforms for digital spectatorship, including in-venue UHF broadcasted "Fanvision" devices that provided in-venue spectators with the data streams and multiple camera angles available on broadcasts. Other technologies included Raceview, a subscription service that provided a digitally streamed simulation of a race rendered in real-time using telemetry data from race teams. Racebuddy, a non-subscription digital streaming service that provided digital spectators with limited multi-angle views from in-car cameras. A number of smartphone applications are in development to further develop digital spectatorship as a source of revenue.

The thickening of the diegesis also leads to a phenomena we identify as *progressive decontextualization* of diegetic content. Broadcast spectatorship obviously represented a spatial decontextualization: NASCAR events staged in the rural South were viewed by a diverse, geographically dispersed audience. As sponsorship shifted to national and global consumer brands, NASCAR expanded its racetrack circuit to the Midwest, West, Canada, Mexico and even, in one instance, to Japan, to solidify its national and international audience. Demographic and cultural decontextualization followed: NASCAR's legendary diegesis (outlaw, southern, white, male) matched its audience in the 1970s, but by the 2000s NASCAR sought to expand spectatorship to match sponsor's desired audience. In the 2000s, NASCAR began to consciously reconstruct its diegesis to attract more diverse spectators. New drivers were cultivated who were young, educated, and non-Southern. NASCAR further launched a "Drive for Diversity" program to cultivate a new generation of women drivers and drivers from diverse racial backgrounds.

Once global consumer brands became deeply invested in NASCAR sponsorship deals and advertising buys, NASCAR was compelled to reconstruct its broadcast spectacle to displace unprofitable in-venue spectators with a much

FIGURE 25   *Camouflaged Seating to Mask Empty Stadium, Daytona Motor Speedway, 2012*
            SOURCE: PHOTOGRAPH BY AUTHORS.

larger and lucrative audience. In-venue activities and imagery offensive to the national audience, such as the carnivalesque partying, right-wing authoritarian politics and Confederate Flags, were kept discretely off-screen. Race broadcasts avoided showing mundane in-venue images that ran counter to the carefully controlled diegetic content: aging fans, large sections of beer-swilling white good-ol'-boys, and especially, empty stands devoid of spectators. After 2007, the half-empty grandstands made the declining popularity of NASCAR all-too-apparent to television viewers, so steps were made to mask the absence of spectators by covering large sections of unoccupied seats with tarps and by hiring a military camouflage expert to design seating that appeared identical on-camera whether empty or full (see Figure 25). While white southern rock and country music could be heard in-venue at NASCAR speedways, to attract a younger, more diverse and sponsor-friendly demographic, broadcasts were scored with youthful rock music from diverse bands.

The Structure of the Sturgis Economy of Spectacle

As outlined in Table 7, the Sturgis Motorcycle Rally shared most of the structural features and moving parts that we saw in NASCAR. In-venue spectator

TABLE 7   *Structure of economic spectacles: Modes of spectatorship and triple markets in Sturgis Motorcycle Rally*

Mode of spectatorship	Spectator market: Paying to see the diegesis	Sponsorship market: Paying to be seen in the diegesis	Trophy market: Paying to be seen enjoying
In-Venue Spectatorship:	– Admissions and Spectator Enhancements: – Event Tickets – Premium Access – Cover Charges – Camping and Lodging Fees – Parking – Food – Beverage – Raingear – Medical and wellness services	Sponsorships: – Corporate – Government – Cause/NFP Entitlement/Naming – Rally official sponsors – Event Sponsors – Subsidiary naming and entitlement sponsorships – Advertising Sales	Merchandise Vendors – Collectibles – T-Shirts – Caps – Other merchandise – body painting – tattoos and piercings Photographs and Images
Broadcast Spectatorship:	– Undeveloped – Various Sturgis-themed television specials, mostly cable – Full Throttle Saloon Series	Sponsorships: – Advertising buys on limited Sturgis-themed broadcasting	– Water-Cooler Status Marker
Virtually-Enhanced Spectatorship:	Undeveloped	Undeveloped	– Social Media postings – Retweets and Likes

markets were highly developed: bars, restaurants, saloons and campgrounds collected admissions fee or cover charges for entry. During the Rally, the built-environment of the town was repurposed as profit-making vacation lodging, camping, and vending space. A large portion of the spectator market met creature needs: food and beverages, especially alcohol, were sold throughout Sturgis venues. The sponsorship market was also in full evidence: like NASCAR, the Sturgis Motorcycle Rally generated cross-marketing licensing agreements with official sponsors of the Rally, and corporate branding, logos, banners are replete throughout rally venues. Compared to NASCAR, the Sturgis trophy market assumed greater economic prominence: trophy vending was widespread, with a greater diversity of merchandise, tattooing, body piercing, body painting, and themed wearables. As we detail in Chapter 6, opportunities for digital trophy taking were highly organized and a central activity at the rally. In contrast to NASCAR, broadcast and digital spectatorship were undeveloped at the Sturgis Motorcycle Rally, which remained more participative, carnivalesque event than the butts-in-seats passivity typical of NASCAR audiences.

To conclude, both the diegesis at both NASCAR and Sturgis were not merely enclosed but intensely managed, strategically manipulated, and carefully staged to profitably stimulate spectator's desire, to attract eyeballs and hold them intensely. The progressive decontextualization that accompanies broadcast and digital spectatorship threatens to degrade the collective effervescence, legends and action around which the entire economy of spectacle is organized. As we describe in Chapter 5, cross-marketing licensing networks (CMLNS) intervene to revitalize their intellectual property and immaterial capital through legend work.

Paying to See: Spectator Markets, the Outlaw Biker Legend and the Sturgis Motorcycle Rally

Mature capitalism, theorized by Guy Debord as the age of the integrated spectacle, is marked by an erasure of boundaries separating culture and commodities.[1] Critical theory has framed this effacement primarily as the *spectacularization of commodities*, in which commodity-images circulate as capitalism's most immediate and potent ideological legitimation. The culture industry that produces spectacular commodities has long been analyzed in terms of the "dialectics of enlightenment" (Adorno & Horkheimer, 1972); a source of ideology and legitimation that negates autonomous subjectivity in modernity. In Debord's own words, spectacle is "ideology *par excellence*" (2006 [1967], para. 215; see also Halnon, 2004; Jay, 1993; Kennedy, 2009; Worrell, 2009). The spectacularization of commodities occurs when their surface images are split off and absorbed into spectacle. Reduced to their ideological function, spectacularized commodities are not so much economic objects of consumption as political objects of legitimation.

Late capitalism is marked not only by this *spectacularization of commodities* but also by the *commodification of spectacle*. This chapter explores this other side of spectacle, in which products of the culture industry are exchanged and consumed as commodities in and of themselves. Emphasizing the *industry* in Adorno & Horkheimer's (1972) concept of the culture industry, we conceptualize spectacle and spectacular cultural products as dominant commodities in their own right; as one of mature capitalism's leading growth industries and an increasingly important source of profit.[2] Keeping with Debord's Marxist

---

1   Debord referred to this assimilation of commodity and spectacle in many passages in his writings, often conceptualizing spectacle as "the main production of present-day society" (2006 [1967]a: 15), "the commodity-form in its 'absolute realization'" (2006 [1967]a: 66), "the commodity dominating all that is lived" (2006 [1967]a: 37), and "the commodity [in] total occupation of social life" (2006 [1967]a: 42).

2   The increasing centrality of spectacular commodities to global capitalism is demonstrated by examining lists of the highest valued corporations, many of which produce spectacle or devices that deliver spectacle: Apple, Microsoft, Google, Amazon, Facebook, Verizon, Motorola, Virgin, etc. Expenditures on spectacular commodities and the devices that deliver them constitute a large percentage of consumer spending central to industries including cable television, wireless telephony, streaming content providers, digital gaming, satellite,

FIGURE 26   *Decontextualized spectatorship infrastructure at the Sturgis Motorcycle Rally, Full*
                Throttle Saloon, Circa 2013
                SOURCE: PHOTOGRAPH BY AUTHORS.

lineage (Best & Kellner, 1997; Gotham & Krier, 2008; Jappe, 1999; Worrell, 2009),
our work subjects cultural manifestations of spectacle to materialist analysis
and emphasizes the economics of spectatorship over the society of spectacle.
While others dwell upon political implications of the society of spectacle, we
theorize the political economy based upon spectatorship. In mature capitalism, spectacles have become predominant commodities that are produced,
exchanged and consumed within *economies of spectatorship*. In this chapter,

event tickets, computers, cell phones, travel and tourism. The Forbes list of the 400 wealthiest Americans includes many founders and owners of spectacular businesses (*Forbes 400*,
2013). As we find in our study of Sturgis, the expenditures upon "cruiser" v-twin motorcycles
constitutes spectacular consumption (i.e. participation in outlaw narratives) rather than
"automobility" (a much overused concept in the analysis of motoring). Even durable-goods
manufacturers have become increasingly "spectacularized": the "value" of many American
manufacturing corporations resides in their "brand equity" and "goodwill" rather than in
their manufacturing facilities, workforce or management. The aftermath of corporate mergers is often the complete shutdown of actual, tangible manufacturing as the valuable "brand"
is attached to other, cheaper products—the fates of Sunbeam Corporation (Krier, 2005) and
Maytag Corporation (Krier, 2009a, 2009b) are two particularly clear examples.

alterations in what we term *spectacular diegesis* (projected cultural content within spectacle, its narrative reality[3]) are caused by dynamics internal to the economy of spectatorship (and not the other way round). Our economic focus leads us to explain changes in spectacular diegeses, including the integration of diverse corporate, political and religious elements, as ancillary to profit extraction. Thus, rather than focusing upon spectacle as a late stage of capitalism (Debord, 1988, 2006 [1967]), a contested realm of politics (Gotham, 2002, 2012; Kozinets, 2002; Langman, 2012; Lundskow, 2012) or a consumer culture exploited for marketing and advertising (Gottdiener, 2001; Ritzer, 2005, 2013; Schouten and McAlexander, 1993, 1995), we conceptualize economies of spectatorship as relatively autonomous economic circuits whose dynamics are primarily determined by their own cycles of production, exchange, and consumption.

This chapter contributes to critical theories of spectacle in several ways. First, we develop disciplined terminology (essentially Weberian ideal types) to describe and analyze geographically and temporally bounded economies of spectatorship. Our concepts were refined through case analysis of *one* concrete instance of such an economy that manifests dynamics consistent with Debord's integrated spectacle: the Sturgis Motorcycle Rally. The material specificity and clear temporal and spatial boundaries of the Sturgis Rally render visible the complex developmental processes and inherent contradictions hidden beneath sweeping generalizations of spectacle as a universal ideological system or stage of capitalism.

Second, economies of spectatorship extract profit by commodifying a unique spectacular diegesis, a privatized legend that spectators pay to see and sponsors pay to be seen within. In our case, the predominantly upper middle-class desire for spectatorship in a spectacular diegesis so famously degraded as the Sturgis Motorcycle Rally seemed counterintuitive. To account for it, we refine Goffman's (1967) theory of action to explain spectators' desire for the Sturgis legend. As the Sturgis Motorcycle Rally became increasingly infused with outlaw biker legend, organizers produced and marketed the diegesis as *consumable character gamble:* an opportunity for law-abiding consumers to find action by playing outlaw biker. Selling action and "ephemeral debasement" also predominates in other economies of spectatorship that produce

---

3 We borrow the concept of diegesis from film theory and literary studies, where it is used as a heuristic to separate the narrative world taken as real by characters from extra-narrative voice-overs, titles, musical scores and the like (Walker, 2006: 418). A spectacular diegesis is the narrative that is produced as the primary cultural commodity of an economy of spectatorship. Spectators pay to see (consume) the spectacular diegesis and sponsors pay to be seen within it.

narratives associated with the violence and machismo of the rural working class—for example, the National Association of Stock Car Racing (NASCAR).

Third, we conceptualize the dialectical, self-negating dynamic inherent to economies of spectatorship as *progressive decontextualization*. Strategies pursued to maximize profits within economies of spectatorship inevitably lead to diegetic incoherence as increasingly unrelated spectators, sponsors, and cultural content are layered upon the original commodified legends. The progressive decontextualization of spectacular times, locations and themes reaches a crisis point when the commodified diegesis becomes so muddied (see figure 26) that profitable spectatorship is threatened. In our case, as organizers and promoters of the Sturgis Rally sought to maximize profit from spectators, they coupled the Rally to law-abiding corporate, religious and political themes that contradicted its outlaw biker legend. This progressive decontextualization produced a level of diegetic incoherence that required active maintenance and capital investment by Rally organizers in order to stabilize declining attendance and sustain the circuit of profit.[4]

We begin by tracing the historical development of the Rally's commodity: its spectacular diegesis themed with outlaw biker legend. We then explain spectators' desire to see and sponsors' desire to be seen within outlaw biker culture as an action filled consumable character gamble. After 1980, the Rally achieved near total commodification as its diegesis was exploited by highly diverse corporate sponsors and vendors. In addition, as the Rally entered Debord's age of the integrated spectacle divergent religious and political themes were overlaid upon its outlaw biker legend. We argue that such progressive decontextualization and diegetic incoherence is not unique to the Rally, and we conclude by conceptualizing such contradictory processes as inherent to economies of spectatorship.

---

4 NASCAR and America's Cup are both undergoing similar diegetic incoherence that remains puzzling to their organizers. In America's Cup and NASCAR, the technological developments within racing have progressed so far that the optics of the spectacle have strayed away from legend: in America's Cup, the boats bear little resemblance to the yachts of sailing lore nor to the boats owned by the spectators. Navy blue blazers, brass buttons, dock shoes and beautiful wooden sloops have been replaced by exoskeleton, padded floating armor, helmets, wearable technology and boats made of kevlar with fixed wings and hydrofoils. The sailing strategies, techniques and dynamics are unique to hydrofoils which limit the capacity for subjective identification of spectators with their avatars inside the diegesis.

The Origins of the Sturgis Diegesis: From Heritage Motorcycling to Outlaw Biker Legend

At present, the town of Sturgis, South Dakota has achieved near global brand recognition as the site of motorcycle legend, conjuring images of tattooed bikers in leather amidst crowds of roaring Harley-Davidsons. Today, the Sturgis Motorcycle Rally annually draws up to 500,000 participants who spill over from downtown Sturgis (population 6000) into campgrounds and motels throughout Meade County and the greater Black Hills region. Tracing its roots to 1937, the Rally began as a series of dirt-track motorcycle races and Black Hills "gypsy" rides that exploded into a mass "outlaw biker" spectator event in the mid-1960s.

The Sturgis Motorcycle Rally originated in the Black Hills Motorcycle Classic (BHMC), a weekend race sanctioned by the American Motorcycling Association and hosted by an official club, the Jackpine Gypsies (see Table 8). Unlike typical "on brand" elements of the Rally today, this early event mirrored the traits of heritage motorcycling culture of the early 20th century, in which respectable, remarkably "square" middle-class participants joined formal clubs that were more akin to civic associations than outlaw gangs (Williams, 2009; Wooster, 2010). The BHMC grew slowly for three decades, attracting fewer than a thousand spectators to a wholesome, family oriented celebration of motorcycling (American Motorcycling Association, 2002). In short, BHMC weekends manifested high levels of active participation in an intimate setting with people bonded together by shared enthusiasm for racing and motorcycle touring—more a society than a society of spectacle.

The mid-1960s marked a turning point of the transition of the BHMC into the Sturgis Motorcycle Rally. Fueled by prominent representations of outlaw biker culture in the popular media of the day, the event gradually shifted away from dirt-track motorcycle racing to become a counter-cultural gathering. This new mass of rally-goers largely ignored the formal Jackpine Gypsy dirt-track racing[5] in order to engage in a form of movie-induced tourism (Connell, 2012; Kim & Richardson, 2003; Riley, Baker & Van Doren, 1998), playfully immersing

---

5　Arguably the Jackpine Gypsies racing and hill climb events that once marked the center of the original Black Hills Motor Classic have been in steady decline to the present. Although the name of the event was changed to the Sturgis Rally and Races in 1992, the telephone survey that prompted the change revealed that the event was more widely known to the public as simply the Sturgis Rally. The reference to "Races" was only added at the request of the Jackpine Gypsies, who discontinued their participation in Sturgis Rally and Races, Inc., in 1994 (US District Court: District of South Dakota, 2000).

TABLE 8 *The progressive decontextualization of an economy of spectatorship: the Sturgis Motorcycle Rally, 1938–2013*

	Heritage Motorcycling	Counter-Cultural Gathering	Integrated Spectacle	Diegetic Incoherence
Time Period	1938–1965	1965–1985	1985–2000	2000–
Name of Spectator Event	Jackpine Gypsies Black Hills Classic	Black Hills Motorcycle Classic	Sturgis Motorcycle Rally	Sturgis Motorcycle Rally
Primary Activities	Dirt-Track Motorcycle Racing	Non- Commercialized Gathering of Bike Enthusiasts (Anti- Establishment)	Commercialized, Corporate Organized Integrated Spectacle	Ephemeral Debasement and Degraded Milling in a Decontextualized Diegesis
Approximate Attendance	200–1000	1000–60,000	60,000–633,000	550,000–400,000
Annualized Growth Rate	10.52%	295%	63.67%	(2.4%)
Length of Event	1–2 Days	5–7 Days	10 Days	10+ Days
Taxable Sales	Negligible	$150,000 -	$3m-$14.3m	$10.8m–14.3m[i]
Annualized Growth of Sales	Negligible	95%	26.67%	(2.4%)
Vendors	Negligible	9–117	117–943	943–675
Participants	Respectable, Middle-Class Racing Enthusiast	Anti- Establishment Outlaw/Hippie Biker	Respectable, Monied Middle-Class Consumer of Character Gamble	Digetically Incoherent Target Markets

SOURCE: THE CITY OF STURGIS RALLY AND EVENTS DEPARTMENT (2013A).
[i]Per conversation with Sturgis city officials, taxable sales are severely underreported by vendors to avoid paying state and local sales taxes. The actual revenues generated during the rally are many times this amount but cannot be determined. To provide some idea of the scale of this understatement, if each attendee spends $200 at the rally, this figure rises to $80,000,000.

themselves in the alternative biker lifestyles that they had seen depicted in newly popular outlaw biker films.

Economies of spectatorship emerge by producing a spectacular diegesis that fascinates spectators, holding their attention long enough to extract profit.

The spectacular diegesis of outlaw bikers that was produced by the Sturgis Motorcycle Rally was rooted in the outlaw biker activity of the mid-20th century.[6] Just after World War II, a wave of motorcycle clubs was founded outside of the governing norms of the American Motorcycle Association (AMA). In the 1950s, these "outlaw" clubs became notorious for disrupting AMA sanctioned events, causing civil disruption and challenging civil authority. News reports spread the infamy of outlaw bikers (Reynolds, 2000; Shellow & Roemer, 1966) while a new genre of biker-themed cinema became widely popular. Especially important was the 1969 film, *Easy Rider*, that depicted motorcycle touring as an expression of the rising youth movement. To young people disenchanted with establishment values, the outlaw/hippie biker embodied countercultural desire for freedom in an authoritarian world. These films and media sensationalism about alleged outlaw biker activity fueled hysterical notoriety and a "moral panic" over outlaw bikers (Cohen, 1980; DeYoung, 1998; Reynolds, 2000; Yates, 1999). Over time, the moral panic subsided but the "legend" of the outlaw biker remained.

By the 1970s, the legend of the outlaw biker had become firmly established as the spectacular diegesis of the Sturgis Rally, and drew new types of rally-goers who desired an experience of countercultural lifestyle that they had seen on screen (Schembri, 2009). These new spectators were younger, and as images from the period clearly depict, dirtier and hairier than members of the heritage motorcycling clubs. Collared shirts, dress slacks and dresses were replaced with collarless and often sleeveless T-shirts (the better to display tattoos), denim jeans, leather vest and jackets, engineer boots, skull caps and bandanas as the de rigueur rally costume, a clear case of the tribalization of consumption (Antonio, 2000; Cova & Cova, 2002). Clad in the regalia of outlaw bikers, the spectators increasingly became part of the spectacle, so that the Rally began to mirror a classic Bakhtinian carnival (Bakhtin, 1968; Krier & Swart, 2012; Langman & Ryan, 2009) marked by sexualized play, unfocused interaction, drinking, brawling, and milling along Main Street or camping rough in the Sturgis City Park. Gazing upon each other, imaging themselves within the spectacular diegesis of the outlaw biker, while participating in consumption rituals (McCracken, 1986), rally-goers transformed what had been a gathering of motorcyclists focused upon the ride into a "society of spectacle" both analytically and temporally congruent with Debord's 1967 essay. Debord's society of the spectacle was defined by consumption of a spectacular diegesis: spectators

---

6 A full account of the rise of outlaw biker culture lies beyond the scope of this chapter; however, a brief discussion is warranted (for a full exploration see Austin, Gagne, & Orend, 2010; Nichols and Peterson, 2010; Reynolds, 2000).

mimicked its content while psychologically identifying with the imaginary images projected before them; images that stupefied them while picking their pockets.

Rally attendance and its economic output grew dramatically during this period. Attendance swelled at an annualized growth rate of 295 percent, from 1000 to 60,000; the length of the rally increased to a full week; and the rally spread outside the city limits and into neighboring towns to accommodate the increasing crowds. Rooted in the sale of its spectacular diegesis, the Rally became a full-scale, diversified economy as temporary vendors set up to cater to the needs of rally-goers. Taxable revenues grew at a 95 percent annualized rate, from $150,000 to $3,000,000.

Unlike the BHMC heritage cyclists, these new rally-goers were not bonded by cross-cutting social ties, deeply shared community or political interest. Instead, they shared little more than a desire to purchase access to a spectacular diegesis replete with media disseminated images of an outlaw biker counterculture. By the end of the 1970s, the heritage motorcycling enthusiasts of the BHMC had been supplanted by spectators who were no longer motorcycle club members or outlaw bikers, but consumers purchasing access to the outlaw biker diegesis at the Sturgis Motorcycle Rally.

The Sturgis Diegesis as Commodity: Spectator's Desire and Consumable Character Gambles

Economies of spectatorship produce profit by commodifying unique diegeses that spectators pay to see and within which sponsors pay to be seen.[7] Like all commodities in late capitalism, the value of spectacular diegeses are conditioned by the willingness of spectators to buy them. Without spectators' desire to see and to be seen within its diegesis, an economy of spectatorship collapses.

On the surface, the spectacular diegesis of outlaw biker legends does not appear to be very desirable or valuable. It seems counterintuitive that lawful citizens with respectable middle-class habitus and significant disposable incomes would desire to see and to be seen within a diegesis so famously degraded as the Sturgis Motorcycle Rally. What value (in the common rather than Marxist

---

7 Commodification of the spectacular diegesis of Sturgis Motorcycle Rally, like that of many other economies of spectatorship, takes the form of an enclosure of the cultural commons (Boyle, 2003, 2008). Most of the iconic images and slogans of the Rally were not created by the organizers of the Rally or by the new cinematically inspired spectators but had already been circulating in the public sphere before being trademarked and branded.

vernacular) do consumers realize in their attendance at Sturgis? What value (in Marxist terms) is realized through the production of this particular spectacular diegesis?

To explain the value of the outlaw biker diegesis, we draw upon Erving Goffman (1967), a sociologist not typically associated with critical theory.[8] To Goffman, "action" occurs when a person voluntarily assumes risk in chancy situations, those that involve potential losses and gains that are consequential and fateful. Many scenes of action place physical bodies at risk, but the most important type of action places social reputations or "character" at risk. Positive character traits—bravery, courage, intelligence, persistence, poise—can only be socially realized when openly displayed in risky situations. To Goffman, only character that has been gambled has value because it is "visible" and socially real.

While action was unavoidable among pre-modern people who were faced with dangerous, difficult *work* tasks that provided ample opportunity to display character, action has been lost to most modern workers. Except for a few high "action" occupations (military, police, firemen, high-rise construction, stock-trading), most modern jobs have become too safe and mundane for action. This lack of opportunity for action is not accidental but structurally necessary to modern capitalist existence: modernity domesticates and administers existence in safety-conscious public spaces, Taylorized workplaces, and "nanny-state" social welfare. While the often-repressed desire for risky, fateful situations remains, it is displaced from work-life onto the after-work world of leisure (Goffman, 1967; Lyng, 1990). Hence, opportunities for action become valuable.

Goffman's theory of action accounts for spectator fascination with the outlaw biker lifestyles and images of the Sturgis Rally's diegesis. In contrast to Debord's spectacle, where leisure is unserious, temporary relief from boredom and vicarious stimulation that quickly fades, Goffman's concept of action presents modern leisure as extremely serious and played for high stakes (see Celsi, Rose & Leigh, (1993) for a discussion of "high-risk leisure consumption" through skydiving). Since leisure is "where the action is," modern people—like rally-goers at Sturgis—use leisure to search for and consume valuable pre-packaged action that simultaneously tests and displays character.

---

8   We continue critical theory's long-standing open-ended incorporation of ideas developed outside Marxist orthodoxy. Note that Goffman's 1967 essay was written contemporaneously with both Debord's *Society of the Spectacle* and the rise of outlaw biker culture in media and film.

While the habitus of lower and working-class people fits the outlaw biker diegesis of the Rally's and its corporate partner, Harley-Davidson, demographic analyses of Harley-Davidson buyers and motorcycle rally-goers reveals a predominance of white-collar workers (Thompson, 2012a; 2012b).[9] Like the "real life" of Thurber's character Walter Mitty, the work of these well-to-do occupants of offices and desks lacks a narrative of action. These are precisely those that figure so prominently among the consumers of ready-made action at motorcycle rallies because they highly value opportunities to purchase action by playing at outlaw biker in their leisure time.

Goffman noted that many moderns consume action through "ephemeral ennoblement," temporarily occupying high-prestige settings typically occupied by elites (or at least by social classes higher than one's own). Action comes from "fancy milling" within these spaces, proving positive character traits (daring, intelligence and presence of mind) by successfully managing the role distance required to pass as someone normal to that setting. What seems clear in our study of motorsports spectacles, however, is that action is found not only from reaching up, but also from slumming down. Thus we propose that *ephemeral debasement* is an equally applicable mechanism by which moderns seek action, one that more clearly captures the consumable *character gamble* that results from degraded milling at contemporary motorcycle rallies. In ephemeral debasement, action is found by demonstrating the prowess necessary to temporarily abandon middle-class norms, successfully navigating role distance and to simulate potentially disreputable identity characteristics. While spectacles that stage diegeses infused with ephemeral ennoblement have proliferated in recent years (all-inclusive upscale resorts, cruise-lines and spas), the rapid growth of Sturgis and other motorcycle rallies suggests that the market for ephemeral debasement has expanded even faster. For Sturgis rally-goers and a growing number of other spectators, the purchase of temporary disreputable identities stands alongside fancy milling as another source of action.[10]

Consumer desire underlies Rally's transformation from a participatory social event into a producer and purveyor of outlaw biker diegesis. The diegesis

---

9   Harley-Davidson's 2012 SEC Form 10K reveals that the median income of those who purchase Harley-Davidson motorcycles is nearly $90,000, an income figure that excludes the bulk of the working and lower classes.

10   Globalization has further reduced the number of cowboy-like, action-dense jobs in our economy. As foundry work, heavy manufacturing and mining have been increasingly outsourced, an increasingly wide swath of modern workers no longer find action on the job and desire action in leisure to prove their character. We think that this explains the rapid growth of spectacles of action that produce, package and sell ephemeral debasement as consumable character gamble to meet this growing market.

scripted a disreputable character for paying rally-goers to playfully enact; one that allowed them to display the dark character virtues that could not otherwise be realized in post-industrial employment. The Sturgis Rally, NASCAR and highly-sexualized carnivalesque settings like Mardi Gras produce diegetic scenes of ready-made action, commodified character gambles marketed to and particularly valued by upper middle-class spectators. Thus, Goffman's concept of "action" explains *why* the Rally's spectators desired ephemeral debasement with sufficient intensity to immerse themselves at high cost in the Sturgis diegesis.[11]

Marketing the Sturgis Diegesis to Spectators and Sponsors

A spectacular diegesis becomes a commodity when it is produced for sale in a consumption market. Beginning with appealing content often originating in the cultural commons (Boyle, 2003), producers transform narratives into commodities by producing and selling them to spectators and sponsors, transforming public domain content into trademarked property. Producers generate revenues from spectators primarily by charging admission to view the diegesis, though substantial secondary revenues are typically generated from parking, lodging, food, beverages, merchandise and premium access. In addition, producers generate revenue from sponsors by charging cross-marketing licensing and advertising fees for the right to appear within the diegesis.

To effectively stage the diegesis for a growing market while profitably servicing the assembled crowds, producers of the Rally made extensive capital investments in the infrastructure of spectatorship. During this period, the City of Sturgis and Rally organizers designated prime real estate along Sturgis's main street and traffic corridors as marketing space for vendor stalls. The City of Sturgis facilitated this commercialization in a variety of ways, providing vendor manuals, city vending regulatory guidelines, Internal Revenue Service

---

11   Capitalism in the age of the integrated spectacle refuels itself by rapidly reformulating emergent countercultural images into cool corporate brands and logos to promote establishment products and services. Concepts such as "rebellion," "revolution" and "outlaw" were increasingly hijacked after 1985, when these iconic and dangerous concepts were digested by the spectacle and widely deployed as marketing slogans and advertising campaigns to boost consumption by coating products with a gloss of cool. Further, these countercultural concepts were adopted as slogans for conservative, establishment and right-wing political groups and causes (Gladwell, 1997; Hale, 2011).

assistance, and State Department of Revenue information to small businesses participating in the Rally.

Rally organizers also worked to ensure that massive crowds of rally-goers maintained an ongoing experience of immersion in the produced diegesis. Property developers constructed massive campgrounds, music venues, grand-stands, stages, and subsidiary infrastructure of parking lots, cafeterias, snack shops, bathrooms. New biker bars were constructed, open only during the weeks of the Rally and saturated with outlaw theming, including names like Broken Spoke, Easy Rider, One Eyed Jacks; the Knuckle, and the Full Throttle. City officials closed Main Street to automobile traffic, transforming downtown into a rumbling showcase of chopped bikes congruent with iconic images of the Rally (preferential motorcycle parking at most Rally venues served the same function). Corporate marketers and event promoters installed tempo-rary signage, street banners and store facades that repeated outlaw biker imag-ery. In meme-like fashion, imagery from biker outlaw cinema, especially *Easy Rider* and *The Wild Ones*, appeared in saloons, restaurants, campgrounds and gas stations, and were echoed in the costuming, leather and chains hawked by Rally vendors and worn as a uniform by milling crowds. Imitating scenes from outlaw biker films, some venues allowed motorcycles to be ridden inside, permeating the atmosphere with rally-themed sounds, vibrations and exhaust.

Like other economies of spectatorship (Mardi Gras, NASCAR, Collegiate and Professional Athletics), sponsorship revenues were essential to the Sturgis Motorcycle Rally.[12] The earliest and most important sponsor of the Rally was Harley-Davidson Motorcycles, Inc., a corporate brand whose profits were tied to intensive commodification of the same outlaw biker diegesis as the Rally.[13] In 1969, the Harley-Davidson Corporation had been absorbed by conglomerate American Machine and Foundry (AMF) who treated the motorcycle manufac-turer as a "cash cow," draining money from the division while under-investing in new technology and innovative design. While other motorcycle brands swept the US market (Honda, Suzuki, Husqvarna and Yamaha) by selling ef-ficient, comfortable, reliable, and powerful transportation, Harley-Davidson's uncomfortable, poor-handling, low-powered machines lost market share (Aus-tin, Gagne, & Orend, 2010; Reynolds, 2000; Schembri, 2009).[14] After a leveraged

---

12   See Worrell (2009) on commercial exploitation of spectacle.

13   This analysis of the economic circuitry of motorsports spectacles contrasts with one-sided emphasis upon political ideology and cultural legitimation sometimes associated with Debordian cultural theory, such as Newman and Giardina's (2011) book on NASCAR.

14   The animosity that existed between Harley-Davidson motorcycle owners and riders of Japanese motorcycles was heated during this period, manifested in partisan slogans on

buyout in the early 1980s, Harley-Davidson's owners recast the firm to cash in on its strongest asset: public association of the brand with popular, mostly cinematic, portrayals of outlaw bikers. Harley-Davidson reformulated into a marketer of branded apparel and motorcycles consciously styled as facsimiles of the choppers and bobbers ridden by iconic cinematic outlaw bikers (Schembri, 2009). The Sturgis Motorcycle Rally was central to Harley-Davidson's rebranding: in the early 1980s Harley-Davidson released a bike "in honor of the historic Sturgis motorcycle rally" and took out a trademark on the "Sturgis" name (US Patent and Trademark Office, 1982). From this period to the present, Harley-Davidson intensively projected its brand into the Rally diegesis, annually occupying the premium vending space at the Rally (a large multi-trailer display on the high-traffic intersection along the main cruising route through town).

The Sturgis Rally's sponsorship also allowed Harley-Davidson to feature Sturgis Rally footage, images and activities in its advertising and promotional activities throughout the year and on its website. Harley-Davidson augmented its marketing effort by managing "customer experience," ensuring the ongoing association of the brand with "cool" outlaw biker diegeses like the Sturgis Motorcycle Rally (and to a lesser degree Daytona Bikeweek and the annual rally at Laconia). In 2012, Harley-Davidson's annual report disclosed that 23 percent of the company's revenues were derived from non-motorcycle sales of parts, accessories, branded merchandise, branded apparel and revenues from cross-marketing license agreements that placed the Harley-Davidson's brand on a surprising array of consumer products (including fountain pens, teddy bears and underwear). Managers of Harley-Davidson, as sponsors of the Sturgis Rally, paid for their branded products to be seen within the outlaw biker themed diegesis, forming a "subculture of consumption" (Schouten and McAlexander, 1993, 1995; Schouten, Martin, & McAlexander, 2007), or "brand community" (McAlexander, Schouten & Koenig, 2002; Muniz & O'Guinn, 2001) in which rally-goers practiced "consumption as play" (Holt, 1995: 8). The success of this cross-marketing for Harley-Davidson was reflected in its dominant 57

T-shirts and tattoos such as "I'd rather ride my Rice-Burner than push your Harley" or "If it Ain't a Harley, it Ain't a Bike." During this period, Harley riding Sturgis-goers paid money for the opportunity to beat a Japanese motorcycle with a baseball bat. What is clear, and widely acknowledged even by Harley devotees, was the inferiority of 1970s HD motorcycles as "automobility" or transportation vehicles. To ride a Harley required a gear-head's skillset; part of the "allure" and "authenticity" of ownership. Harley's success eventually led Japanese manufacturers to produce memetic "copies of the copies"– Honda, Suzuki, Yamaha and Kawasaki now market simulated HD cruisers.

percent share of the large displacement motorcycle market in the USA (*Harley-Davidson Annual Report*, 2012).

Other sponsors paid to promote their brands by merging them into the Sturgis Rally. Many of these brands were similar to Harley-Davidson in that they were so closely aligned with the outlaw biker legend that their presence intensified the Rally diegesis. Victory Motorcycles, a division of Polaris Industries that manufactures Harley-Davidson-like motorcycles, was a recurring sponsor of the Rally. Jack Daniel's Whiskey sponsored a variety of venues within the Rally, explaining the fit between their brands and the Rally as follows: "Jack Daniel's Tennessee Whiskey ... has stood for authenticity, Americana, Independence and freedom. And that's exactly why Jack Daniel's is proud to be part of the annual Sturgis® Motorcycle Rally" (City of Sturgis Rally and Events Department, 2013). FX's Sons of Anarchy, a television series that reproduced "legendary" outlaw biker images and narratives, has become an official sponsor of the Sturgis Motorcycle Rally. Sonny Barger, the infamous leader of the Hell's Angels, reinforced the diegetic coherence of the 2002 Rally while he exploited it for gain by promoting his new brand of beer ("Sonny's Lean and Mean Lager") while selling copies of his newly published biography during the Rally (Horsey, 2002).

Dialectical Development of the Sturgis Diegesis: Progressive Decontextualization in Economies of Spectatorship

In economies of spectatorship, organizers maximize profit by growing the size of audiences and expanding the network of sponsors paying cross-marketing licensing fees. In initial stages of growth, organizers reach culturally related spectators and sponsors by stretching the original diegetic content. Eventually, organizers must seek target markets further afield to sustain growth. Reaching these culturally distant spectators and sponsors requires production of less coherent narratives that introduce new themes, images and legends that obscure the original content. Thus, economies of spectatorship develop in a dialectic process that we term *progressive decontextualization.* Beginning with a focused diegesis produced for a culturally coherent market of spectators and sponsors, the growth imperative forces organizers to produce internally inconsistent cultural content to reach audiences from distant market segments and to sign sponsors from diverse industries. As economies of spectatorship integrate sundry elements, the produced narrative loses its coherence, reducing its audience appeal by destabilizing spectator's desire. Just as a coin debased with impurities diminishes in value, so too does a fully commodified diegesis.

The progressive decontextualization of spectators, sponsors and diegetic content was evident as the Sturgis Motorcycle Rally grew. Spectatorship at the Rally increased from 60,000 attendees in 1985 to 633,000 attendees in 2000, an annualized rate of growth of 65 percent (see Table 8). After 1985, the expansion of spectatorship incorporated market segments of high-dollar spectators that were culturally distant from the low-dollar outlaw biker diegesis of the Rally. These new spectators were disproportionately "off brand" middle-class professionals, women, younger riders, families, and minorities. Such demographically diverse rally-goers were unified by their high disposable incomes, their desire to see the Sturgis diegesis and their willingness to spend thousands of dollars purchasing factory-chopped bikes and outlaw costuming essential to the Sturgis scene. To make these highly profitable rally-goers comfortable, Rally organizers and Sturgis City officials began regulating those activities most directly congruent with the outlaw biker diegesis. Unpaid rough camping by "hippie freeloaders" in city parks was officially suppressed in 1984, and public drinking and overt public nudity became heavily regulated during the ensuing decade. As a form of progressive decontextualization, these new regulations increased spectatorship and profit flows by cleaning up the "outlaw" content of the Sturgis diegesis to make it more palatable to middle and upper middle-class spectators.

Sturgis Rally organizers inked cross-marketing licensing agreements with sponsors increasingly off brand from the outlaw biker themes of Sturgis.[15] Revenues from commercial vendors and corporate sponsors increased from $3m in 1985 to $14m in 2000, an annualized growth rate of 26 percent (see Table 8).[16] The number of vendor licenses grew even more rapidly from 117 in 1985 to 943 in 2000, an annual growth rate of 47 percent. Some new sponsors and vendors were consistent with the leather, skin and steel imagery attributed to legendary outlaw bikers. On-brand sponsors and vendors included tattoo artists, body painters, motorcycle parts and accessories, motorcycling apparel and insurance, carnivorous food and low-brow alcohol. But, an increasing group of vendors sold "off-brand" products and services to the rapidly diversifying demographic of rally-goers. Many of the sponsors who

---

15   Other economies of spectatorship, such as America's Cup, Formula 1, NASCAR and Collegiate and Professional Athletics and, increasingly, cinematic productions depend upon profits from diverse corporate sponsors to augment spectator admission revenues.

16   Taxable sales figures are almost certainly understated by a wide margin. Sturgis city officials and event organizers readily admit that vendors have an interest in the underreporting of taxable sales while vendor licenses include few penalties for doing so. Nevertheless, the magnitude of change in taxable sales is an indicator of rally growth.

signed sponsorship agreements paid to display brands and icons at the Rally that had little connection with outlaw biker theming. The Sturgis Economic Development Corporation, the Sturgis Chamber of Commerce, and the South Dakota Department of Tourism were prominent Rally sponsors, signaling intensive injection of legitimate state-business coalitions into the outlaw biker diegesis. Corporate sponsors who paid to be seen within the diegesis of the Rally included Ford Motor Company, Sony Electronics, GEICO, AMSOIL, Pak-Mail, Budweiser, South Dakota Lottery, Coca-Cola, Knowlogy, Pork—The Other White Meat, and Alltel. Rally organizers indicate that these diverse sponsors "found the Sturgis Motorcycle Rally to be a productive investment and one on which they proudly place their brand" (City of Sturgis Rally and Events Department, 2009). Marketing managers of Sony Corporation believed that their Rally Sponsorship would not only "lure bikers from checking out fast rides to our sponsor booth filled with the latest electronics" but would "build a brand connection with attendees" (City of Sturgis Rally and Events Department, 2009).

Professional marketing firms were hired by Sturgis city officials to facilitate the diverse commodification of the Rally and to manage the Rally's increasingly complicated corporate sponsorship contracts and cross-marketing licensing agreements. Prior to 1992, these contracts had been administered by not-for-profit agencies—the local Chamber of Commerce or its subsidiary, the Black Hills Motor Classic Board (BHMCB). The BHMCB was reincorporated as the *for-profit* Sturgis Rally and Races, Inc. to better "plan, organize and promote the rally and races and return significant tangible financial benefits to the residents of Sturgis" (US District Court: District of South Dakota, 2000). The City of Sturgis changed promotional firms three times, with each succeeding contract written to better realize returns to interested parties. For example, in 2013, the City of Sturgis terminated its contract with Motoring USA, Inc., in order to put rally publications out for bid and regain control over vendor leases on city owned properties (Ganje, 2013; Holland, 2013, 29 Januaky). Highlighting the goal of profit expansion to a global audience, city officials sought a new agent that better "matched the City's long-term goals in marketing the Rally; one with global reach for the development of one of the world's leading lifestyle brands—at one of the world's most well-known events, the Sturgis Motorcycle Rally" (Ganje, 2013). Additionally, the City of Sturgis Rally and Events Department produced an *Official Sturgis Motorcycle Rally Magazine* and the *Schedule of Events Pocket Guide*, as well as a widely circulated *Rally Visitor Information CD*, which promoted the Rally to diverse audiences with advertising space sold to diverse sponsors.

Politics, Religion and the Sturgis Diegesis in the Age of the Integrated Spectacle

Progressive decontextualization of the Sturgis Motorcycle Rally diegesis also occurred through the integration of sponsors and thematic elements drawn from politics and religion. Such diegetic thickening of economies of spectatorship was anticipated by Debord in 1988, when he revised his already bleak theory to herald capitalism's descent into an even darker era: the "integrated spectacle."[17] Debord (2006 [1967]) had always conceived of the society of spectacle in political terms: spectacular images redoubled alienation, leaving viewers unenlightened and distracted from the real conditions of social life. As individuals cathected strongly with their consumer brands—automobiles, home appliances, clothing and favored forms of entertainment—they became progressively distracted, socially estranged, and politically impotent (Debord, 2006 [1967], para. 28). Debord added the adjective "integrated" to his concept of spectacle to highlight the synthesis of consumer oriented "diffuse spectacles" with "concentrated spectacles" that serve as political theology (Debord, 1988, para. 4). Consequently, the integrated spectacle floats "above real society," combining the pacification and distractions of consumer capitalism with the ideological power of religion and politics. Hence, the consumer economy in the age of the integrated spectacle is always also ideological since political and religious themes are overlaid upon and blended within profitable diegetic content.

To Debord, even oppositional politics and revolutionary actions were flattened into images that safely and impotently circulated within the integrated spectacle, generating profit at particular moments but nowhere organizing effective political opposition to the system. This helps account for the counterintuitive integration of conservative religion and politics into economies of spectatorship like the outlaw biker themed diegesis at Sturgis. The liberatory qualities of spectacular consumption have often been noted (see Firat & Venkatesh, 1995), but, as discussed in Chapter 6, the Rally's diegesis was closer to authoritarian politics and "repressive desublimation" (Marcuse, 1964) than to "liberatory postmodernism." Leftist politics and liberatory symbolism rarely appeared at the Rally or related motorsports events like NASCAR, monster truck rallies, or other motorcycle rallies, but these venues featured imagery

---

17   The standard translation of Debord's essay stylizes his concept as "the integrated spectacular." Under the assumption that two adjectives do not make a noun, we prefer the more grammatical phrase, "integrated spectacle."

and symbolism of right-leaning politics. Significant military presence infused the Rally, including flyovers by military aircraft, veterans' rides, a traveling facsimile of the Vietnam War Memorial, and memorials to Iraq/Afghanistan war casualties. American flags festooned public streets, private campgrounds, and biker apparel. Pro-American slogans such as "Try Burnin' this one, Asshole" and "These Colors Don't Run" appeared on T-shirts and bumper stickers while right-leaning acts such as Ted Nugent, Toby Keith, Charlie Daniels and Molly Hatchet dominated music venues. Images and candidates from the Republican Party, the South Dakota Tea Party, and The Young Obama Haters appeared within the Rally diegesis. In 2007, the Sturgis Motorcycle Hall of Fame officially inducted the "Bush Bike," a customized chopper, complete with the preamble of the US constitution, commissioned by the Republican National Committee to commemorate G.W. Bush's 2004 campaign (Maverick, 2007). The rally annually incorporated a "Governor's Ride" in which state and local politicians dressed up, without consciously registered irony, as outlaw bikers to ride with celebrities and music artists to Mount Rushmore, the ur-monument of American imperial power.

A tableau portrait of political integration at Sturgis occurred during the 2008 rally, when Republican candidate for President, John McCain gave the "Tribute to the Vets" speech at the Buffalo Chip Campground. McCain's campaign was struggling at this time, and while Sarah Palin drew large crowds to her campaign events, McCain's were noticeably smaller. Thus his campaign staff sought already assembled audiences; in this case, the assembly gathered for the Kid Rock concert on the Wolfman Jack Memorial Stage at the Buffalo Chip campground. His glamorous power-elite wife Cindy introduced him by claiming that her husband was "the only man who can keep us free." After he received the microphone, McCain then famously offered her up to the raucous crowd as a competitor in the Miss Buffalo Chip beauty pageant (a notorious wet T-shirt/banana licking/strip contest) with the comment, "With a little luck she could be the only woman ever to serve both as First Lady and Miss Buffalo Chip." Below are some vivid quotes from this speech which capture the ultra-establishment McCain covering himself in outlaw biker theming:

> …not long ago a couple hundred thousand Berliners made a lot of noise for my opponent. I'll take the roar of 50,000 Harleys any day … I recognize that sound … it's the sound of freedom.…
>
>   …we're not gonna pay $4 a gallon for gas because we're gonna drill off-shore and we're gonna drill now … and we're gonna drill here and we're

gonna drill now. My opponent doesn't wanna drill ... he doesn't want nuclear power, he wants you to inflate your tires.

...you're the heartland of America and you're the heart and soul of America ... you provide the men and women who serve our military.

BECKYCHR007, 2008

Following Debord, most critical theorists have viewed spectacle primarily through the lens of politics, and would interpret McCain's stumping as confirmation of spectacle's ideological power. The cultural phrasing that permeated motorsports spectacles—free-grace Christianity, neo-conservative politics (pro-military, anti-welfare state) and neo-liberal economics—does serve an ideological function in that it encouraged spectators to recast global capitalism's hazards as character proving lifestyle choices.[18] Unlike progressive politics which encourage risk pooling and the organized reduction of chance (Amidon & Sanderson, 2012), right wing politics places risk and chance squarely upon the shoulders of individuals. The parallel to Goffman's concept of action is unmistakable: the spectacular diegeses of motorsports encouraged spectators to voluntarily reject safety and security in multiple regions of life (religion, politics, work, consumption), while embracing risks to mind, body and bank account. Motorsports and other contemporary spectacles of "action" allowed spectators to pretend that they were voluntarily choosing the risks and meta-anxieties forced upon them by global capitalism (Žižek, 2009).

However, on balance, our observations at Sturgis lead us to conclude that ideological considerations were secondary to money-making. The Rally's diegesis was primarily determined by economic forces (the desire for profit) rather than political forces (the desire for ideological control), especially after action seeking consumers had supplanted countercultural rally-goers. As an economy of spectatorship, what appears as ideological theming within the Sturgis Rally was the unintended byproduct of profitable diegetic production (see also Bonilla, 1988; Endres & Ferrar, 2002; Gottdiener, 2001; Gottdiener, Collins, & Dickens, 1999). Organizers incorporated commercial, political and religious motifs into the diegesis to enhance profits rather than to induce ideological control. Whatever ideological power McCain's appearance may have generated was immediately dissipated by other ideologically discrepant events produced by the Sturgis Buffalo Chip staff for consumption by paying

---

18   The combination of these ideological features are prominent throughout the political right in the USA, especially the contemporary Tea Party Movement. See Langman (2012) and Lundskow (2012).

spectators: "Women of Wrestling's Wringing Wet and Wild Throwdown," Buf-falo Chip's "Fake Orgasm" contest, "Homemade Bikini" contest, "Beers and Burps" contest ("how loud can you blast a burp out ... while still keeping the important stuff down ?"), midget bowling ("toss Short-Sleeved Sampson down the greased-up lane"), or "Beer Belly" contest. Our field observations lead to the conclusion that political appearances are not ontologically distinct from these other, profit motivated events. In contrast to many readings of Debord, the cultural content of economies of spectatorship like Sturgis was materially, not ideologically, determined.

In the age of the integrated spectacle (Debord, 1988), not only political el-ements but also religious themes blend into spectacular diegeses. In recent times, religious imagery, leadership, and practices have become commonplace at sporting events, political gatherings, military exercises and other public set-tings, conceptualized by Ritzer (2005) as the re-enchantment of consumption. As a hedonistic spectacle themed with outlaw biker imagery, however, Sturgis seemed an unlikely forum for religiously themed images and activities. Amidst the conspicuous, posed sinning of rally-goers, ascetic matters of faith were at least mildly out of place, if not jarringly discrepant. Mundane religious inte-gration occurred in the background of the rally, as local churches in Sturgis hosted a variety of biker events including pancake breakfasts and special ser-vices. Additionally, the largest private venue at the Sturgis Rally, the Buffalo Chip Campground, prominently displayed a fifty-foot tall, metal fabricated "battlefield cross" at its main entrance.

The Sturgis Rally was a hotbed of more pronounced religious activity, to the considerable profit of Rally organizers. Described as a "modern-day Sodom and Gomorrah" and "Vanity Fair" by the Dakota Baptist Convention, this group nevertheless spent $10,000 for vendor space at the 2009 rally, and recorded 125 professions of faith (conversion experiences), which was described by one mission volunteer as "not a bad day's work in hell" (*Christian Index,* 2009). In addition to such delegations from mainstream Christian denominations, nu-merous specifically biker-themed evangelical ministries purchased vendor space and were observed selling religiously themed merchandise while pass-ing out literature. These ministries included the Wheels of Faith Motorcycle Ministry, Hog Wild for Jesus Ministry, Soldiers for Jesus Motorcycle Club ("Ride with Jesus"), Jesus Loves Bikers, Motorcycle Ministry ("Reaching Out to the De-pressed, Oppressed, Addicted, Convicted and Just Plain Lost"). Apart from of-ficial ministries, many rally-goers purchased and displayed T-shirts or patches sewn onto leatherwear that implicitly or explicitly connected them with Chris-tianity (crosses, bible quotes, "Jesus Saves") or to Christian biker clubs.

In classic cross-marketing fashion, the motorcycle themed devotional litera-ture distributed by biker ministries blended together Christian iconography with outlaw biker imagery. For example, multiple variants of a "Biker's Prayer" appeared in ministry materials, including the following taken from their websites:

> Jesus A Biker? Let's look at the facts. He had long hair and a beard. He hung around regular people, not the church types. The government did not care for him.
>
> BIKERS FOR CHRIST: ORANGE COUNTY CHAPTER, n.d.

> 60 miles an hour with the wind in my face, hands up on the grips and my feet up on the pegs going down the road for a ride somewhere ... I say a biker's prayer ... For me it's not about the chrome, the leather, or the steel. It's all about connection to something beautiful and real when you're balanced on two wheels.
>
> BIKERS FOR CHRIST: EAST BAY CHAPTER, n.d.

> If Jesus appeared today in the flesh he would be here, parked right next to you on his motorcycle ... He would be seen on his motorcycle at biker rallies telling others what he told you. Jesus loves bikers because he is one of us ... Get on your ride and follow him.
>
> *JESUS THE BIKER*, n.d.

This cultural mash-up of Jesus and chopper riding bikers not only inspired Christian ministries, but generated devotional commodities in the form of artwork, music and even "Jesus as Biker" action figures that were sold at the Rally, biker websites and eBay. The Freedom Rider Action Toy was molded in the form of Jesus as an outlaw biker astride a chopped cruiser with robes flowing, helmetless but with a crown of thorns (see Figure 27), and was "inspired by the thought of what Jesus might do in modern times." The description further

FIGURE 27
Cross-Marketing at Sturgis Motorcycle Rally:
Jesus as Outlaw Biker, circa 2010
SOURCE: EBAY LISTING.

stated that the action figure symbolized Jesus's message as "I Am Freedom" (eBay, n.d.)—a reformulation of the gospel in terms consistent with the outlaw biker legend, the newly formulated brand slogan of the City of Sturgis, and all three elements of the current integrated spectacle: the free-market neo-liberalism of global capitalism, the political ideology of the Tea Party and the free-grace theology of Christianity.

Progressive Decontextualization, Diegetic Incoherence and Diegetic Maintenance

As economies of spectatorship decontextualize, the produced diegesis loses coherence and destabilizes spectators' desire. Like a hurricane, the Sturgis Motorcycle Rally grew as spectators and sponsors circulated about the "eye" of its outlaw biker diegesis, absorbing ever more distant and inconsistent spectators and corporate sponsors. Spectacular diegeses possess a certain degree of elasticity and organizers of the Rally attempted to stretch its outlaw biker tropes to accommodate discrepant corporate sponsors and commercial vendors. In 2012, this led to strange pairings of biker outlaws and legitimate cross-marketed partners like casualty insurance, massage services, homeo-pathic health aids, soft drinks, home electronics, pharmaceuticals, and the History Channel. Carnivalesque commercial activities entirely unrelated to the outlaw biker legend were also incorporated within the Rally: greased midget bowling, machine gun demonstrations, zip lines, and atonal performances by aging 1980s hair bands. Atop this already discrepant commercial content, Rally organizers layered additional, highly discordant themes of "law and order" politics and religious salvation.

Such progressive decontextualization of a founding diegesis is inevitable as organizers integrate ever more divergent corporate tie-ins, cross-marketing agreements, political ideologies and religious themes. Consistent with Ritzer's (2007) "globalization of nothing" thesis, progressive decontextualization is also temporal and spatial. As economies of spectatorship develop they sprawl out over calendars and maps until they appear everywhere at all times. For ex-ample, NASCAR attracted spectators and profit flows year-round from virtually (literally "*virtually*") all locations on its digital platforms including Raceview 360, iRacing, and the Speed Channel. Similarly, the two-week Rally gener-ated nearly continuous, nearly global "doubles" in streaming videos, online images, cable television programming and websites, as well as in copycat ral-lies deploying Sturgis brands and imagery. These McDonaldized (Ritzer, 2013) rallies reproduced Sturgisesque outlaw biker diegeses across North America and Europe. For example, Jay Allen, a self-proclaimed "pioneer in the art of motorcycle entertainment" (Allen, n.d.), also owned major Sturgis venues, the Broken Spoke Saloon and the Broken Spoke Campground. Allen also operated Broken Spoke Saloons in other biker-themed locations like Daytona Beach and Laconia, each reproducing images and narratives drawn from Sturgis. Allen developed a traveling version of the Sturgis diegesis, The Jay Allen Road Show, that produced outlaw biker diegeses sold to spectators throughout the USA. Allen was the principle organizer of the 2012 Iowa Grand Rally, a ready-made Sturgis-style motorcycle rally staged at a NASCAR track in Newton, Iowa. This rally featured many of the same performers and celebrities featured at Sturgis (including cast members from FX Network's *Sons of Anarchy* series) and was timed to capture spectators and sponsors en route to and from the Sturgis Rally. A similar McDonaldized Sturgisesque diegesis was produced by the owner of the Sturgis Buffalo Chip campground, who staged a travelling version of his campground's regulated raunch called the "Sturgis Road Show" (held in April 2011 in Hershey, Pennsylvania). Finally, the towns of Sturgis, Mississippi and Sturgis, Kentucky have each cashed in upon the notoriety of the Sturgis Motorcycle Rally by staging small-scale simulations of the outlaw biker diegesis, demonstrating the relevance of Baudrillard's most famous concept to spectacular economies (Baudrillard, 1983a; Krier & Swart, 2012).

As economies of spectatorship progressively decontextualize they draw in spectators, sponsors and content in a self-negating developmental process that results in diegetic incoherence. Diegetic incoherence proceeds as the founding images and legendary narratives that launched spectatorship and sponsorship are lost amid a swirling kaleidoscope of unrelated products, decontextualized activities and diversified locations. At the Rally, excessive promotional tie-ins, brand elasticity, unrelated carnivalesque activities, and dispersed McDonaldized reproductions of the Rally threatened the audience appeal and value of its underlying commodity: the outlaw biker diegesis. As it became stretched and incoherent, spectator desire to view and be viewed within the diegesis eroded, destabilizing the spectatorship and the sponsorship revenues that were predicated upon it.

Diegetic incoherence is inevitable in mature spectacular economies. To counteract it, producers of spectacular diegeses engage in ongoing maintenance, active management, and reinvestment to restore profits to the economic circuit.[19] At Sturgis, declining attendance at the Rally in the 2000s

---

19   We recognize that Harley-Davidson and Sturgis (as Victory and other motorcycle brands and Daytona, Laconia and other rally cities) form a relatively coherent "subculture of

prompted organizers and civic leaders to increase capital investments to re-associate the Rally with the outlaw biker brand and restore coherence to the Rally's activities. These efforts to restage the authenticity (MacCannell, 1973) of the Sturgis Brand included contemporary fabrication of heritage motorcy-cling T-shirts, "retro" souvenirs and the future construction of a "Sturgis Expe-rience Museum" intentionally designed to reconnect the visual space of the Rally with its historic "aura" (Goss, 2004; Rickly-Boyd, 2012). In recent years, the degradation of the "authentic" Old West built environment of Sturgis as the themed backdrop of the Rally required diegetic maintenance. Main street buildings had been bulldozed by developers to increase vending and parking space to accommodate larger crowds and more diverse vendors, motorcycle themed street signage, cobblestone walkways, Old West and biker public art. Sturgis officials increased regulation of absentee-owned downtown buildings, specifying that facades be maintained to restore and maintain the town's "Old West" appearance. Owners of the Buffalo Chip Campground, the Broken Spoke campground, the Full Throttle Saloon and other Rally venues erected facades, fittings and furnishings that reinforced both Old West and outlaw biker them-ing diegetically consistent with the Rally.

Such active maintenance in response to diegetic incoherence parallels Gottdiener's (2001) writings on theming and Ritzer's (2005, 2007) theses on "re-enchanting a disenchanted world" and "globalization of nothing." In econo-mies of spectatorship, spectacular themes do not just enchant commodities, they are the *primary* commodities produced and sold. In other words, spectac-ular diegeses are more than just theming or enchantment that fuels the sale of commodities produced elsewhere, but are commodities in and of themselves that generate profit through sponsorship and spectatorship.

Retranslated into Ritzer's (2005, 2007) terms, spectacular diegeses possess the power of enchantment, attracting paying spectators and sponsors seek-ing to market other goods to them. Progressive decontextualization forces managers of economies of spectatorship to travel a road that begins with an enchanted diegetic "something" and moves toward "nothing," a consumption market that is decontextualized, incoherent and disenchanted. In economies of spectatorship, growth of spectators and sponsors requires the incorporation of ever more diverse and off brand commercial, political and religious motifs into an originally enchanted diegesis. Managers of spectacular economies do

---

consumption" associated with a motorcycling lifestyle (Schouten and McAlexander, 1993, 1995), but we see decontextualization and loss of coherence as structurally necessary to the growth of these markets. Much of the work of organizing and managing these subcul-tures involves periodic reinvestment in the diegesis to ensure coherence.

not traverse a random walk of enchantment, but actively intervene to maintain the coherence and value of the enchanted diegesis, thereby forestalling full decontextualization, disenchantment and nothingness.

Conclusion

This chapter has conceptualized economies of spectatorship that produce diegetic content for sale to spectators and sponsors, marking late capitalism's increasing commodification of spectacle. Spectacular cultural products have emerged as dominant commodities in their own right, a growth industry and an important source of profit. As one of the largest and longest running mega-spectacles, the Sturgis Motorcycle Rally provided bounded case materials that enabled clear conceptualization of the structure and dynamics of economies of spectatorship. The Rally's outlaw biker diegesis drew spectators ripe for commercial exploitation, attracting ever expanding audiences seeking action through consumable character gambles. As the spectators and sponsors at Sturgis decontextualized, commercial, political and religious elements were cross-marketed with legends of outlaw bikers. The resulting diegetic incoherence threatened the circuit of profit, leading rally organizers to control cultural content, regulate the built environment and make extensive capital investment to maintain diegetic coherence and profit flows.

Economies of spectatorship have grown dramatically in recent years, as industries and local communities have responded to globalization and deindustrialization. In the USA, local growth coalitions (political leaders, development agencies, business groups) have increasingly turned to spectator events as engines of economic development (Delaney and Eckstein, 2003; Swenson, 2010).[20] Recognizing that an economy of manufacturing is unlikely to return and thrive, they have pinned their hopes for new jobs and prosperity upon economies of spectatorship. Economic development of spectatorship often involves financing massive privately owned infrastructures with public dollars. We confirm the findings of other social scientists who study publicly financed sports stadiums and entertainment venues: the economic benefits promised to the public in these types of ventures are rarely realized (Delaney & Eckstein,

---

20   One pronounced illustration of a de-industrialized town turning to motorsports spectatorship for economic development is Newton, Iowa. After Maytag Corporation was sold to Whirlpool (Krier, 2009a, 2009b), local economic development groups floated public financing for the Iowa Speedway which has yet to deliver on the promises made to Newton citizens (Swenson, 2010).

2003; Fellrath, 2009; Swenson, 2010; Thornton, 2012). Furthermore, the private interests that promote and build these facilities are often consolidated in power relationships that lie outside of democratic decision making processes. Arranged with little public input or awareness, these financing deals escape public oversight and accountability.

While poor returns to public investment in spectator events was partly due to expropriation of profits by private owners, our study points to another, more profound, reason for the disappointing economic impact from spectacular development. Just as Marx explained the falling rate of profit in mature industries due to rising organic composition of capital, with machinery and other fixed capital investments overwhelming the profit making capacity of living labor, we see a similar process under way in the economies of spectatorship we studied. The *organic composition of spectacle*—investments in infrastructure, marketing, promotion and diegetic maintenance—is increasing as this region of the economy matures. While massive growth in information technology has equipped spectators with micro-scale spectacle delivery devices, producing diegeses for these spectators requires enormous capital outlays for physical, broadcast and digital infrastructure as well as large promotional budgets in order to break through the crowded spectacular field. The immense competition for spectators' bodies and eyeballs, and the scale of capital investment necessary to deliver profitable diegeses to spectators, means that even after a half-decade of diegetic maintenance and heightened capital investment, profit flows at Sturgis, NASCAR and other motorsports spectacles remain stalled.

Conceptualizing such dialectical dynamics and self-negating contradictions of economies of spectatorship adds materialist nuance to Debordian cultural studies. Economies of spectatorship produce a diegetic commodity whose audience appeal and value is destabilized as it is scaled for mass spectatorship and sponsorship. Mapping the evolving circuitry of revenue and profit at Sturgis revealed that developmental dynamics of spectacular economies have little to do with external political pressures or heroic local activism, but instead hinge upon internally generated economic contradictions.

CHAPTER 5

Paying to be Seen: Sponsorship Markets, Branding, and the Management of Legends

> The realm of freedom begins only where labour determined by necessity and external expediency ends; it lies by its very nature beyond the sphere of material production proper... The true realm of freedom, the development of human powers as an end in itself, begins beyond ...[the realm of necessity], though it can only flourish with this realm of necessity as its basis. The reduction of the working day is the basic prerequisite.
>
> MARX [1894]1991, pp. 958–959

In this passage from Volume Three of *Capital*, life outside of work appears to Marx as a potential realm of human freedom and spontaneous, self-directed living. Critical theory, following Marx's lead, paid special attention to capitalist developments in time-out-of-work, tracing its degeneration from a hopeful sphere of flourishing praxis into consumptive leisure that was dialectically coupled with the production process, forming an alienating "complex of activities and passivities" (Lefebvre, 1991, p. 40). Frankfurt School critical theorists, especially Adorno, viewed degraded leisure and consumption as a result of a culture industry that "transfers the profit motive naked onto cultural forms" (1991, p. 99). The products of the culture industry were "no longer *also* commodities" but were "commodities through and through" (1991, p. 101).

This chapter analyzes the economic significance of the culture industry and economies of spectacle in contemporary global capitalism, an era in that has capitalized the products of the culture industry. Capital has increasingly "flown" from fixed assets (property, plant and equipment) to take on the pure symbolic form of fictitious capital, backed by intangible assets such as intellectual property, copyrights, patents and trademarked brands (Jameson 1997; Krier 2008, 2009). The products of the culture industry, brands, advertisements, themed experiences, have become a primary form of capital. Trademarked brands are particularly important as capitalized culture: brand equity is now the largest and most rapidly growing component of *goodwill* (the accounting mark of fictitious capital on corporate financial statements). Speculative financial markets capitalize the products of the culture industry by awarding premium stock values to corporations with valuable brands. A recent report on brand equity and market capitalization found that the percentage of market

FIGURE 28   *Brands, Sponsorships, and Legends at Sturgis: Easy Rider Saloon, Circa 2012*
SOURCE: PHOTOGRAPH BY AUTHORS.

value of corporations covered by material assets has fallen sharply in recent decades. Tangible assets accounted for 80% of the market valuation of corporations in 1980 but only 25% of in 2004: the bulk of value is now fictitious, attributed to intangible assets, especially brands (2010, p. 529). As speculative financial markets award premium security values to corporations with valuable brands, the work of brand managers and other professionals in the culture industry is increasingly important.

We theorize brands as global capitalism's most valuable product of the culture industry. The most prominent approach to the analysis of brands is Consumer Culture Theory (CCT). Lying at the intersection of sociology, anthropology and marketing (Arnould & Thompson, 2005), CCT investigates complex dynamics of consumer lifestyles and consumption identities amidst the fractured sign-systems of postmodern culture (Holt, 1997). Organizing concepts guiding CCT include: the aestheticization of consumption (Featherstone, 1991), brand communities (Muniz & O'Guinn, 2001), subcultures of consumption (Schouten & McAlexander, 1993, 1995), tribal marketing and consumptive *communitas* (Cova & Cova, 2002; Cova, Kozinets, & Shankar, 2012) and the re-enchantment of formerly-disenchanted markets (Firat & Venkatesh, 1995;

Ritzer, 2005). Gender identities have become increasingly staged through consumption, and analyses of symbolic masculinity and gender performativity appear in much of this work (Kimmel, 1994; Mort, 1996; Belk & Costa, 1998; Martin, Schouten & McAlexander, 2006; Thompson, 2012a). We critique the approach and findings of consumer culture theory by analyzing the process of branding and brand management in a prominent contemporary consumer culture: large displacement motorcycling.

Large-displacement motorcycling, motorcycle rallies and consumer cultures associated with motorcycling (clubs, owners groups) have been heavily analyzed within CCT (Alt, 1982; Schouten & McAlexander, 1993, 1995; Muniz & O'Guinn, 2001; Holt, 2004; Holt & Thompson, 2004; Martin, Schouten & McAlexander, 2006; Schouten, Martin & McAlexander, 2007; Thompson, 2008; Schembri, 2009; Thompson, 2012b). Researchers have returned to motorcycling as a forum to examine changes within consumption cultures over time. For example, Schouten, Martin & McAlexander (2007) noted increasing commodification and upscale marketing at American motorcycle rallies. Thompson (2008) and Quinn & Forsyth (2009) noted similar changes in motorcycling club culture, in which the more distasteful and unmarketable vestiges of motorcycling's outlaw, misogynistic past have been displaced by "pseudo-deviance," inclusiveness and heightened self-definition (Martin, Schouten & McAlexander, 2006, Thompson, 2008). Schembri (2009) documents the emergent consumption culture and playful bonding among Harley-Davidson Owner's Group (HOG) members in Australia; as well as the dynamics of gender in such motorcycling scenes (see also Martin, Schouten & McAlexander, 2006; Thompson, 2012a).

The large displacement motorcycle market in the United States is tied closely to motorcycle rallying (see Figure 28). The three American motorcycle manufacturers—Harley-Davidson, Victory and the reorganized Indian Motorcycles—are the most important corporate sponsors of motorcycle rallies and use these events as a major forum to promote their products. Manufacturers display images from major motorcycle rallies, especially Sturgis, in their promotional materials and include links to rallies on their product homepages. In an 2011 interview, Steve Piehl, Harley-Davidson's director of Customer Experience, emphasized that Sturgis was "ground zero" for Harley's marketing program, because it was "real," "authentic" and unreservedly "on brand" forum for HD (S. Piehl, personal communication, 8 August 2012). Other motorcycle rallies lacked the global name recognition (Laconia), the Western "Easy Rider" landscape (Daytona), or more than seventy years of continuity (Republic of Texas).

The centrality of rallying to the large displacement motorcycling market allows us to utilize critical theorists who study the culture industry (Best &

Kellner, 1997; Gottdiener, 2000) by analyzing it as "spectacle" (Debord 2006 [1967], 1988; Gotham & Krier, 2008). To Debord, consumptive experience generates momentary *communitas* among spectators fleetingly aligned with their fellows in joint attendance to spectacular scenes. Joint consumption of spectacular products does not reinforce social and political organization (labor unions, professional associations, political party activities), but cuts across them, ultimately alienating and isolating consumptive spectators while reducing their capacity for creative action. Consumer cultures are a mode of social control that pacifies spectators with mesmerizing images and stupefying forms of entertainment. Authentic social relationships—warm, genuine, cooperative or at least politically effective—are replaced with shallow, passive, temporary co-consumption of administered experiences and profitable exchange of spectacular images and commodity forms. The energy expended upon cultures of consumption are withdrawn from more durable and satisfying forms of associated living, degrading social life further as consumers search for compensatory meaning in shopping and entertainment.

Legend Work in the Development of Sponsorship Markets

We analyze the Sturgis Motorcycle Rally as a capitalized product of the culture industry: an *economy of spectacle*. An economy of spectacle emerges from the enclosure of legendary images and action circulating within the cultural commons (racing, fist-fighting, stick-and-ball games, folk performances, carnival, festivals, motorcycle rallying). The enclosure privatizes, transforming collective life into a form of immaterial capital. The enclosure enables several intertwined economic circuits to develop: spectator markets (payments to see the privatized spectacle), sponsorship markets (payments to be seen within the privatized spectacle) and trophy markets (payments to obtain valorizing proof of attendance).

We studied the Sturgis Motorcycle Rally as an economy of spectacle because the Rally reveals how privatized legends enclosed from the cultural commons promote profit by sustaining spectator, sponsor and trophy markets over time (Hyde, 2005; Boyle, 2003, 2008; Holt, 2004). Economies of spectatorship are a form of immaterial production (Hardt & Negri, 2005, pp. 109–115; 2008, pp. 132–137; DeAngelis, 2007, pp. 165–172) created through privatization of culture using intellectual property law to reappropriate value (Boyle, 2003) created under conditions of "co-production" using the immaterial labor of working consumers (Cova & Dalli, 2009), many of whom produce the very show they pay to view (Kozinets et al., 2004). Analysts who study the unpaid labor of consumers point to a condition of double-exploitation (Cova & Dalli, 2009, p. 29) that consumers rarely understand with clarity. Originally part of public-domain popular culture, these images are refreshed, reproduced and embedded with value by consumers in economies of spectacle. Once produced and privatized, these enclosed legends stimulate consumers with desire for additional expenditure of time and money to dwell within the cultural space taken from them. Legends orient the behavior of participants and spectators within the consumptive scene, hence economic spectacles become disoriented and disrupted when their legends lose clarity and focus.

Because of this, managers of brands enclosed from the cultural commons must actively engage in *legend work* to administrate public perceptions of legendary origins on the enclosed culture while promoting continuity between current activity and a storied past. In our study, we have found that legend work can rarely be accomplished by a single corporate sponsor or brand manager, but must be undertaken by *Cross Marketing Licensing Networks* (CMLN), communities of interest composed of corporate, civic and state actors with an interest in sustaining the value of privatized legends and the brands they infuse. In the case of the Sturgis Motorcycle Rally, the CMLN is composed of rally profiteers and civic leaders who often simulate and fabricate legendary content to ensure that bodies, eyeballs and dollars continue to circulate within the spectacle.

Heritage Motorcycling: Racing and Gypsy Touring

The large displacement motorcycle market in the United States utilized two distinct enclosures of the cultural commons: club-organized touring and adventure motorcycling (which we refer to as *"heritage motorcycling"*) and outlaw-biker culture, the subject of mass hysteria and low-budget films in the 1970s. Though both of these enclosures involved large-displacement motorcycles, they shared little else, as their underlying legends were located in mutually hostile regions of popular culture, separated by a yawning generation gap and unbridgeable social divisions. Indeed, outlaw bikers and organized heritage motorcycling clubs were stigmatizing to each other.

Heritage motorcycling, like other forms of *automobility* (Urry, 2004) emerged as middle-class phenomena as manufacturers promoted a new and unfamiliar region of consumption. Motorcycling was pursued as an avocation of respectable citizens who remained within their workaday identity while joining well-run, organized motorcycle clubs. Early motorcycle clubs were tightly coupled to manufacturers and dealers and constituted a culture of consumption: club members reviewed brands and models, gave advice on modifications and accessories, kept careful track of attendance and participation in events, arranged for professional photographs of tours and other events, and were as organized as hierarchically as a military battalion.

The growth of large displacement motorcycling in the United States was fostered by an early privatization of heritage motorcycling. After World War I, gypsy touring was the focal point of motorcycle culture, and included racing, camping, and gaming at designated watering holes and stopping points. Motorcycle rallies evolved from club-organized gypsy tours, in which groups of motorcycle enthusiasts travelled point-to-point, often following carefully mapped routes. Because gypsy touring covered long distances, participants often camped along the way; in city parks or farm fields. Despite the vagabond nature of this experience and its gypsy label, these tours remained within the well-defined middle class cultural space that was central to pre- and post-war *automobility*. Tours were respectable events, officially sanctioned and promoted by motorcycle associations like the Federation of American Motorcyclists and later the American Motorcycle Association. Participants in these events practiced mutual surveillance and informal social control to keep each other in line. Heritage motorcycling kept their gypsy tours clean: prizes were awarded for good demeanor, neat attire and for winning a variety of homely motorcycle games: such as "riding the plank," (a kind of tight-rope walk with a bike), "biting the wiener" (men would drive their wife under a hanging hot dog at speed while she attempted to bite it off) and "whacking the murphy" (a sort of joust). Gypsy tours were led by a "tourmaster," with lieutenants and captains assigned in a hierarchy to closely monitor riders, help repair breakdowns and keep the tour on schedule and within respectable morality. Heritage motorcycling was a family activity: the rider was not an independent "loner," but an organization man or woman: middle class, respectable, concerned with reputation and public morals, worried about sexual license (there is a preponderance of commentary in early motorcycling magazines about the inappropriateness of women wearing skirts or not riding side saddle). Heritage motorcycling did not travesty bourgeois morality: it *was* bourgeois morality.

The emerging popular culture of pioneering motorcycle adventuring, gypsy touring and races was enclosed by manufacturers, promoted in their marketing materials and "restaged" during the sponsored gypsy tours. Racing was especially important to generate desire for bikes: the legendary, daredevil excitement drove sales of machines and gear.

Economies of spectacle develop when authentic activities in the social commons are enclosed and privatized as a capitalized product of the culture industry. In stock car racing, for example, small-scale beachfront and county road races were the initial attractor of bodies and eyeballs, and once enclosed (literally enclosed with grandstands and sight-barrier fencing—indeed, some of the earliest enclosures of auto racing repurposed the infrastructure of horse-racing tracks) generated attendance ticket sales, sponsorship sales and eventually grew into NASCAR, whose races dominate lists of the largest spectator events in the United States. The enclosure of gypsy touring and races such as those at Sturgis served as an initial enclosure of the motorcycling commons, infusing the culture of consumption with legends of adventure, freedom and good-clean bourgeois fun. The Sturgis Motorcycle Rally began as one of these small-scale enclosures of heritage motorcycling, with well attended dirt-track races, trail rides, road tours and hill climbs along with product trials aimed at promoting the sponsor's Indian Motorcycle dealership. For its first three decades, the event remained small, as did the market for large displacement motorcycles in the U.S. that plummeted during this period. When Indian Motorcycles went bankrupt in 1954 including Indian Motorcycles, which went bankrupt in 1953, Harley-Davidson remained as the sole American manufacturer serving an anemic market.

The Second Enclosure Movement: Privatizing the Legend of the Outlaw Biker

During the 1970s, motorcycling expanded rapidly as a second enclosure of cultural legends, symbols and imagery associated with the countercultural lifestyles of outlaw bikers spurred fresh interest in motorcycling and its associated branded commodities. Television and film depictions of legendary biker outlaws, especially the award-winning hippie-biker film Easy Rider, lured a wave of film-induced consumers into the culture of consumption. These new consumers were not actively recruited by either motorcycle rally organizers or by the marketing staff at the sole remaining American manufacturer of motorcycles, Harley-Davidson, but began attending rallies en masse as a countercultural escape from workaday life. They were in fact initially viewed as a detriment to the culture of consumption: film-induced consumers rode astride chopped and bobbed used bikes and seemed unlikely to purchase a new Harley-Davidson from dealers still marketing bikes branded for club-organized heritage cyclists.

Film-induced consumers spurred rapid growth in motorcyling, Privatized spectacles, enclosed from the cultural commons, provide consumers with momentary communitas and identities, a point frequently made in consumer culture theory (see Schembri, 2009) depiction of the Australian Harley-Davidson owners group and Belk & Costa's (1998) analysis of mountain men rendezvous. Harley-Davidson and rally organizers were slow to realize that these new legends circulating in popular culture—legends of outlaw bikers—had eclipsed *heritage motorcycling* themes, activities and brands. In the 1980s, Harley-Davidson and other purveyors of motorcycle gear began enclosing this now widespread popular culture, privatizing legendary narratives and iconic outlaw biker images into brand identities, advertising campaigns and marketing slogans.

By 1985, motorcycle touring and rallying had been almost entirely overshadowed by the spectacle of consumers restaging legendary scenes. Clad in the regalia of outlaw bikers, these new attendees came for the party, not the races or tours. Their activities mirrored a classic Bakhtinian Carnival (Krier & Swart, 2012) marked by sexualized play, unfocused interaction, drinking, brawling, milling and mesalliance or camping rough (see Ferrell, 1999, who views the spread of criminal-motifs in popular culture as "cultural criminology"). Motorcycle rallying became a venue of "film-induced tourism" (Riley, Baker & Van Doren, 1998; Kim & Richardson, 2003; Connell, 2012). Gazing upon each other, imagining themselves within the legendary world of the outlaw biker, the rally was not just "tourism," but a carnival whose participants formed an economic spectacle.

Large displacement motorcycling and the Sturgis Rally first grew by enclosing club racing and touring but expanded rapidly upon enclosure of legends associated with outlaw bikers. It had a particularly distorting impact upon Sturgis because its initial legend was discontinuous and culturally discordant with the legend of outlaw and hippie The original racing events receded into the margins of the spectacle as a minor sideshow hardly attended by the masses of rally-goers playing at being outlaw bikers. This particular pattern of development may be unique to the Sturgis Rally. Other spectacles may not experience such displacement of legend in the course of their development.

We expect that a graphical depiction of spectacular development for most major spectacles (including other motorsports spectator events that we have studied) would approximate a series of concentric circles growing around a stable, relatively unchanging center, where original events and founding legends remain the focus of spectatorship in each development stage. The mediated images of outlaw bikers that caused rapid growth at Sturgis, however, were not rebroadcasts of Jackpine Gypsy dirt-track races but imaginary screen depictions of outlaw and hippie biker culture that viewers sought to recreate in the real at Sturgis. Unlike NASCAR, which retained its original enclosed legends as they developed, the Sturgis Motorcycle Rally grew when an external legend attracted new spectators, fascinated with media-generated images of outlaw bikers, searched for a forum in which they could immerse themselves in this world of fantasied countercultural enjoyment. The outlaw biker legend did not become the Sturgis brand or the Harley-Davidson brand as a result of internal "legend work": but was a fortuitous unplanned externality (Holt, 2004, p. 187).

Parallel to our case, Holt (2004, pp. 155–188) analyzed Harley-Davidson who had a windfall when their brand became identified with outlaw biker legend. A complex sequence of events (disruptive activity of actual outlaw bikers, media-fuelled moral panic, growing youthful rejection of establishment culture and heroic depictions of outlaw bikers in the media) established Harley's equation with outlaw bikers by 1970. Though initially a drawback for Harley-Davidson, the outlaw biker legend as Harley brand paid off when Reagan-Era intervention in the motorcycle industry, continuing positive film placements (Holt singles out Schwarzenegger's riding of a Harley in *Terminator 2* as a signal moment), and the rise of consumer masculinity focused upon symbols of the "gunfighter" man-of-action hero (Holt 2004, p. 175).

Similar to Harley-Davidson, once branded as a celebration of the outlaw biker legend, the Sturgis Motorcycle Rally grew explosively, peaking at 633,000 participants in 2000. This massive crowd of spectators formed a critical mass of bodies and eyeballs ripe for commercial exploitation. After 1985, property developers, corporate marketers and event promoters swept in and professional rally organizers and event promoters began to actively manage the Rally's logistics and content in line with spectator tastes (Cluley, 2009).

As the Sturgis Rally grew, it became a scene of capitalist profit-making, establishment power and traditional religious values. The legend of the outlaw biker was lost amidst the "swarming forms of the banal" (Adorno 1991, p. 34) in the economic, political and religious integration of the Sturgis spectacle. This outlaw rally had become entirely lawful and exceptionally profitable: a multi-centered, swirling carnival of brands with uncoordinated activities spread out over dozens of locations in downtown Sturgis and other venues outside of the city limits. Pickle-licking contests, midget bowling, welding demonstrations, assault rifle ranges, History Channel displays, political speeches by conservative politicians, religious ceremonies, concert appearances by aging 1980s hair bands, and various memorial rides were among thousands of activities that developed around the Rally. Off-brand products and services appeared in bizarre juxtaposition alongside on-brand products and services aligned with the leather, skin and steel of the outlaw biker legend. Marketing representatives for major insurance companies (GEICO), automobile manufacturers, motorcycle attorneys, various consumer products from soft drinks to meat, pain relievers, cigars, wines, vacation package tours, various sellers of jewelry vied to attract the disposable income of rally-attendees. The proliferation of such myriad activities—especially those unrelated or even hostile to outlaw biker legend—eventually destabilized the value of the enclosed cultural legends, muddying the water sufficiently to generate a crisis of authenticity. Indeed, few outlaw bikers or countercultural experimenters could be seen within the rally, and those that remained viewed the upscale consumers of bike culture with disdain as poseurs (Austin, Gagne & Orend, 2010, p. 58).

Managing Enclosures: Cross Marketing Licensing Networks and the Outlaw Biker

The enclosure of popular culture associated with outlaw bikers, the transformation of edgy rebellion into cool brands, devalued the capitalized culture associated with the Sturgis Motorcycle Rally. In the 2000s, this crisis of authenticity could be discerned in a number of ways (compare to the literature on authenticity in tourism such as MacCannell, 1973; Rickly-Boyd, 2012). The built environment of the town of Sturgis no longer looked like the town of old: it had been (re)constructed to effectively stage a gathering of 500,000 simulated outlaw bikers. This small western town featured expansive sections of asphalt to accommodate vendor tents and booths, a large inventory of commercial buildings with partitioned space suitable for vendor rental, several square-mile campgrounds, and multi-tiered plywood saloons. During the two weeks of the rally, the town filled with vendors, display booths, bikers and visitors but looked remarkably bleak during the rest of the year. Much of the prime rally real estate had long since passed into the hands of out-of-state owners who allowed historic buildings to sit vacant, sometimes bulldozing them to free up space for high-profit rally use.

By 2000, the political culture of the State of South Dakota, as well as the citizenry of Sturgis, became politically conservative. The rally's displays of counter-cultural lifestyles—sexualized frolicking, public intoxication and drug use—met with increasing administrative and police resistance. Most notably, city and county officials prohibited bikers from camping in city parks and open space, forcing rally-goers into expensive hotels or large campgrounds outside city limits. The city also began enforcing nudity laws, mandating pasties and arresting those who displayed statutorily-prohibited pieces of skin.

Finally, the quality of the "spectacle of other spectators" declined: there were fewer rally-goers to look at (attendance was lower in most years after 2000) and, as widely acknowledged and decried by Rally organizers, those who continued to attend were clearly aging. Current rally-goers no longer had that lean, aggressive look characteristic of cinematic outlaw bikers: they tended to be arthritic, out of condition, and balance-challenged, driving self-supporting three-wheeled trikes rather than hard-to-hold-upright Harley-Davidsons. Like Wilde's *Picture of Dorian Gray,* Sturgis spectators aged while the image of the outlaw biker remained forever young. The resulting discrepancy between the brand image of the biker and the reality of rally attendees signified, rather jarringly, that the biker base of Sturgis had aged itself off-brand.

Powerful images of outlaw biker culture—leather, skin and steel—had long infused rallies with thematic imagery, branding the spectacular space. This branding was ontologically legendary, not real. Actual flesh-and-blood outlaw bikers were not necessary to ground the Sturgis brand; what was necessary were easily-recognizable, attractive and reproducible legends of them. This powerful on-brand legend sustained and shaped spectatorship even while the rally worked to negate it. But eventually, commercialization of the rally, the crackdown on transgressive behavior, the aging of the biker demographic, and the bizarre commingling of on-brand and off-brand cultural forms proved overwhelming: the outlaw legend lost its orienting force.

Depleted, over-enclosed legends undergo a crisis of authenticity and a devaluation of brands. Sturgis was in this situation by 2000. When faced by such crises, those who enclose the cultural commons engage in *legend work* to administrate public perceptions of the legendary origins of the economic spectacle (contrast to Mundt 2002 on "myths" in branding). Legend work began in earnest at Sturgis in 2010, as government officials, Rally organizers and the Rally's corporate partners organized to refocus and recharge the value of motorcycle legends. Legend work clarifies and promotes a spectacular brand image not only to attract spectators, but also to structure their behavior and consumption patterns. Luedicke, Thompson & Gieseler (2010) use a parallel concept, "consumer identity work," to reference activity undertaken by consumers to manage competing, contradictory moral demands that emerge within consumption and are mediated by it. Fuchs analyzes such activity as digital labor to develop an "audience commodity" (2014, p. 100). It is likely that consumers engaged in such identity work in and around Sturgis as well, but our focus is on the "legend work" undertaken by the producers of the Rally— civic leaders, event promoters and marketing professionals—to facilitate the alignment of consumer and brand identities.

Legend work seeks to remedy three degradations of legend:

1. *legendary banality* resulting from over-exposure and over-enclosure of iconic images and narratives,
2. *legendary incoherence* resulting from over-extension of cross-marketing into unrelated cultural regions, and

3.   *legendary undesirability* resulting from cultural change that redefines the
      content of legends as excremental objects.

Legend work overcomes these degradations by restoring desire to the original
legendary images and narratives, restoring coherence and clarity of legendary
images—often by policing and removing incongruent cross-marketing from
the cultural space and in the face of legendary undesirability, replacing the degraded legend with new content freshly enclosed out of the cultural commons.

At Sturgis, organizers paid special attention to establishing and promoting
continuity between the legendary origins of the rally and its current activities. To facilitate legend work, Sturgis civic leaders recently terminated their
promotional contract and cross-marketing license agreements with Motoring
U.S.A. They also engaged the services of an architectural design firm (Four
Square Design, Rapid City) and marketing consultants to clarify, refocus and
promote the Sturgis brand and to mediate between advocates of different origin myths.

Legend work at Sturgis revealed a *politics of legend* involving two factions of
rally organizers: CMLN divided into two subgroups:

1.   *Civic Leaders:* officials representing permanent residents of Sturgis
      interested in promoting a vibrant, year-round economy; many of these
      leaders sought to decouple Sturgis' fortunes from that of the Rally by
      spurring non-rally tourism and economic development; wished to main-
      tain civic control over the rally—ensuring that it remains domesticated,
      controlled, safe and advantageous for Sturgis and its citizens.[1]
2.   *Rally Profiteers:* officials representing extra-local real estate, commercial
      and corporate enterprise interested in extracting profits from annual
      Sturgis Motorcycle Rallies; economic interest of these officials is entirely
      rally-focused (growing it, promoting it, profiting from it; while minimiz-
      ing fixed investments and taxes); many of these officials travel the circuit
      of other motorcycle rallies.[2]

---

1   Several agencies are merged in our concept of civic leaders, including City of Sturgis officials
     (mayor, city manager, Rally coordinator), the Sturgis Area Chamber of Commerce and the
     Sturgis Economic Development Commission.
2   Several entities are merged in our concept of rally profiteers, including officials representing
     the Buffalo Chip Campground, the Broken Spoke Saloon and Campground, the Full Throttle
     Saloon and various organizers and promoters of multiple motorcycle rallies around the U.S.,
     such as Motoring U.S.A. Our use of "profiteers" as a concept is descriptive rather than legal.

In light of this political situation, legend work at Sturgis was doubled. Rally profiteers, with the full cooperation and assistance of civic leaders, worked to promote legends of the outlaw bikers while civic leaders, acting mostly on their own, worked to promote legends of heritage motorcycling. Through 2012, the legend work of rally profiteers was more straightforward than that of civic leaders. Both parties acknowledged the outlaw biker legend as foundational to the Rally, and willingly branded Sturgis with the outlaw biker legend since it stabilized desire for attendance among its biker base.

Civic leaders and rally profiteers, alone or in partnership, promoted the legend of the outlaw biker in a variety of media to bring the Sturgis brand to distant spectators. Broadcast programming included Sturgis themed episodes of Cops, Sturgis themed episodes of Pawn Stars and American Pickers on the History Channel, several Sturgis based specials on the Travel Channel, and a Sturgis-based reality-television series entitled Full-Throttle Saloon on TruTV. Rally profiteers also encouraged (at least tacitly) the production of sexualized DVD's with titles like "Sturgis Gone Wild," "Sturgis Uncensored," and "Girls of Sturgis." Civic leaders and rally profiteers promoted the outlaw biker brand in multiple online forums, including city and business websites, online rally schedules, promotional websites and user-submitted photo and video galleries.

Legend work serves as a masking device, covering off-brand changes to the rally with on-brand imagery. For example, prior to 1983, rally-goers had camped in city parks and other public spaces during the rally. The city of Sturgis closed the park to camping in 1982, a move that shifted the wildest parts of the Rally outside city limits to open undeveloped campgrounds. These campgrounds were often owned by rally-profiteers rather than civic leaders and quickly grew by unabashedly embracing the outlaw biker legend, promoting it in their advertising copy, such as the Full Throttle Saloon's trademarked "The world's biggest biker bar" or The Buffalo Chip Campground's trademarked "the best party anywhere." Rally profiteers profited from their own post-1983 legendary reputations as venues for counter-cultural behavior and sexual license. Advertised as adult-only playgrounds, these venues promise the "authentic Sturgis experience" in which those who pay the entrance fee can party like an outlaw biker amidst the backdrop of wild-west libertarianism.

However, the imagery of outlaw biker culture that pervaded these "authentic" Sturgis venues masked the reality that they are quite fake—simulations (Baudrillard, 1983a, 1983b) of a legendary Sturgis rather than a real one. These "authentic" Sturgis experiences did not take place in tolerant, old-west towns but in renovated cow pastures, whose metal sheds are covered with plywood "old-west" facades. Their swimming holes were, in reality, stock ponds with trucked-in sand beaches, and their musical venues feature upgraded VIP seating. While the wild, raucous and rough camping of Sturgis outlaw legend was certainly available, many aging rally-goers—accustomed to high-thread-count sheets and good mattresses—opted for a better class of accommodation. These facilities provided air conditioned cabins, RV-parking sites with full hookups and "ready-made" camping kits prepared by staff for those unable or unwilling to manage their own camping gear. Thus legend work at these venues masked the discrepancy between the Sturgis brand that stimulated rally-goers desire for attendance and the reality of the built environment that accommodated them.

Legend work also masked the reality that the aging demographic of rally-goers were off-brand regarding sexualized display. With careers, families and reputations at risk, responsible rally-goers were increasingly hesitant to flaunt their aging charms before audiences equipped with digital cameras and 4G connectivity. Thus rally profiteers routinely hired attractive young women to work as bartenders, waitresses and ticket-takers; their primary function was to simulate the sexualized transgression associated with outlaw bikers but no longer engaged in by establishment rally-goers. More sex-worker than laborer, these young women wore costumed regalia, mimicked the "girls gone wild" of Sturgis DVD lore, and displayed as much skin as legally permissible in a finely-tuned game of regulated raunch. Such intentional on-brand theming sustained the legend of the rally by providing ample (yet simulated) evidence that countercultural activities continue at the center of Rally activity. Legend work allows rally-goers to safely maintain their morality and modesty while imagining themselves in the legendary world of the outlaw biker.

All of this extensive legend work, conducted cooperatively by rally profiteers and civil leaders, addressed the *banality* and *incoherence* of the outlaw biker legend (due to over-exposure, over-enclosure, over-extension, cross-marketing). These activities sought to infuse outlaw biker legends, images and narratives with desire by restoring coherence, clarity and authenticity.

Managing Enclosures: Civic Leaders, Rally Profiteers and Heritage Motorcycling

Civic leaders addressed their legend work to a second, more profound degradation of legend: the *undesirability* of outlaw biker culture for economic development. These leaders promoted a *return to the original legend underlying the rally associated with heritage motorcycling* of the Jackpine Gypsy variety: respectable, formally-organized, bourgeois. Civic leaders recognized that the outlaw biker legend had sustained the rally but constrained options to attract new industry, develop year round tourism and to promote new economic development. They sought to replace the degraded outlaw biker legend with fresh enclosures of the cultural commons and *heritage motorcycling* emerged as a legend that business-minded leaders in a conservative political culture could build upon, safe for families and potential investors in the local economy.

Museums institutionalize legend work: they create, refine and represent legends of the past to contemporary audiences. Legendary museums are widespread in cultures of consumption based upon privatized legends. For instance, hall of fame museums perform legend work for most major spectator sports (National Football League, National Baseball, Basketball, Hockey, NASCAR, America's Cup Yacht Racing) and many non-sports spectacles (Rock & Roll, Country Music, Blues). In recent years, a new genre of legendary museum has emerged: dedicated experience museums that commemorate events and other ephemeral happenings (Daytona 500 Experience; Harley-Davidson Experience, NASA Experience, Scotch Whiskey Experience) and travelling experience exhibits that routinely tour traditional museums (Sixties Experience, Vietnam Experience, Woodstock Experience), transforming these general cultural spaces into workshops of focused legend work. Through artifacts and interpretive exhibits, these cultural institutions forestall crises of authenticity and mitigate them once they begin, selectively displaying images that reinforce the image of legend desired by promoters of spectacle.

The legend of *heritage motorcycling* as the foundation of the Sturgis brand was nurtured in the Sturgis Motorcycle Museum and Hall of Fame. Located in downtown Sturgis, supported by civic leaders, the museum showcased dozens of motorcycles and featured images from pre- World War II Jackpine Gypsies events, including the Black Hills Motorcycling Classic. The Sturgis Motorcycle Museum de-emphasized outlaw and counter-cultural themes—in fact, no images from the rebellious decade between 1975 and 1985 was on display or in their collection. Instead, the museum collection focused upon heritage motorcycling, especially the respectable Jackpine Gypsies portrayed as founding fathers of the Sturgis legend, with Clarence "Pappy" Hoel cast in the role of George Washington, and his wife as a motherly Betsy Ross (compare to "Legendary Gypsies, Sturgis, South Dakota" t-shirts featuring clean-cut riders on un-chopped bikes).

In 2012, civic leaders unveiled plans to dramatically enlarge the Sturgis Motorcycle Museum and Hall of Fame into a destination attraction, housed in a new, Disneyesque building featuring a 40-foot tall, rider-less motorcycle (depicted in an architectural rendering as a vintage Indian, not a chopped Harley Davidson) rising out its roof (see Figure 29). This museum extension does not prominently feature outlaw biker imagery nor countercultural theming. Rather, it is linked to a broader revitalization aimed at reformulating a cleaner

Sturgis brand ("Sturgis Freedom" is the current choice for a brand slogan favored by civic leaders) to better attract year-round, family-friendly tourism. Sturgis City officials have drawn three additional motoring events to the city with this more general brand image—including family oriented owners rallies for Ford Mustangs, Chevrolet Camaros, and Cushman Scooters. During the 2013 rally, the reorganized Indian Motorcycle company (a division of Polaris) launched its new range of retro-motorcycles, with prominent styling cues of heritage-motorcycling, brand managers selected the Sturgis Motorcycle Museum and Hall of Fame as the site of their product launch. Event organizers staged gleaming heritage-styled machines on top of the roof (mimicking the artists' conception above). Indian Motorcycles, like Sturgis Civic Leaders, chose to move away from the over-enclosed outlaw biker legend to re-enclose the culture of heritage motorcycling, basing product design, marketing and advertising campaigns upon the legend of adventurous, heritage pioneers.[3]

The legend of the outlaw biker as an anchor of the Sturgis brand was promoted in a variety of locations owned and controlled by rally profiteers: in 2012, the most prominent being the "Motorcycle as Art" exhibit at the Buffalo Chip Campground (or, as billed in its advertising, the "Legendary Buffalo Chip"). This exhibit brought together representative custom motorcycles, historical photographs of outlaw and countercultural bikers and visual artwork featuring choppers, bobbers and subsidiary regalia outlaw biker culture. Notably absent: any reference to the square, Jackpine Gypsy heritage motorcycling featured in the museum downtown.

Despite their divergent interests, the two factions of the CMLN functioned effectively as a unified team, as evidenced in their joint willingness to add the words "legend" and "legendary" to recent trademarks and signage, including "Legendary Sturgis Mainstreet," "Legendary Sturgis Area Chamber of Commerce and Visitors Bureau," "Legendary Buffalo Chip" that sponsors an annual "Legends' Ride." This cooperation extended to partnerships between the civic-minded Sturgis Motorcycle Museum and the profiteering Buffalo Chip to organize joint exhibitions to flesh out and refine legendary images favorable to both factions. In 2011, the Buffalo Chip hosted one of the museum's exhibits on the history of women in motorcycling, entitled "Paving the Way." Still, the imagery displayed throughout the visual space of the Buffalo Chip and other

---

3   While Indian is resurrecting the legend of heritage motorcycling, it is doing so selectively, entirely abandoning the word "gypsy" or any images that include gypsy imagery. Enclosure of cultural legends creates capitalized culture through ongoing cultivation and domestication of captured legends, rather than by a single act of plunder.

large Sturgis Rally venues almost exclusively conjured the legend of the outlaw biker as the Sturgis brand.[4]

In neo-liberalism, privatized legends are vulnerable to re-appropriation, piracy or rustling by outsiders to the CMLN. By the 2000s, the outlaw biker legend became a free-range global brand transferred to a wide variety of scenes and products. Even the specific brand packaging of Sturgis' outlaw biker legend was re-appropriated. The name "Sturgis" was trademarked by a group of local and non-local businessmen (Sturgis Motorcycle Rally, Inc.): the City of Sturgis paid royalties to use its own name (Wagner, 2013) in conjunction with its own rally. Other towns named Sturgis rustled the Rally's immaterial capital: Sturgis, Mississippi (population 254) staged a knock-off rally, an annual "Too Broke for Sturgis" Rally was held in Arizona, an annual "Sturgis on the River" rally was held in Davenport, Iowa. Legendary images and icons rustled from the Sturgis enclosure reappeared in myriad motorcycle rallies, sporting the same carnival of brands, consumer product managers, event marketers, rally personnel, and itinerant vendors. The Hell's Angels carved enclosures from outlaw biker legend and maintained active intellectual property litigation to protect their marketed product lines (Kovaleski, 2013). The ingredients of a Sturgis-style outlaw motorcycle rally were widely known and accessible to key players in the motorcycle event industry who efficiently assembled the components of a ready-made motorcycle rally with a few spins of their Rolodex. The 2012 Iowa Grand Rally was a case in point—a McDonaldized rally (Ritzer, 2013) fully saturated with Sturgis-style theming, situated in a new venue and timed to capture biker traffic en route to the Sturgis Rally. In a similar fashion, Rod Woodruff, owner of the Buffalo Chip campground, hosted the 2011 "Sturgis Road Show" in Hershey Pennsylvania—cloning the Sturgis Motorcycle Rally down to its very name. The capital invested to build the outlaw biker-themed Sturgis legend created a global commodity with portable "cash value" that was captured by those who did not create it.

Conclusion

Spectacular economies, not only motorcycle rallies like Sturgis but also NASCAR and professional stick-and-ball sports, are inherently self-negating. Privatized

---

4   The political division in the Sturgis CMLN deepened in Spring 2015 when Ron Woodruff, owner of the Buffalo Chip, successfully incorporated his campground and rally-venue as a city over the political opposition of Sturgis' civic leaders (Holland, 2015, 20 February). The incorporation of the east campground region as a separate political entity will further enable rally profiteers to forestall and engross rally markets.

legends, carved from the cultural commons, and transformed into capitalized products of the culture industry, are marketed as brands that generate profitable growth, but eventually become degraded, buried under their own reproduction as commercially-exploitable commodities. To Adorno, the culture industry was "dominated by the distribution and mechanical reproduction" of reified culture (1991, p. 101). Following Benjamin (1936), Adorno argued that the "aura" of traditional culture disappears in the culture industry, which is "defined by the fact that ... it conserves the decaying aura as a foggy mist" (1991, p. 101). The aura of legends in the commons, captured, privatized and conserved as trademarked brands, nevertheless is subject to decay. When the foggy mists of enclosed legend dissipate, aura is recharged through managed gleanings of the commons.

Simulation, reproduction and mass distribution debases capitalized culture, no matter how fascinating its original aura. The culture of consumption surrounding motorcycling, including the Sturgis Rally, was threatened with devaluation from a depleted, over-enclosed brand. Motorcycling's cross-marketing licensing network sought to restore value to their degraded enclosure through legend work that restored desire, coherence and authenticity to outlaw biker culture while re-enclosing the heritage motorcycling that preceded it. It appears that for Sturgis, at least, legend work was successful and the Sturgis brand remains capable of stimulating a half-million well-off vacationers to forgo the pleasures of luxury resorts in favor of an uncomfortable journey to a crowded, inconvenient rally of dubious repute for a week of debauched slumming.

This chapter analyzed brands as products of the culture industry, capitalized and managed through ongoing "primitive accumulation" and enclosures of the cultural commons. From this perspective, marketing professionals do not create iconic brands *sui generis* but instead capture and enclose them from the cultural commons. The crucial question for analysts of contemporary capitalism is not to understand how "brands become icons," but rather how legends in the commons become private brands when they are hunted, captured and enclosed by marketers and practitioners of intellectual property law. The analysis of enclosed brands as immaterial capital reveals that primitive accumulation is not a one-time act of cultural piracy, but an ongoing cultivation and management of enclosed legends, closer to ranching than hunting.[5] The second enclosure movement is not mere expropriation, but coproduction of legendary value by extracting unpaid living labor from working consumers that is embedded within immaterial products enhancing corporate values.

---

5 Compare to Wallerstein's (1980: 160) analysis of state-supported, hence legally-defensible, piracy and plunder as a technique of primitive accumulation in the 17th century.

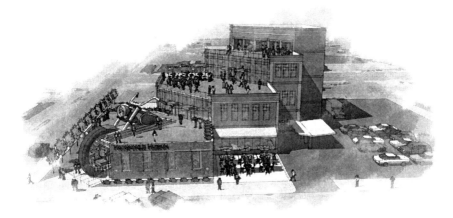

FIGURE 29   *Legend Work at Sturgis: Architectural Rendering of the Proposed Sturgis Experience*
Museum, 2012
SOURCE: ARCHITECTURAL RENDERING CREATED BY FOUR FRONT DESIGN,
INC., RAPID CITY, SOUTH DAKOTA FOR THE STURGIS MOTORCYCLE MUSEUM
AND HALL OF FAME, STURGIS, SOUTH DAKOTA. COPYRIGHT STURGIS MOTOR-
CYCLE MUSEUM AND HALL OF FAME.

The economy of spectacle is structured parallel to speculative financial markets. Enclosures of the cultural commons operate like initial public offerings,
in which surplus value is captured and extracted in a strategic, legally-backed,
one-time market operation. The value of legends, like corporate securities,
once capitalized, fluctuates based upon managerial action. Under conditions
of immaterial production, cross-marketing licensing networks emerge as powerful and important actors who engage in legend work to intervene in the value
of degraded legends by countering the effects of banality, incoherence and the
consumer nausea that arises when legends lose their cool. CMLN manage the
value of legends in a process parallel to speculators who manage the value of
corporate stock through organizational restructuring, mergers, acquisitions
and other interstitial reshufflings (Krier, 2005). Initial acts of enclosure and expropriation must be technically differentiated from the ongoing management
of value. Critical political economy allows us to see the work of marketing professionals and brand managers in a brighter, but more sinister, light. These actors capture value not only by engaging in cultural piracy through enclosures
of the public domain but also by coordinating the unpaid, immaterial labor of
working consumers. Primitive accumulation under conditions of immaterial
production depends upon a special dynamic, in which value is not captured by
hunting and killing in the wilds of culture, but rather by domesticating brands
and fattening them in the legendary commons like a herd.

CHAPTER 6

Paying to be Seen Enjoying: Trophy Markets, Display, and Surplus Enjoyment

Contemporary sociological theories have addressed *megaspectacles* as intensified scenes of consumption (Best and Kellner, 2001; Ritzer, 2008). Mixing entertainment and tourism with retail marketing, megaspectacles are related to a number of other theoretical constructs, including "mega-events" (Roche, 2000), "new forms of consumption" (Gottdiener, 2000), "new means of hyperconsumption" (Ritzer, 2005), subcultures of consumption (McAlexander, Schouten & Koenig, 2002), and economies of spectacle (Krier & Swart, 2014a). Megaspectacles have also been analyzed as a manifestation of a broader Bakhtinian "carnivalization of society" (Langmann & Ryan, 2009). Following Bakhtin (1968), contemporary carnivalesque scenes include highly participative, yet often commodified gatherings such as Burning Man (Kozinets, 2002), Mardi Gras (Gotham & Krier, 2008), the Occupy movement (Langman & Lundskow, 2012), music festivals (Flinn & Frew, 2014), and historical reenactments (Belk & Costa, 1998).

This literature shares an underlying assumption about the experiential foundation of megaspectacles as venues of fun and pleasure. To quote Collins, large-scale spectator events are interaction rituals in which attendees desire "the experience of being at a successful ritual" structured to enable "the occurrence of strong emotion in a setting where it can be amplified by bodily interaction within the crowd" (2004, p. 59). From this perspective, megaspectacles appear as *markets of spontaneous enjoyment.* By spontaneous enjoyment we mean something akin to *jouissance* (Lacan, 2006 [1966], pp. 694–695),[1] translated as "satisfaction" or "enjoyment" that is immediately realized in situ. Current framings of megaspectacles maintain a commonsense notion that spectators do, in fact, experience intensified *jouissance* while in these settings, and we anticipated these dynamics during our multi-year study of motorsports megaspectacles. We expected to see high levels of spontaneous enjoyment in

---

1   Enjoyment, satisfaction and other chaste words fail to capture *jouissance's* sexual connotations (one translation of *jouir* is to have an orgasm). We concur with Fink (1997: 225–227), who suggests that the phrase "getting off," though crude, is a more accurate translation. The embodied pleasures and sexualized raunch that is central to the legend of motorcycle rallies and speedway infields seems to conform to Lacan's usage: it is not purely or primarily a bodily discharge, but a spark of moral energy that flies like a "symptom" between spectators (see Lacan, 2006 [1966]: 431).

FIGURE 30   *Trophy Hunting in Downtown Sturgis, Circa 2012*
               SOURCE: PHOTOGRAPH BY AUTHORS.

the form of carnivalesque activities, excessive public drunkenness, rowdy rebellion, brawling, mixing of genders, classes and generations and participative
sexualized display. We also expected to find "action" in Goffman's sense: participants immersed in risky, consequential and fateful activities that gave them
the opportunity to prove "character" by willingly undertaking danger and peril
(Goffman, 1967, pp. 149–270).

    While we observed spontaneous enjoyment, conspicuous *jouissance* and ac-
tion during the megaspectacles we studied, their magnitude fell far short of
their description in the literature. Attendees at these events appeared patently
de-animated, physically uncomfortable and passive: spectators more than participants. The conditions necessary for "fun" in social settings, specified by Goffman as unselfconscious joint engrossment and "spontaneous involvement" in
shared activities (1961, pp. 37–41, 80; 1967, pp. 113–114; see also Collins, 2004,
p. 48) were typically not met. Instead, attendees were often unfocused and "out
of play," disconnected from one another yet awaiting with mild anticipation

the occurrence of something worthy of their attention. Further, we observed a preponderance of obviously unpleasant experiences: gruelling walks, extensive wait times, traffic jams, long lines, unsanitary toilets, crowded venues, and uncomfortable environmental conditions. If these negative experiences were subtracted from the pleasures of the event, too little *jouissance* remained to account for spectatorship in terms of a market for spontaneous enjoyment.

But while spontaneous enjoyment was understated at motorsports megaspectacles, these events were predominated by a different type of market; one that we conceptualize as *markets of surplus enjoyment*. Unlike markets of spontaneous enjoyment that are structured by sales of in-venue experiences (access to which is obtained by purchase of admission tickets, cover charges, and event passes), markets of surplus enjoyment are structured by sales of trophies in the form of souvenirs, themed apparel, wearable merchandise, and staged opportunities for amateur photography (see Figure 30). These trophies were not intended to be enjoyed during the event but when they were taken away from the event and displayed elsewhere. The overwhelming preponderance of trophy markets within the space of megaspectacles and the dominance of activity revolving around trophy hunting masked the relative absence of in-venue spontaneous enjoyment. Spectators at the events we studied seemed so distracted by shopping for symbols of enjoyment that they forgot to actually enjoy. When carried away from the event and displayed to non-attendees, these trophies triggered an illusion of in-venue spontaneous enjoyment that masked the absence of its reality. Thus spectator's enjoyment was evidential not experiential: megaspectacles did not immediately "pleasure" their attendees, but enabled them to bask voluptuously in the delayed, reflected glory of their trophies fueled by the envy of those who did not attend.

To summarize, theories of megaspectacle (in all of their varieties) either explicitly or implicitly point to enjoyment within the immediate moment as the primary commodity produced and sold to spectators. Our observations of economies of spectatorship, in which spontaneous enjoyment was scarce and trophies plentiful, challenge this assumption. With liminal pleasures sidelined, the collection of trophies for the purpose of invidious consumption and surplus enjoyment became the central social activity. What drives participation in these events is the hunt for artifacts and documentary evidence that can be used to extract envy from those not present. From this perspective, markets of surplus enjoyment represent a central feature in economies of spectatorship.

In what follows, we develop a sociological model of trophies, trophy hunting and trophy display based upon the theoretical foundations of Veblen (1934 [1899]), Goffman (1967), Lacan (2006 [1966]), and Žižek (2008 [1989]).

We argue that trophies are charged with moral energy by in-venue ritualistic activity, transforming them into collective representations of the megaspectacle from which they were extracted (Collins, 2004; Durkheim, 1965 [1915]; Goffman, 1967; Marshall, 2002, 2010; Worrell, 2005, 2008b). We theorize three different ideal-type forms of trophies, each charged with different kinds of moral energy: status trophies (charged with envy of symbolic prowess), action trophies (charged with envy of imaginary risk taking) and trophies of *jouissance* (charged with envious yet repressed desire for libidinal pleasure). Surplus enjoyment does not arise in the moments in which trophies are charged, but rather emanates from the reflective prestige and envious after-effects of their display. Following Veblen (1934 [1899]), trophies are invidious: they generate few primary gains for possessors, but important secondary gains from the reflected dissatisfaction they induce in others.[2] Trophies are hunted, purchased and displayed in order to disturb the libidinal system of those who view them, forcing these others to envy the trophy possessors' superior status, character and access to *jouissance*.

Megaspectacles and the Lack of Spontaneous Enjoyment

The theoretical approaches to megaspectacles that emphasize spontaneous enjoyment most strongly are those rooted in Bakhtin's (1968) analysis of the writings of Rabelais. Bakhtin developed the concept of the "carnivalesque" to interpret transgressive forms, sexual liberties, and celebratory functions of medieval feasts, festivals and carnival. Many theorists view megaspectacles as modern forms of carnivalesque activities that perform the same social functions as traditional carnival: regenerating social energies, discharging repressed sexuality, relieving aggression, and enabling alienated spectators to experience, however briefly, liminality and communitas (Celsi, Rose, & Leigh,1993; Cova & Cova, 2002; Holt, 1995; Langmann & Ryan, 2009; McAlexander, Schouten & Koenig, 2002; Muniz & O'Guinn, 2001; Turner, 1969; Wang, 1999). Others theorize megaspectacles as large-scale carnivalesque gatherings that allow participants a temporary "second life" to provide reprieve from the repressive constraints of the "first life" of work, school and church (Eco, 1984; Justice, 1994; Langmann & Ryan, 2009). Finally, some theories of the carnivalesque view it more as a repressive than an emancipatory social force and frame megaspectacles as a source of elite social control (Brandist & Tihanov, 2000;

---

2 Veblen's conception of invidious consumption resonates with analyses of mimetic desire (Cassano, 2014; Girard, 1965; Kojeve, 1969: 6; Mauss, 1967).

Camille, 1992; Humphrey, 2001) or repressive desublimation (Langman, 2008; Marcuse, 1964). This darker view of carnivalesque spaces echoes Debord's (1988, 2006 [1967]) *Society of the Spectacle*, where spectacles distract spectators with quickly vanishing pleasure while immersing their consciousness in ideology (Andrews, 2006; Cassano, 2008; Gotham & Krier, 2008; Krier & Swart, 2012; Newman & Giardina, 2011).

Motorsports megaspectacles such as motorcycle rallies and stock car races have a notorious reputation for carnivalesque activity: drinking, fighting and sexual carousing are legendary in these venues and are elemental to their audience appeal. Promotional materials for these events prominently feature imagery of carnivalesque licentiousness as central motifs of event activities. Counter to these expectations, however, we documented little in the way of participatory sexualized activity, raucous transgression or effervescent revelry at the events we studied. Instead, we witnessed a preponderance of decidedly un-carnivalesque behavior: passive, bored spectators engaged in mundane activities as they shopped or manipulated their digital devices. Spectatorship was highly regimented—security workers and staff dictated parking locations, corralled milling, and funneled attendees through a gauntlet of vending. While enthusiasm periodically erupted at races during restarts, military flyovers, or crashes and at motorcycle rallies during concerts or "burn outs," such "peak experiences" represented a small percentage of spectators' time within the event.

Much of the "unfun" of megaspectacles derives from an extreme level of social density that stretches travel and tourism infrastructure to a breaking point. In the crush of dense crowds, even the most basic activity becomes more difficult. Travelling to venues, traversing immense parking lots, setting up camps, negotiating through scrums of spectators, waiting between scheduled events and other work-like activities consume large blocks of spectator time. The events themselves, held outdoors and exposed to the elements, were often physically uncomfortable. Noise levels were often so extreme as to require earplugs or noise-canceling headsets and precluded conversation and interaction. Security personnel enforced assigned seating, separating spectators into stratified categories (skyboxes, bleachers) while limiting carnivalesque milling. The pleasures of eating and drinking were often curtailed by long lines, limited selection and dubious quality. Sleeping was difficult for many spectators due to cramped accommodation and excessive noise. Meeting other creature needs, especially those requiring toilets, was often difficult, inconvenient or at least unpleasant: we often observed spectators (especially women) queuing in long lines before rudimentary and odiferous facilities.

In addition to the unpleasantnesses of social density, several other factors limited carnivalesque experience at megaspectacles. First, the demographic characteristics of attendees at motorsports megaspectacles differ markedly from the types of people who populate their legends. The legends underlying both motorcycle rallies and stock car racing feature young, risk-taking, devil-may-care outlaws with voracious sexual appetites. Actual attendees, however, represent a graying, risk-averse and generally law-abiding demographic with sufficient disposable incomes to make them appreciate the creature comforts lacking in event venues. Even if they desired to engage in the carnivalesque activities of motorsports legend, attendees often had reputations to protect and relationships to lose. Unable to throw caution to the wind, these establishment attendees were often unwilling to make a spectacle of themselves, thus limiting the spectacle of spectators central to authentic carnivalesque events.

Further, the experience of attendees was often interrupted by the distractions of digital technology. The use of smart phones was ubiquitous and intrusive at all venues we studied. Additionally, major speedways (and other major professional sporting leagues) have introduced their own revenue-generating digital technologies to augment spectatorship, including FanVision, a personalized digital radio and video feed that provides enhanced in-venue coverage to audiences. Such devices individuated spectators, drawing their attention into a variety of particularized data streams, limiting their capacity for interactive behavior and spontaneous enjoyment.

Finally, the spectacle staged at racetracks and rallies was often monotonous and frankly boring. Exciting action seemed perpetually forestalled and spectators were patiently waiting for something to happen. The oval tracks of NASCAR, as many critics have noted, reduce auto racing to a highly repetitive, almost numbing series of perpetual left turns by cars whose livery transforms them into rolling billboards. The most depressed appearing group of people that we observed in our research were racing spectators, ears-ringing, pouring out of the stands at the end of a race, the vast majority having just watched their "driver of identification" get defeated, facing the hours-long slog through jammed traffic before reaching home after a de-animated and disappointing day. Similarly, navigating the epicenter of most motorcycle rallies often involves slow rides through stop-and-go traffic astride hot, loud, vibrating v-twin motorcycles. The bulk of the daytime hours during the event are spent standing in the heat listening to second or third rate musical entertainment, aimlessly milling through vendor stalls and motorcycle expos, or wandering around looking at other people's rides.

Thus, while carnivalesque fun and spontaneous enjoyment were central to the legend of motorsports megaspectacles, and while signage, advertising and display screens marketed carnivalesque fun as an icon of these events, we encountered precious little of it in our research. Together, high social density, demographic mismatch, distracted attention and boredom limited the carnivalesque qualities and spontaneous enjoyment of megaspectacles. These events lacked high levels of observable fun and conspicuous pleasure. They were populated by a majority of middle-aged, establishment attendees, and permeated with commerce: "consumers gone mild" more than "girls gone wild."

Despite this, attendees functioned as volunteer customer experience managers, defending the legends of spontaneous enjoyment when we pointed out their absence. Attendees covered over the all too apparent lack of immediate enjoyment with stories of legendary fun that maintained the fantasy of spontaneous enjoyment for themselves and others. When questioned, attendees we interviewed consistently displaced enjoyment to other places and times: "You should have been at last year's Daytona 500," "You should attend next year's Republic of Texas Rally," "You should have been at the Buffalo Chip last night at 2:00am." Throughout our fieldwork we were never in a place that was identified by attendees as the epicenter of spontaneous enjoyment. We do not believe that this was due to an error, oversight or lack of luck on our part. Instead, we see this as symptomatic of participants' desire to maintain the legend of spontaneous enjoyment, which, as we argue below, is crucial to the value of trophies of surplus enjoyment.

Motorsports Megaspectacles as Trophy Markets

To naive observers, NASCAR races, motorcycle rallies and other motorsports megaspectacles could readily appear as vast schemes for the marketing, distribution and sale of themed merchandise; an elaborate traveling flea market full of itinerant vendors working the motorsports circuit. Clearly the built environments of these megaspectacles were optimized for merchandising. At major motorcycle rallies, main traffic thoroughfares, crossroads, and parking lots were transformed into vending spaces. Leases for prime commercial property in downtown Sturgis, South Dakota required that they be vacated for the month of August and converted into retail space for Rally vendors because the rental income from the ten day Rally far exceeded that from the rest of the year. Major clubs, restaurants and bars subleased merchandising stalls in front of and inside of their buildings, layering vendor upon vendor in a somewhat disorganized jumble. Recent litigation over the use of the "Sturgis" registered trademark on apparel has drawn attention to the immense scale of the market for themed T-shirts, motorcycling leathers and other apparel as cheap, mass-produced trophies of "outlaw biker" culture. The retail sprawl of the Rally spreads out from Sturgis to encompass the entire western portion of South

Dakota and rally-themed merchandise is sold at watering holes for hundreds of miles in each direction.

A similar scene was on display at NASCAR megaspectacles. On race weekends, semi-truck trailers filled with racing-themed and sponsor-branded merchandise rimmed the entrance to speedways. Most prominent were merchandising trailers assigned to popular drivers, each hawking driver-and-sponsor themed clothing and collectibles. Other trailers sold highly visible scanners and "FanVision" systems that provided access to premium racing content. Speedways also served as marketing platforms for major automobile and motorcycle manufacturers, hunting and fishing equipment retailers, and military recruiting. Major restaurant franchises often established satellite storefronts within these events, selling racing-themed food and souvenir merchandise. Further afield, outside of the controlled ring of the speedway, laminations of gray economy, unincorporated "Pop Yokum" vendors lined roads and parking lots selling more downmarket, unofficial and unlicensed wares. NASCAR races, like motorcycle rallies, appear on the surface as an elaborate pretext to generate an intensive market for T-shirts.

If the preponderance of trophy markets makes megaspectacles appear as flea-markets, the omnipresence of amateur photography at these events could readily lead casual observers to interpret them as gatherings of amateur documentary filmmakers. Cameras were quite literally everywhere at the events we attended, and the calculating, dogged, purposeful manner with which participants filled their cameras with images means it is almost impossible to overstate the prevalence of digital image taking within megaspectacular venues. At present, the social media forums that host these images contain millions of amateur images from these events. Further, many of these images inadvertently capture other people taking pictures of the same activity: essentially capturing other trophy hunters within the trophy itself. The general ubiquity of digital photography at these events demonstrates that new social media has at least partially eroded the value of traditional, physical trophies while stimulating demand for new forms of digital trophies.

Omnipresent smart phones not only captured images but enabled their instant transmission to online locations and geographically dispersed people. Again, these devices signal that attendees remain tethered to their everyday social networks even while immersed in spectacle events. In addition, their use provides further evidence that attendees were not immersed in spontaneous enjoyment. Camera-wielding attendees were neither active participants in the photographed scene nor spectators immersed in vicarious, scopophilic enjoyment. Instead, they were fully removed from the scene that they were shooting and occupied a role outside the frame of the shot.

Legend confirming photo opportunities were often actively stage-managed by organizers of the megaspectacles we studied. Carnivalesque behavior was prominently on display, but in commodified not authentic form. At the most notorious venues (motorcycle rallies at Sturgis, South Dakota and Daytona Beach, Florida), scantily-dressed, tattooed, or body painted waitresses and barmaids doubled as professional subjects of trophy photography. Blending the roles of wait staff, model, and sex worker, these women hawked beer and food while posing for pictures with attendees. Being photographed with one of these professionals was one of the most widely sought trophies at large motorcycle rallies, and in several cases, women actually posed next to signs welcoming both photographers and tips. Such commercially supplied simulations of raunch were necessary to spice up notoriously wild events that had gone mild. The growing demographic of aging, upscale, and responsible attendees were reluctant to participate directly in transgressive behavior, but still wanted to document that they were surrounded by it.

These two trophy hunting activities—purchasing themed merchandise and capturing legendary images—point to fundamental alienation from spontaneous carnivalesque interaction (Goffman, 1967, pp. 113–136). In short, *having a good time was less important than proving that a good time was had.* This distinction is critical to the dynamics of trophy markets. Trophy hunting often blocks spontaneous enjoyment in-venue but generates a different form of *jouissance* that is extracted from others outside the event. Themed merchandise and images of revelry prove that participants were "really there"—enjoying the extraordinary satisfactions denied to those who were not present. These objects and images function as the envy inducing and status conferring trophies of what Lacan refers to as "surplus enjoyment" (Lacan, 2007 [1969], pp. 19–20). Organizers of NASCAR events, motorcycle rallies and other carnivalesque spectacles that we observed understood that attendance was motivated by the desire to obtain trophies, and profitably met that demand with simulated photo opportunities and massive volumes of themed merchandise. Thus, from our perspective, the primary commodities produced and consumed in megaspectacles are trophies, and economies of spectacle are structured as trophy markets.

We accept Veblen's (1934 [1899]) radical reconstruction of the psychological foundations of consumption as essentially invidious: the psychic life of consumers is infused with envy, both their own envy and the imagined envy of others (see also Cassano, 2009, 2014). Invidious consumption is, at core, trophy acquisition and operates through a series of perverse displacements.[3] First,

---

3 Benjamin's distinction between cult and exhibition value cuts across our argument in that
   cult value derives from structured ritual while exhibition value derives from specularity.

invidious consumption displaces and inverts pleasure. Trophies are not purchased to be pleasurably consumed but to be displayed to others with the intent of causing them envious displeasure. As theorized below, trophies return the envy extracted from viewers to their owners in inverted form, as surplus enjoyment. Second, invidious consumption displaces and inverts the situation of pleasure. Pleasure is derived not from the moment of the trophy's purchase, but from the realization of surplus enjoyment in another place and time. Thus, invidious consumption signifies the psychological interpenetration of situations in which immediate conduct is structured by the anticipation of *jouissance* in future situations. Third, invidious consumption displaces and inverts the subject position of the consumer, who "takes the role of the other" (Mead, 1934, pp. 160–161) or identifies with the "other" in an "other showplace"—literally Freud's *andere Schauplatz* (see Lacan, 2006 [1966], p. 462). The subjectivity of invidious consumers is fundamentally decentered in that their own desires are structured by the desires of others. The hunt for trophies is in essence a search for collective representations that resonate with other people's fantasies and repressed desires. All of this rather intense shopping during events is for the acquisition of objects that will make others envious rather than directly pleasure the purchaser.

In sum, as economic markets, megaspectacles are structured by the thrill of the hunt, not the pleasure of transgression. As such, trophy markets, trophy hunting and trophy display are central to megaspectacles. Though these events are often theorized as quintessential "time off," bounded regions of transgressive activity that are fundamentally removed from consequentiality and fatefulness (Goffman, 1967, p. 185), we argue that trophies keep these events tightly coupled to attendees' everyday life. We find that attendees perpetually reference their everyday lives and remain tethered to their "time on" roles even while staging the vacating of them. People travel long distances, endure discomfort and invest their discretionary income in the pursuit of trophies of surplus enjoyment that will augment their prestige in their everyday lives. As such, these apparently unserious and fun events have incredibly serious, even fateful, consequences.

Benjamin argues that modernity stripped objects of their aura, annihilating their cult value while promoting exhibition value. Megaspectacles, as postmodern economic forms, ritually re-enchant (Ritzer, 2005) commodities that have been technologically reproduced, attaching a legendary aura and cult value to them, transforming them into trophy objects (Benjamin, 2002 [1936]: 106–108). Hence, trophies of surplus enjoyment possess both kinds of Benjaminian value.

Trophies and the Sociology of Envy

The sociology of trophies can be traced to Veblen's *Theory of the Leisure Class*, where he argued that trophy hunting and trophy display are the essential economic activity of elites (1934 [1899], p. 28). Trophies originated as booty extracted by victors after battle (1934 [1899], p. 24) and signified the "prowess" of warriors who had proved their exploitative superiority (1934 [1899], p. 27). Because perpetual displays of prowess (in battle, sports, debate, fighting) were difficult and costly to sustain, trophies were sought as durable and portable signs of prowess. Trophies served as warehouses of valor, storage batteries of exploitative superiority proven in previous contests (1934 [1899], p. 24) that are displayed to obtain prestige when not performing honorific activity. Trophies take the pressure off the demand to prove prowess, literally allowing possessors to "rest on their laurels." Under capitalism, Veblen argued, all property takes on trophy value, signifying prowess, superiority and prestige (1934 [1899], p. 28).

The demand for trophies is endemic to modernity because the density, anonymity and mobility of modern life destroys the efficacy of directly associated systems of honor (Veblen, 1934 [1899], pp. 102–114; see also Simmel, 1950, pp. 409–424). Few know one's character, but all can see and be envious of one's trophies. Hence, attendees at contemporary megaspectacles have little incentive to prove their prowess in combat: it is far simpler to purchase a trophy. At best, many spectacles, like NASCAR, encourage fans to identify strongly with a contestant who functions as the fan's champion within the diegetic reality of the event. Attendees register their identification by purchasing ready-made trophies that mark both their solidarity with the contestant and their attendance at events where prowess was proven. Attendees' trophies secure, in their term, "bragging rights" for spectators when displayed before envious others in the wake of the event.

The value of commodities is determined in Marxist economics by the socially necessary labor worked up in them (Marx, 2010 [1867]). Veblen's trophies are an odd economic object, in that their value does not derive from the labor embedded within them but rather from their sign value (Baudrillard, 1996 [1968]) or exhibition value (Benjamin, 2002 [1936], p. 106).[4] This explains why

---

4   Klein (1963 [1932]: 326–368) argues that the acidity of envy is so overpowering that infantile efforts to cope with it form the basic psychic structure, or "rough draft" of the ego (Lacan, 2006 [1966]: 286). In the effort to expel, control and manage envy, the child is launched into the long process of psychic development. To Klein, envy remains a fundamental socially relevant emotion throughout adult life (see the analysis of the child "Erna" in Klein, 1963 [1932]:

counterfeit trophies are worthless and even discrediting. Though Veblen was a noted though sympathetic critic of Hegelian/Marxist economics (see especially Veblen, 1906), his theory of trophies was clearly influenced by Hegel's master and slave dialectic (Hegel, 1967 [1910], para. 178–196). Veblen's trophies have value for what they signify: prowess and superiority over others. As such, trophies mediate the Hegelian dialectics of recognition, in which the dialectic between master and slave is short-circuited by trophies that evidence the prowess and status of the master.

Trophies are sublime objects: their physical substance is overwritten by their social substance. This sublime substance of social power is ritualistic moral energy, literally a Durkheimian "collective representation" of prowess that has been stored in the trophy, creating a mirror-like surface that reflects prestige onto its possessor when enviously viewed by others (Cassano, 2009; Collins, 2004; Durkheim, 1965 [1915]; Marshall, 2010; Veblen, 1934 [1899]; Worrell, 2008b). The value of trophies varies with the prowess required to obtain them: the greater the vanquished enemy, the larger the field of battle, the larger the "audience" to this battle, the greater the moral energy embedded within. As such, Veblen's trophies are coextensive with a society's symbolic structure: like law and language (Lacan, 2006 [1966]; Levi-Strauss, 1963, 1976; Žižek, 2008 [1989]), the prestige codes of trophies are obdurate structures that form primary status conferring systems of a society.

Finally, trophies reflect socially sanctioned superiority, forcing an invidious distinction to be made between the trophy possessor's superiority and the trophy viewer's inferiority. Veblen's envy is more than mere Hegelian recognition of superiority, however; the envious trophy viewer manifests destructive desire for the good or goods possessed by the trophy possessor and fantasizes that these objects have been robbed or dispossessed from them. Viewers of trophies are not merely inferior to trophy possessors, but have had something *taken* from them (social honor, at least, but often something more tangible). Envy has long been recognized as a particularly corrosive, dark emotion; a "green-ey'd monster, which doth mock the meat it feeds on," as the triadic form of envy, jealousy, is described by Shakespeare (*Othello* Act 3, Scene 3). Veblen's theory of trophies aligns with Klein's (1963 [1932]) psychoanalytics of envy; both recognize the destructiveness of invidious distinctions in social life and explain the pervasiveness of invidious consumption as a major economic category. By equating trophies with the booty robbed from the vanquished, Veblen fundamentally linked acidic envy to dispossession, exploitation, and

---

78–80). A complete sociology of envy would require fuller confrontation with the literature on narcissism, which manifests itself by a fixation on envy.

trophies. Similarly, Klein argues that the envious person is driven by "destructive impulses" to either repossess the object or destroy it (Klein, 1963 [1932], pp. 276–282; Klein, 1975 [1957], pp. 176–235).[5]

Lacanian Objects and the Envy Dynamics of Trophies

Veblen's analysis of the invidious underpinnings of trophies can be specified in greater detail by viewing them through Jacques Lacan's psychoanalytic triad of objects (Lacan, 1997, pp. 109–114; Žižek, 2008 [1989], pp. 206–212). The trophies of megaspectacle instance all three Lacanian forms: *objet petit a* (imaginary semblance of desire), *phallic signifier* (symbolic markers of prohibited *jouissance*) and *das Ding* (the Freudian thing, a materialization or stain of unsymbolized *jouissance*) (see Lacan, 1997, pp. 83–100; Worrell & Krier, 2012; Žižek, 1992, p. 135, 2008 [1989], pp. 206–210, 2010 [1992], pp. 1–12). These are not mutually exclusive categories into which trophies can be neatly divided, but ideal-types that are used here to trace envy's complex dynamics in trophy markets. A single trophy can manifest all three of these dynamics, though often in unequal proportions.[6]

Objet petit a is an unobtainable object that causes desire, launching desiring subjects into symbolically structured motion. As imaginary fantasy projections, these sublime objects play an essential role in constituting reality as a consistent field of meaning, bridging gaps and masking inconsistencies in the symbolic order (Žižek, 2008 [1989], pp. 45–49). Though often conceived of in terms of romantic desire, Žižek's archetypal *objet petit a,* the primary sublime object of ideology that he analyzed in his first book, is the anti-Semitic figure of "the Jew." The Jew is a "fantasy-construction" or "illusion" that makes the world of symbolic relations appear meaningfully seamless by masking "insupportable" and "impossible" inconsistencies in the anti-Semite's world (2008 [1989], p. 45). The characteristics of the fantasized Jew—financially exploitative, sexually lascivious, dirty—are exteriorizations of the repressed wishes

---

5 See Worrell and Krier (2012) for analyses of cinematic objects (the shark in Jaws and James Bond) as figures that shift between all three Lacanian objects depending upon the subjectivity that views them.

6 The concept of the organic composition of spectacle is developed by the authors in other work to analyze the expansion of public and private capital investment in megaspectacle infrastructure (speedways, event centers, sports complexes, stadiums, shoppertainment complexes, parking and transportation infrastructure, etc.). The concept and the dynamic it references are drawn from Marx's organic composition of capital (Marx, 2010 [1894]).

and disavowed desires of the anti-Semite, a pure semblance "invested with ... unconscious desire" (2008 [1989], p. 48). By projecting their own dark desires onto the out-hated image of the Jew, anti-Semites domesticate their repressed wishes and fantasies, allowing everyday life to maintain a consistent, meaningful texture. When envy-potential takes the form of *objet petit a*, subjects project their repressed desires onto emotionally cathected fantasy objects represented by trophies. At motorsports spectacles, such trophies represented both positive objects (adored racers, sexually attractive celebrities, idealized folk heroes) and negative objects (scorned liberal politicians, pacifists, illegal immigrants, demonized racial minorities). The potential envy in these trophies is realized when such trophies are displayed before subjects who recognize in the trophy a staging of their own unconscious desire.

Phallic signifiers are symbolic markers of the "barred other," remnants of *jouissance* that were cut off from subjects when they were installed within the symbolic order (Žižek, 2008 [1989], p. 174). These leftovers lack an official place in the symbolic system and circulate from subject to subject in exchange relationships (Žižek, 2010 [1992], pp. 6–7). Phallic signifiers are "little pieces of the real," literally an excess of *jouissance* or surplus enjoyment, that mediate between positions in a symbolic network so that relationships between subjects assume the form of fetishistic relationships between things (2008 [1989], p. 31). The externalized surplus enjoyment, cut off from the subject, takes on a free-floating life of its own within the subject's symbolic network. When envy-potential takes the form of phallic signifiers, the enjoyment denied to subjects reappears in expropriated form as someone else's trophy. Quite literally, the trophy takes the form of enjoyment that has been robbed from the subject, often intermixed with the congealed enjoyment dispossessed from other subjects. These trophies of surplus enjoyment are substantially parallel to Veblen's invidious objects, and examples of these trophies are analyzed throughout this chapter.

The final Lacanian object, *das Ding* refers to a "massive, oppressive" materialization or "embodiment of an impossible *jouissance*" (2008 [1989], p. 208–209). Whereas the phallic signifier takes on the form of a symbol, *das Ding* cannot be symbolized. It is a materialization of raw *jouissance* that no signifier can be found to mark. As realized *jouissance*, it cannot be sublimated into an object of desire. These bizarre, surreal eruptions of pleasure "stain" the world but cannot be domesticated within it, disturbing subjects and social relations with their all too real, pulsating presence.

Our reading of Lacan and Žižek's descriptions of *das Ding* leads us to equate this pulsating *jouissance* with raw Durkheimian collective effervescence, free-floating moral energy not affixed to a totem. Megaspectacles present subjects with amorphous sensations of energized substance whose dimensions, contours and textures they can neither quite imagine nor symbolize. Submersion of the ego within such a pulsating mass teeming with inchoate *jouissance* both stimulates and repulses the subject. Subjects experience this as a disorienting flood of spontaneous enjoyment (*jouissance* in Lacan's multiform meaning) that quickly spends itself in uncoordinated excitations unless focused upon a totemic object. To Durkheim, this is the fundamental function of the totem: it transforms the *das Ding* of collective effervescence into a lasting *objet petit a* in the form of the totem. Without the totem, collective effervescence as *das Ding* immobilizes and stupefies subjects absorbed in *jouissance*. When transferred to totemic *objets petit a,* collective effervescence launches subjects in desiring-action upon the pathways of the symbolic network.

Megaspectacles may be the only events in modernity with the capacity to commodify *das Ding,* to load trophies with this form of potential envy. Motorsports spectacles conjure sensations of noise and vibrations from revving engines, intermingled smells of alcohol, exhaust and fried food that are both sickening yet oddly seductive. Subjects of such trophies find themselves in the presence of coagulated, amorphous sexualized pulsations: greased midget bowling, jello-wrestling, pickle-licking contests, burnout pits, automatic weapons trials, mechanical bull-riding and ceaseless, disoriented milling of carnivalesque bodies. These entities are experienced as an indistinct conglomerate of oppressive, grotesque yet enticing sensations.

In sum, Veblen, Lacan and Žižek theorize the profound role played by bizarre, disruptive objects as a mediating force in social life. Megaspectacles produce and market a class of such bizarre objects, trophies of surplus enjoyment, loading them with disruptive potential envy. The Lacanian objects closest to Veblen's trophies are phallic signifiers, markers of enjoyment that have been expropriated from subjects and accumulated into trophies of surplus enjoyment, the owners of which become the ultimate "subjects supposed to enjoy" (Žižek, 2008 [1989], p. 212). Lacan's conception is the precise analogue of Marx's surplus value: and we argue that the two concepts are brought close together within the trophy markets of megaspectacle.

The Mediating Role of Legends in Trophy Markets

In this section, we specify how megaspectacle trophy markets, filled with disruptive objects charged with envy-potential, relate to their legends. Legendary narratives and imagery depicting scenes of spontaneous enjoyment are the primary income producing asset of megaspectacles. Legends operate as a capital fund that is built up when spectacular events are staged and drawn down when mass-produced, geographically distributed trophies are charged with potential envy. Trophies are rarely charged directly during immediate moments of megaspectacle. Instead, each successful staging of a spectacle pays into a legend fund and trophies are charged indirectly as withdrawals from this fund. The envy that disturbs viewers of trophies results from their awareness of the megaspectacle's capitalized legend—its fund of narratives and images of spontaneous enjoyment—not from their cognizance of the specific event attended by the trophy possessor. In the mutual determination of trophies and legends, trophies are charged *by* megaspectacles but not necessarily *during* them.

The outsized, durable trophy markets of megaspectacle develop upon the bankable foundation of their legend fund. By contrast, small-scale events lack generalized notoriety: outsiders to them do not possess a fantasy image of their activity. Trophies from these events are restricted to those vividly depicting sexualized and carnivalesque spontaneous enjoyment, scenes that require no legendary support to stimulate desire. As a result, the trophy markets of small events remain underdeveloped relative to megaspectacle (these small events market trophies of *jouissance*, see below). The value of trophies is stabilized by the widely diffused awareness of their legend rather than the direct experience of their events.

Veblen's analysis of goodwill, capitalism's quintessential intangible asset, provides insight into the hard economic realities of something as soft as a legend (1915 [1904]). As an intangible asset, legends are managed as a fund whose balance depreciates without ongoing investment. Just as Durkheim argued that collective representations erode "after the assembly has ended" and require ongoing ritual action in order to reignite them, since "when left to themselves, [they] become feebler and feebler" (Durkheim, 1965 [1915], p. 265), we argue that legends require similar ritual reenactment to prevent their decay. Such investment in the intangible asset of the legend is required to stabilize and protect the solvency of megaspectacle trophy markets.

Unlike corporate brands that are internally manufactured and precisely controlled, megaspectacle legends are difficult to manufacture or to control with specificity. They are diffuse narratives authored by "many hands," like early Bible translations, with obscure origins, indeterminate evolution and imprecise contours all of which lie outside the capacity of any single corporate actor to control. Legends are "crowd-sourced" assets of great value to event organizers, corporate marketers and trophy sellers but these actors can only expropriate, not generate, them. Found in the wilds of social life, legends are sought as a "free gift" to be privatized by marketing managers and domesticated in the service of brands as a sublimated form of primitive accumulation (Marx, 2010 [1867]).

Marketing professionals in our motorsports study varied in their approach to legends. Recognizing the impossibility of managing and controlling legends single-handed, they established complex networks of cross-marketing partnerships to better expropriate, privatize and tame legends. A growing focus of marketing professionals emphasizes the management of customers' in-venue experience of the legend, rather than management of the legend itself. These *customer experience managers* seek maximum expropriation of megaspectacle's legend to augment the value of their brand (Harley-Davidson at Sturgis, Chevrolet at NASCAR races). Benefitting from a legend that they did not create, marketing professionals nevertheless seek to increase legend awareness while managing customer experience, an action we denote as legend work.

Legend work includes a host of activities. Event organizers promote legend awareness with direct marketing campaigns and indirect promotions, including staged or documentary representations of the megaspectacle in film or television programming that double as mechanisms to reinforce and disseminate a megaspectacle's legend. Event organizers often invest in durable memorials (museums, visitor centers, etc.) to the spectacle to sustain legends between megaspectacular events. Ultimately, the most important investment comes from staging in-venue activities consistent with the legend, at least in appearance. For example, NASCAR's 2013 marketing campaign focused upon infusing its race broadcasts with images and icons from its legendary past. In 2013, NASCAR commercials featured peak moments in NASCAR history, retro video footage and overlay of current drivers with legendary heroes of the past. Rules changes were instituted to bring current races in line with NASCAR legend: closer racing, frequent crashes and a "boys have at it" policy encouraged rivalries to spill over into pit-row brawls. The Sturgis Motorcycle Rally engaged in similar legend work to manage attendance experiences and public awareness of its legend, marketing and "branding" activity to maintain its legend as an "outlaw biker" venue. Plans were formed to construct an outlaw biker-themed "Sturgis Experience Museum," and the word "legendary" was appended to the names of numerous rally events and venues (Legendary Sturgis, Legendary Buffalo Chip, the Sturgis Legends Ride, the Legendary Sturgis Main Street, Legend Lane, Legends Suites Bed and Breakfast) as well as a host of Sturgis trademarked goods. Such legend work was partially aimed at managing customer experience in-venue by creating the illusion of real-time spontaneous enjoyment. It was also directed at increasing the potential envy of trophies while building legend awareness with non-attendees by confronting them with graphic evidence of missed events that had lived up to their fantasized expectations.

In financial accounting, goodwill represents the surplus of the purchase price of a company over the value of its tangible assets. Goodwill is usually parsed as the prestige value of a brand, the "discounted present value" of future recurring revenues resulting from consumer recognition of logos, registered trademarks, brands, patents and other intangible assets. In Veblen's time, mergers and acquisitions often resulted in corporations whose value was mostly goodwill, a tendency that has only escalated in recent decades with asset-light corporations floated on speculative financial markets (Krier, 2009a, 2009b). Megaspectacles are rarely organized by a single, hierarchically managed corporation but by cross-marketing coalitions of asset-light, post-Fordist businesses (Edwards, Alderman & Estes, 2010; Harvey, 1989), many of which are essentially nests of contracts: light to the point of gas. They invest in few fixed assets and the value of their contracts floats upon legendary brand-recognition or goodwill in the form of legend awareness. As evidenced by recent financial crises, the goodwill of asset-light firms is highly unstable and can vanish overnight (Krier, 2005). Maintaining a vibrant legend is critical to the economic stability of these events and is a central focus of managerial activity.

If a legend becomes devalued, so do its trophies. Just as myths decompose into legends when they become disconnected from a tightly organized ritual order (Levi-Strauss, 1976, pp. 256–268), legends disconnected from actual staged events similarly decompose, generating crises of authenticity or "degradation of aura" (Benjamin, 2002 [1936], pp. 103–106, 119). For these reasons, organizers of megaspectacles expend considerable resources supporting, broadcasting and protecting their envy inducing legend. Legends provide a fantasy construct that fills gaps and covers inconsistencies of attendee experience within the venue, generating a relatively seamless consistent experience. As such, legends are essential to maintain both the surplus enjoyment produced in events and the surplus value of the goods sold in their trophy markets; this theoretical analogue between surplus enjoyment and surplus value is developed by Lacan (2007 [1969], pp. 19–20, 44–45, 80–81) and Žižek (2008 [1989], pp. 50–55).

Legend awareness preloads trophy viewers' fantasy space with invidious emotion. Hence, the surplus enjoyment of trophies is an after-effect of a legend awareness that preceded the moment when the trophies were viewed. The situations that charge trophies and the situations in which they are displayed are linked, but not tightly coupled in temporal chains, in which one situation immediately feeds into the next (Collins, 2004, p. 202). Instead, trophy situations may be separated by large expanses of space and time. Such inverted temporality and teleological causation are typical of trophy markets: events that have not yet happened (trophy displays) determine activity in a present scene (trophy hunting and legend work). Hence, subsequent situations cause previous ones, a dialectically reflexive, trans-situational effect that Goffman described as having one's "world played backwards" (Goffman, 1971, p. 319).

The codetermination of events and legends provides one answer to a fundamental question of megaspectacles: if they are markets for trophies, why stage the spectacle? Why make huge capital investments that increase the organic composition of spectacle[7] rather than simply sell the trophies? Trophies, though tangible commodities, have negligible value unless charged with the intangible asset of legend. Since a spectacle's legend is an externality that cannot be internally controlled, it depreciates unless ongoing megaspectacle events replenish the legend fund. In an era of new media, evidence of the discontinuity between events and legend can "go viral," spreading instantly and exponentially, threatening the potential envy of the event on a mass scale. Hence the imperative to manage customer experience, providing simulated photo opportunities in venues artificially papered over with legendary images.

Megaspectacles, Rituals, and Trophies as Social Objects

The relationship between myth, ritual and totem in classical anthropology is parallel to the relationship between the legends, events and trophies of megaspectacle. Rituals embody and enact myths while sacralizing totems, overwriting their physical substance and charging them with social energy (Collins, 2004, pp. 81–87; Durkheim, 1965 [1915]; Hubert & Mauss, 1964; Levi-Strauss, 1963, pp. 232–41, 1976, pp. 65–66; Mauss, 1967; Worrell, 2008b). Megaspectacles, despite their highly profane qualities, are sacralizing quasi-ritual events that generate and sustain their legends, while loading their trophies with envy-potential. Megaspectacles are closer to the conception of modern interaction ritual than to notions of pure ritual derived from classical anthropology (Collins, 2004; Goffman, 1967). As interaction rituals, megaspectacles generate social energy by aggregating individuals, aligning them into a momentary moral community and agitating them into collective effervescence (Collins, 2004, pp. 48–49; Durkheim, 1965 [1915], pp. 250–265). To prevent collective effervescence from dissipating when the crowd disperses, interaction rituals project the group's precarious current of social energy onto objects or totems, charging them with a moral force that Durkheim equates to "electricity" (1965 [1915],

---

7   As noted above, our distinction between totems and trophies cuts across Benjamin's distinction between objects with cult value and objects with exhibition value, in that trophies possess both (Benjamin, 2002 [1936]: 106–108).

pp. 215, 322, 419). By connecting ritual energy with "something that endures [totem], the sentiments themselves become more durable" (1965 [1915], p. 265). Thus the totem serves as a storage battery of social power (Worrell, 2005, 2008b); "energy in a bottle" (Lacan, 2007 [1969], p. 49) that preserves collective effervescence beyond the place and time of its production (Collins, 2004, p. 87; Marshall, 2010).

The totems of traditional ritual differ from the trophies of megaspectacles in several important ways. A totem operates as an obdurate representation of the collective, making society effectively "real" when its members are not co-present. Totems operate by "constantly bringing [collective sentiments] to mind and arousing them … assuring the continuation of this consciousness" (Durkheim, 1965 [1915], p. 265). Both totems and trophies mediate social relationships, totems by objectifying shared identity and reverence for normative system, trophies by objectifying envious distinctions and expropriation of the goods of life. Trophies generate differential, yet interconnected subject positions that are mirrored but inverted. Totems bring people together in moral community while trophies divide social consciousness by extracting surplus *jouissance*. Trophies force fantasy images to consciousness; images that excite and disturb trophy viewers by flooding their consciousness with repressed *jouissance* and envy. The impact of trophies for possessors and viewers is not the same: the disturbing invidious energy is dispossessed from the viewer and reflected back to its possessor in inverted form, as surplus enjoyment (*plus-de-jouir, mehrlust*) (Lacan, 2007 [1969], p. 44). Trophies and totems are distinct social objects: each is reflexively charged with moral energy in ritualistic activity. However, totems are *collective* goods that belong to the group as a whole and generate and preserve social identification (Collins, 2004, p. 49) but do not produce envy. Trophies, by contrast, are private property that divides collective sentiments, generating envy in viewers and prestige for possessors.[8]

Megaspectacles produce potential envy that is realized as surplus enjoyment when viewed through the mediation of legends. Megaspectacles vary in their ritual formality, from almost high-church stadium settings (spectator sports, concerts) to disorganized, sprawling venues (motorcycle rallies). Events with greater ritual-formality, as well as those with large numbers of attendees, collective effervescence and focused ritual expression will more effectively

---

8   Even Durkheim, whose emphasis upon shared sentiments underlies sociological ritual theory, was aware of the emotional energy generated by ambivalence, such as the "veritable disorder" of emotion generated by inconsistent conventions (1984 [1893]: 53–54), and the strong delayed reactions when ambivalence leads to neglect of piacular rites (Durkheim, 1965 [1915]: 455).

charge trophies with surplus enjoyment (Collins, 2004; Marshall, 2010). We would like to suggest four additional propositions regarding the magnitude of surplus enjoyment charged in trophies.

The Sacrifice of Spontaneous Enjoyment

Sacrifice is a central component of ritual and refers to burning that sublimates and transfers moral energy onto objects (Hubert and Mauss, 1964, pp. 19–49). Megaspectacles vary in their level of sacrifice, roughly indexed by the in-venue ratio of spontaneous enjoyment to masochistic displeasure demanded of their attendees. Spontaneous enjoyment at spectacles often dissipates within momentary revels, while the sacrifice of spontaneous enjoyment generates a "surplus" transferred to trophies. As noted above, attendance at megaspectacles is often a veritable potlatch of time, money and comfort. Just as Durkheim, Hubert and Mauss theorized that religious sacrifices are essential to sacralizing objects, we argue that sacrifices of spontaneous enjoyment are essential to trophies of surplus enjoyment. *Events with high levels of sacrifice will load trophies with greater surplus enjoyment.* In Marx's terms, such sacrifice constitutes socially necessary labor-time to acquire a trophy charged with spontaneous enjoyment: the greater the sacrifice required (the more elaborate the "war stories" associated with trophy acquisition), the greater the social value.

The Importance of Emotional Ambivalence

While some theories of ritual emphasize one-sided and uniform emotional intensity or "emotional entrainment" as essential to ritual (Collins, 2004, p. 119; see also Durkheim, 1965 [1915], pp. 255–256, 1984 [1893], p. 61), the events that charge trophies of surplus enjoyment manifest intense emotional *ambivalence* (Adorno, Frenkel-Brunswik, Levinson, & Sanford, 1950, pp. 884–889; Freud, 1950 [1919], pp. 18–74; Marshall, 2010, p. 65; Smith, 1998; Worrell, 2008a, pp. 9, 19, 91).[9] Events infused with intense, uniform feeling-states and unidirectional emotional alignment discharge their moral energy in orgiastic or even chiliastic spontaneous enjoyment: moral energy burns bright but brief in a "useless dissipation of energy" (see Durkheim, 1984 [1893], p. 57). In contrast, events infused with intense emotional ambivalence, in which strong positive emotions (pleasure/love) pulsate with equally strong negative ones (displeasure/hate),

---

9   Collins (2004) suggests that "forced rituals," in which the emotions of participants are not aligned with normative expression, are "energy draining not EE [emotional energy] creating" (2004: 53). Such rituals fail to generate spontaneous enjoyment (which we think is close to Collins's EE), and under certain conditions the energy that is "drained" is actually repressed, concentrated and projected onto trophies.

often sanction the expression of only one of these bivalent poles. Hence, the appearance of group solidarity and emotional entrainment is more widespread than its reality, as group members project an "illusion of unanimity" that masks their ambivalence and underlying diversity (Turner and Killian, 1987, p. 26). Repression of emotional energy contrary to mandated expression leads to its concentrated projection onto social objects (Freud, 1950 [1919], pp. 67–71; Marshall, 2010, pp. 73–74). In other words, *social objects are charged with the energy of taboo, repressed emotion, not a morally sanctioned, consciously expressed emotion.*[10] Hence, the greater the suppression of emotions and desires contrary to sanctioned expression, the greater the moral energy available for projection onto trophies of surplus enjoyment.

The Importance of Moral Ambiguity

We have argued that surplus enjoyment is produced in megaspectacles but realized upon display of trophies before envious others. These others, the *subject of the trophy*, must know what the trophy represents, they must be cognizant of the event's legend.[11] Legend awareness pre-forms the contours of potential envy, but because these contours must lie within the coordinates of the subject's desire, the insidious impact of trophies will not be uniform throughout the trophy possessor's social network. While some subjects of the trophy will overtly express their envious response, we suspect that those whose desires are most aroused by the trophy are least likely to express them. In fact, they may well repress or disavow their arousal and openly derogate the trophy with expressions of disgust, disapproval and moral outrage. The arousal of *jouissance* in the subject is likely to be greatest when the trophy depicts forbidden pleasures, when it gives form to enticing, but disapproved of desires that the subject already expends energy to suppress (Durkheim, 1965 [1915], pp. 434–461). Because the trophy represents "temptation," its emotional impact will be profound but indeterminately expressed (Marshall, 2010, pp. 69–72). The *jouissance* released by the trophy may lead to denials, jokes or scorn and other antinomies of moral ambiguity. The envy is experienced by the subject

---

10   Trophies of *jouissance* are an exception to this, as noted below.

11   Simmel (1950: 34) labels such phenomena "sociological tragedies," in which the individuation of modern society makes individuals incomparable to each other, coarsening mass society by placing high value upon traits shared by all, which correspond to "lower and primitively more sensuous levels." Trophies of surplus enjoyment, especially when rooted in sexualized transgression, are tragically symptomatic of the weak social ties and fractured identities of postmodern society (see Krier & Swart, 2012).

as stolen *jouissance* that has been dispossessed by the trophy holder: it is this invidious disruption, reflected and inverted, that realizes surplus enjoyment.

Carnivalesque Transgression as a Short-circuit of Surplus Enjoyment

Trophies that evidence carnivalesque transgression, especially if direct expressions of sexualized debauchery, are "trump cards" of surplus enjoyment. For such trophies, surplus enjoyment is realized directly: cognizance of the legend need not precede the display of the trophy. Sexual transgression was particularly widespread in the megaspectacles we studied, appearing with great regularity on themed merchandise and in staged photo opportunities. Such trophies transcend the sectoral limitations of most megaspectacular legends by arousing base fantasies and fundamental moral repressions, that are coarse but widely shared. Such trophies short-circuit the mediating role of legends in the realization of surplus enjoyment, as they symptomatically lie within the coordinates of desire of a broad mass of the population.

To summarize, greater magnitudes of surplus enjoyment are produced and transferred to trophies in megaspectacles when these exhibit: large numbers of attendees; collective effervescence; ritual realization of legends in-venue; mass dissemination of legends extra-venue; ritual formality; sacrifice of spontaneous enjoyment; emotional ambivalence coupled with morally sanctioned expression; moral ambiguity and carnivalesque transgression.

Trophies of Surplus Enjoyment: Status, Action and *Jouissance*

Trophies of surplus enjoyment are bizarre objects whose value lies in their capacity to invidiously disturb those who view them. Like all commodities in capitalism, the value of these trophies must, at core, result from the socially necessary labor, or abstract labor, embedded within them (Marx, 2010 [1867]). Because the physical substance of trophies of surplus enjoyment (digital images, T-shirts, trinkets and wearable merchandise) require relatively little labor to manufacture or produce, a large portion of their value derives from the *socially necessary labor of acquisition*. Like the cheap medals presented to winners of sporting events, trophies have value because they are difficult, expensive and time-consuming to *acquire* and not because they are difficult, expensive and time-consuming to *manufacture*. The greater the magnitude of abstract acquisition labor embedded within a trophy, the greater the invidious disturbance when viewed. The value of trophies, then, is a strange form of scarcity value or economic rent, but of a non-transferable kind, since acquisition, not mere possession, is key to social recognition.[12] The secondary market for second-hand trophies is notoriously weak because the value is entailed and is literally not capable of transfer without changing form.

The magnitude of the invidious impact of trophies upon their subjects is determined, at least in part, by the abstract labor of acquisition, but the quality of that impact depends upon the form of surplus enjoyment that the trophy represents. In our study of megaspectacles, surplus enjoyment was transferred to trophies in three distinguishable ideal-type forms: status trophies, action trophies, and trophies of *jouissance*. These distinctions were marked by the nature of invidious comparison aroused in the subject of the trophy. While we discuss each of these forms of surplus enjoyment as a discrete entity, it is important to note that any actually existing trophy may represent a blend all three forms.

Status trophies generate envy by forcing recognition of the possessor's superior social rank, prestigious position, elite standing and wealth. In late capitalism, status trophies signify conspicuous wealth, waste and leisure (Veblen, 1934 [1899]; see also Baudrillard, 1996 [1968], p. 212; Bourdieu, 1984, p. 281; Elias, 2006, pp. 42, 70; Goffman, 1951). For example, an outlaw biker-themed T-shirt, dated by the logo of an annual motorcycle rally, functions as a status trophy despite the negligible cost of the T-shirt as token. As a status trophy, the potential envy lies in its conspicuous display of the superior levels of wealth, waste and leisure necessary to come into possession of it, including wealth to purchase an expensive motorcycle, income to travel and time off work to attend the event. The value of status trophies is affected by the resources and prowess required to obtain the trophy hunter's position in-venue. For instance, digital images of a NASCAR fan posing beside a race-team's pit crew signifies the status connections necessary to obtain such premium access, in addition to displaying disposable wealth. Sending a text message with a photograph of oneself at a sold-out venue that was cumbersome to navigate, expensive and time consuming has greater value than a photograph of oneself at a poorly attended high school event. Charged with the megaspectacle's envy inducing

---

12   Trophies are bought and sold as collectibles and memorabilia, but the original "trophy" is fundamentally altered when acquired by a new buyer. The auction sale of DNA-modeler Francis Crick's Nobel Prize medal (a status trophy marking scientific excellence) for $2.27 million in April 2013 is a case in point: the Chinese biotech magnate who purchased the medal acquired an object with high scarcity value because it is infused with Crick's aura (a status trophy marking wealth and waste of the possessor). The buyer of second-hand trophies comes into possession of a different trophy than the seller sold.

social energy, status trophies mark their possessor's superiority, reflecting the degraded status of the viewer.

Action trophies generate envy by displaying idealized, socially valued character traits of their possessor, especially courage, gameness, integrity and composure in the face of voluntarily chosen danger (Goffman, 1967, p. 185). Character, like trophies, is an after-effect of such situations of action (Goffman, 1967, p. 217). Action trophies signify that their possessors were "where the action" was, and that they engaged in "deep play" for high stakes (Geertz, 1972). In sharp contrast to status trophies, action trophies do not signify conquest, exploitation or status superiority, but simply the courage and fortitude required to willingly face danger. Thus a "duel can be lost but character won" (Goffman, 1967, p. 246). Middle-class suburbs provide little opportunity for action, their residents constitute a large portion of the market for action trophies redolent of legendary danger, violence, and death. Much of the danger at action spectacles is simulated and maintained within safe bounds. At motorcycle rallies, burnout pits, zip-lines, cage-fighting, and midget wrestling provide safe representations of danger to trophy hunting attendees who trailered their recently purchased, factory-chopped bikes to the rally.

Because action trophies do not signal socially sanctioned status but risky, morally suspect activity like gambling, fighting and other forms of chancy behavior, their envy-potential is more fragile than that of status trophies. More so than status trophies that signal socially sanctioned, symbolic superiority or trophies of *jouissance* that are charged directly in-venue with conspicuous carnivalesque pleasure and require no legendary support at all, action trophies are highly dependent upon legend awareness as a source of potential envy. For example, the legend of the outlaw biker is essential to infuse motorcycle rallies with action: motorcycle rally T-shirts are emblazoned with outlaw biker imagery and signify that the wearer voluntarily entered an outlaw biker setting rife with dangerous activities, excessive drinking, and unsavory people. Unlike status trophies, action trophies require strategic impression management. Status trophies signify generalized prestige and honor that reflect positively on their possessors even within professional settings (resumes are notoriously padded with lists of status trophies). Action trophies, on the other hand, must often remain separate from professional activities (purged from resumes, Facebook pages, etc.) in order to prevent potentially negative character attributions that would be stigmatizing in many status conferring settings.

Trophies of jouissance generate envy by representing fantasy scenes of enjoyment, usually with sexual overtones, that lie at the core of a subject's desire. The essence of these scenes is carnivalesque transgression in the form of general laughter, mesalliance and animated, lower "grotesque bodies" (Bakhtin, 1968), the quintessential content of psychological repression in Western society. Hence, desire for such pleasures is often unconscious, or when conscious, openly denied or disavowed. As described above, subjects are most aroused by trophies of *jouissance* when they depict fantasy scenes of forbidden pleasures that the subject outwardly condemns, but inwardly desires. The greater the ambivalence between suppressed desire and moral condemnation, the more the subject is stirred up by the trophy. The expression of this emotional agitation is somewhat indeterminate: the subject may jokingly distance themselves from the scene, display bemused disinterest, or express horror, disgust, or condemnation, especially when such expressions are demanded by social convention. Megaspectacles produce trophies infused with sexual license, frivolity and libidinal pleasures because such pleasures, though strongly condemned, lie deep within the coordinates of unconscious desire in Western subjectivity. Possessors of these trophies realize surplus enjoyment with a high degree of effectiveness because of the extreme ambivalence of subjects.

Because trophies of *jouissance* target fantasies that are the lowest common denominator of Western society (Simmel, 1950, p. 34), their relationship with megaspectacular legends is complex. Crucially, some trophies of *jouissance* so vividly represent fantasy scenes that they require no foreknowledge of the event's legend in order to arouse trophy viewers (photographs, videos). In our study, organizers of small-scale motorcycle rallies that lacked mass notoriety ensured that attendees were provided with overt scenes of sexualized transgression to photograph. The resulting images were effective trophies of *jouissance* that stimulated viewers even without legendary contextualization. On the other hand, the Sturgis Motorcycle Rally's global legend awareness as a notorious scene of carnivalesque raunch meant that G-rated merchandise and photo opportunities were profitably sold that generated X-rated levels of *jouissance* when displayed as trophies. Sturgis' legend was so powerful, in fact, that even the most chaste rally-themed objects operated as trophies of *jouissance*. Megaspectacles with powerful legends require little to ignite full-blown fantasy construction in trophy viewers: objects that provide some small tangible evidence of libidinal action, such as posed photographs of pastied wait staff, serve as complete trophies of *jouissance*.

Character attributions of action (bravery, courage, voluntary acceptance of bodily danger) reflect systems of honor associated with Western masculinity: men find action in dangerous risk-taking while women find action in reputation risking settings that test virtue (Goffman, 1967, pp. 209–214, 234). In our study, photographs of women's sexualized activity was a common artifact of motorcycle rallies, and such scenes were sought by camera wielding men and women alike as trophies of *jouissance*. For the women who appeared in these images, trophies of *jouissance* doubled as action trophies, a sign of daring and risk taking as much as of spontaneous pleasure. Like pure action trophies, such potentially stigmatizing objects require strategic impression management.

Conclusion

This chapter conceptualized markets for a special kind of commodity: trophies of surplus enjoyment. Sociological accounts of spectacles have presented them as sites for the experiential consumption of exciting distractions, fun but fleeting moments of purchased enjoyment that ideologically dupe those who consume them. We acknowledge that megaspectacles sell enjoyment; that their attendees pay the price of admission to access a venue of legendary enjoyment. It is the timing, location and nature of that enjoyment that is at issue. The megaspectacles we studied exhibited subdued in-venue pleasures and surprising amounts of image-making and shopping. Attendees did not just exit through the gift shop but entered through never ending trophy markets whose trade pervaded their every moment. We observed so much activity diverted away from immediate enjoyment into trophy hunting that we were forced to approach megaspectacles from this new angle.

To explain the patterns we observed, we analyzed spectacles as economic circuits that produce trophies of surplus enjoyment rather than sites of ideologically laced consumption. This complex circuit decomposes into several interconnected moments. Megaspectacles produce events that stage envy inducing legends of spontaneous enjoyment. As quasi-rituals, these events produce moral energy, some of which is not dissipated in immediate *jouissance* but is instead transferred to trophy objects as potential envy. Markets are provided for attendees who hunt for these trophies of status, action and *jouissance*. Hunting for trophies that will best represent the event's envy inducing legend is the central focus of activity.

Hence, the value of trophies is begotten outside Marx's primal scene of wage-labor production in the spectacular wilds of consumer culture. Potential envy embedded in trophies is realized upon display in "another showplace," well away from the time and space of the trophy hunt, to subjects who are aroused by them. Trophies function like funhouse mirrors, reflective but distorting surfaces in which viewers (mis)recognize the owners' superior status, action and *jouissance* as their own dispossessed enjoyment. Gazing at trophies, subjects see congealed therein the abundant joys of life that were denied them, that were robbed from them, or that were somehow expropriated as a surplus by the trophy owner. These invidious emotions are strongest when the trophy crystallizes viewers' desire for secret but forbidden pleasures, those fundamental fantasies that provide structure to subjectivity. Trophies reflect subjects' profound invidious energies back upon their owners in inverted form: emotional disturbances of viewers are reversed as the owner's prestige, honor and *jouissance*.

Megaspectacles and trophy markets are widespread in contemporary capitalism (professional and collegiate athletics, cinema, music concerts, festivals), each event promising to deliver legendary, spontaneous enjoyment to attendees. Yet, in the events we studied, spontaneous enjoyment was less conspicuous than legend would have it or than attendees claimed it was at other times and places. Perhaps enjoyment was more subtle than we, as relative outsiders, could discern. But it was clear that trophy hunting was extensive, that spontaneous enjoyment "in the moment" evaporated as trophy hunting escalated and that many spectators played their enjoyment backwards, planning their event entirely around the acquisition of trophies that they imagined would most effectively disturb the emotions of viewers back home.

Digital technology and social media have overcome the space and time constraints that formerly separated the capturing of trophies from their display, dramatically reducing turnover time within circuits of surplus enjoyment (Harvey, 1989). Social networking sites thrive upon the digital fandoms that develop around spectacular productions, in which networked consumers share in-venue "selfies" as well as derivative fan art, fan fiction and devotional discourse, e.g. "NASCAR Nation," H.O.G. (Harley Owners' Group), My Little Pony "Pegasisters" and "Bronies," Harry "Potterheads," "Twi-hards," Dr "Whovians," Star "Trekkies." Beneath fandom's pleasurable surface pulses a dismal joust of trophy hunting as envy inducing images are displayed and instantaneously valorized by others who "retweet," "like," "favorite" or comment upon them. Far from elevating spectators into a carnivalesque sphere, megaspectacles and their trophies digitally redouble the alienation and interpersonal status competition already rampant in everyday life.

CHAPTER 7

Dark Spectacle: Authoritarianism and the Aestheticization of Economics

The association of authoritarianism with automobility dates back at least as far as Hitler's emphasis on mass motorization and the dominance of the Nazi racing program in the 1930s Grand Prix (König, 2004, von Saldern, 1992). Other work on more contemporary American motorsports spectacles, especially Newman and Giardina's (2008, 2010, 2011) analysis of *NASCAR Nation* also emphasizes its affinity of authoritarianism, pointing to themes of patriarchy, militarism, neo-liberalism, evangelical Christianity, white supremacy and government deregulation within these events as evidence of an overt, intentional strategy to produce and disseminate neo-liberal and authoritarian attitudes amongst its spectators. Likewise, there is a developed literature that implies the rise of authoritarian rebellion in post-War American motorcycling. Although they do not reference authoritarianism generally or Adorno, Frenkel-Brunswik, Levinson, and Sanford, (1950) specifically, Austin, Gagne and Orend (2010) point to outlaw and rebel themes in American motorcycle culture, drawn from American cinema and catalyzed by the post-war political climate, yet further appropriated, stylized, polished and amplified by the culture industry (Horkheimer & Adorno, 1972 [1944]; see also Barger, Zimmerman & Zimmerman, 2000; Klinger, 1997; Morton, 1999; Reynolds, 2000; Thompson, H.S., 1967; Wood, 2003).

These works share common ground with Walter Benjamin's (1936) notion of the *aestheticization of politics,* where political leaders produce fascism and other forms of authoritarian politics as a work of art and works of art function as authoritarian politics. Our goal in this chapter is to augment Benjamin's work to recognize that there is also *aestheticization of economics.* We believe there is a fundamental difference between mass spectacles shaped for political control (as in the Nazi spectacles Benjamin studied) and mass spectacles being shaped for profit. What seems clear to us about the history of American motorsports spectacles is that, despite their rather obvious authoritarian overtones, authoritarian structures of control and the diegeses marketed through them served economic as well as political purposes. In our time, it seems clear that the primary goal of these events is profit; thus the staging of these authoritarian diegeses more fully represents an aestheticization of economics than politics.

This chapter explores the aestheticization of economics in the history of American motorsports. We align our analysis of American motorcycle culture with the authoritarianism literature, especially that of Adorno, Frenkel-Brunswik, Levinson, and Sanford, (1950) and Altemeyer (1981, 1988), by exploring two variations of authoritarianism in the history of American motorcycling. Early American or "heritage" motorcycling (1910–1950) exhibited a relatively orthodox authoritarianism that stressed submission and conventionality. These traits were overwritten with the anti-establishment, rebellious, and aggressive characteristics of "rebel" authoritarianism (Adorno, Frenkel-Brunswik, Levinson, & Sanford, 1950, pp. 762–765) during the post-War era (1950–1980). Rebel authoritarianism became the leitmotif of contemporary American motorcycle rallying (1980-present), but has been increasingly coupled with anti-authoritarian themes as motorcycle companies and event organizers progressively decontextualize the event in order to grow them into increasingly profitable megaspectacles (Best & Kellner, 1997; Kellner, 1995).

From its earliest years, the authoritarian structure and culture of American motorcycling were critical to its economic enclosure. The motorcycle industry, subsidiary merchandizers and event organizers used the authoritarian structure of heritage motorcycle clubs to transform groups of informal motorcycle enthusiasts, not into fascists, but into networks of loyal consumers. In addition, they relied upon rigid conventionality and in-group boundaries of heritage motorcycle culture to attract customers and solidify "consumer tribes" (Cova & Cova, 2002, Cova, Kozinets, & Shankar, 2012). When the orthodox authoritarianism of heritage motorcycling was challenged by post-War motorcycle "outlaws," the motorcycle industry enclosed rebel authoritarianism into an outlaw biker diegesis. This diegesis became the central narration of contemporary American motorcycling served as a critical resource for marketing and promotion. We theorize the economic role of this diegesis as "dark spectacle." Dark spectacles transform authoritarianism into cultural commodities and market them to those who wish to see or be seen within an authoritarian themed diegesis.

In what follows, we examine authoritarianism and its role in the spectator, sponsorship, and trophy markets of American motorcycling. In this sense, we focus on authoritarianism as a cultural commodity, not a personality. We have not taken "F" or "RWA" scale measurements of event participants, and while we would infer that authoritarian personality characteristics are present within many American motorcycle enthusiasts, we are not in a position to make claims about their personality structures. Instead, our goal is to analyze authoritarianism as a key element in the broad history of the American motorcycling subculture of consumption (Schouten & McAlexander, 1993, 1995) and an important catalyst to its economic enclosure. We analyze the cultural content of three distinct historical epochs of American motorcycle history—heritage motorcycling (1910–1950), outlaw motorcycling (1950–1980), and contemporary motorcycling (1980-present)—in order to delineate the characteristics of authoritarianism present within each and examine their role in the growing commodification of motorcycle culture in America.

Authoritarianism in Early American Motorcycling

As discussed in Chapter 3, the image of American motorcycling in the contemporary public mind bears little resemblance to the reality of heritage motorcycle culture. Pre-War motorcycle culture, clubs, and activities were generally conventional, establishment, and civic minded—more akin to church socials than the Hell's Angels. Motorcycle enthusiasts of this era were middle and upper-middle class, and their clubs and activities were respectable and family friendly. Early heritage motorcycle events were local and spontaneous, often involving road tours, dirt track races, "tourist trophy" (TT) events or hill climbs that were modestly attended and relatively uncommodified. Cyclists gathered for evenings or weekends to ride and socialize, and events often included family picnics, dances, carnivals and field games with prizes for innocuous distinctions like the most neatly dressed lady and gentlemen riders or those who had come the furthest distance (Wooster, 2010). Even the "gypsy tour," whose name suggests an anti-social or at least vagabond quality, was consistent with establishment lifestyles. During such events, riders logged miles to and from events; "riding gypsy" meant riding self-contained, carrying one's necessities on their bike and camping in city parks or farm fields. Along the way, riders were expected to maintain decorum in an effort to "give the general public a convincing demonstration of the practical transportation and pleasurable possibilities of the motorcycle" (History of Laconia, nd.).

Despite this patina of wholesomeness there is clear evidence of authoritarianism in heritage motorcycle culture. Adorno, Frenkel-Brunswik, Levinson, and Sanford (1950) and Altemeyer's (1981, 1988) conceptualization of authoritarian attitudes provides a useful framework to explore these qualities. These works identify conventionalism, submission and aggression as three attitude clusters critical to the authoritarian personality. Conventionalism involves high degree of adherence to the social conventions perceived to be endorsed by social authorities (Altemeyer, 1988, p. 2); the strong acceptance, commitment, and rigid adherence to traditional social norms (Altemeyer, 1981, p. 153) or middle class values (Adorno, Frenkel-Brunswik, Levinson, & Sanford, 1950, p. 228).

Authoritarians reject individualistic definitions of morality, believing instead that moral principles are obdurate, universal, and pre-defined by religious or political authorities. Importantly, adherence to conventional or traditional values may often be a standard not fully observed by the authoritarian himself; a "code" for how people *ought* to act but not necessarily *how* they act (Altemeyer, 1981, pp. 155–156). Authoritarian submission turns on the trust of and obedience toward established authorities, especially those perceived as legitimate. Authoritarians generally take the statements and actions of authority figures at face value and demonstrate a willingness to blindly comply with accepted authority figures (Altemeyer, 1981, p. 151). They hold strongly to the belief that those in an official capacity know what is best, that their authority should not be challenged, and that they are "owed" allegiance, obedience and respect (Altemeyer, 1988, p. 4). Finally, authoritarian aggression is the intent to harm or produce a negative state in an individual or group that they would usually avoid. Targets of authoritarian aggression are typically those outside the status quo—law breakers, minorities, or others who deviate from rigorously held group norms—thus authoritarian aggression is often coupled with the development and maintenance of rigid in- and out-group boundaries. Aggression typically becomes authoritarian when it is tied to the belief that an established authority approves of it or would be protected by it, and often centers on the drive to punish, isolate or demonize those who lie beyond in-group boundaries. On the other hand, aggression toward out-groups may be held in check under strong social prohibitions or the disapproval of authoritarian leaders (Altemeyer, 1988, p. 106).

We draw Adorno, Frenkel-Brunswik, Levinson, and Sanford (1950) and Altemeyer's (1981, 1988) conceptualization of authoritarianism in our study of American motorcycling. However, while they identify conventionalism, submission and aggression as "attitude clusters" or elements of a personality structure, we conceptualize these characteristics as social artifacts. In what follows, we read these characteristics in the culture and structure of American motorcycling and explore their role in the development of spectator, sponsor and trophy markets.

There was a strong conventional orientation in heritage motorcycle culture. Uniforms, for example, were *de rigueur* in heritage motorcycling and mirrored the conventional dress of the time. Matching shirts and breeches, bow or bolo ties, aviator hats and wing tipped shoes enforced respectability, mass conformity, and traditional values. Clubs mandated uniforms be laid out with specific attention to detail, noting acceptable color combinations and fabrics and identifying the specific location for embroidery, club insignia, and other pins and patches. Event organizers promoted this regimentation by awarding prizes the most neatly dressed and orderly uniformed clubs at tours or parades. They endorsed uniforms as a central element in the legitimation of American motorcycling, noting that "It's the uniformed clubs that get the admiring glances and the favorable comment as they swing down the street and highway" and that uniforms were central to turning clubs into "civic institutions" (*The Enthusiast,* 1939, n.p.).

Conventionalism and submission were also promoted by the formal organization and rigid hierarchies of early twentieth century motorcycle clubs. Structured like branches of the military, clubs elected leaders, designated "ranks" (captain, first and second lieutenant, etc.), and evaluated applicants for membership. Membership typically involved a formal application; once approved, members were given visible club insignia (typically brass or bronze pins rather than patches) required to be worn on club uniforms. Local clubs brought structure to motorcycle events of the day by policing club tours and serving as the final authority for races. They elected "investigation committees" to provide social control during tours and events and to enforce rules for motorcycle competition. They published specific rank orders for riders during tours, and it was considered a violation of club rules for a rider to pass another member of higher rank who might be perceived to be driving too slowly. They employed graded point systems that "scored" members for acceptable participation. Members could earn (or lose) their good standing in a club based points earned for such activities as attending club meetings, participating in and assisting with club events, choosing to ride their motorcycles to club events during appropriate moths of the year, and following club rules and authority. Finally, clubs served as important sources of political organization; like the Harley Davidson Motorcycle Club of Lincoln Nebraska, whose 1912 bylaws stated that their purpose was "to defend and protect the rights of motorcyclists."

Mass conformity and orderly conduct was solidified through the various national associations that evolved to provide structure, oversight, and political organization to early twentieth century American motorcycling. The earliest races, tours, hill-climbs and other events were subject to the rules of local motorcycle clubs, however, they lacked the standardization that was deemed necessary as participation and geographic representation expanded. In addition, the transition from motorcycles to cars as the primary form of automobility in America threatened the legitimacy of motorcycling and created the need for political mobilization for motorcycle rights. The patterns of authority first established by motorcycle clubs were standardized under the fledgling Federation of American Motorcyclists in 1903, who began to regulate motorcycle racing and other forms of motorcycle competition. Over time, the authority of the FAM was transferred to other organizations, including the Motorcycle and

Allied Trades Association (1916–1924) and finally the American Motorcycling Association.

The AMA and its predecessors charged themselves with bringing structure and respectability to American motorcycling, consolidated the authority structures of local clubs into national bodies, and made themselves the final authority on motorcycle competition and recreation. Races and events had to be sanctioned by the AMA if their results were to be official. The AMA controlled the models and engine sizes of motorcycles allowed in competition, and speed and distance records could be challenged or disqualified if not made under the rigid guidelines and supervision of AMA sanctioning bodies. By the late 1920s, clubs were required to register with the AMA in order to be legitimate and recognized, and only clubs and members chartered with the AMA could participate in official AMA tours and events. Club members were expected to abide by the AMA code of conduct, and a club's charter could be threatened if its members did not demonstrate the middle class respectability and decorum required by the AMA (The History of the AMA, 2013).

Early motorcycle associations also saw themselves as political organizations charged with the responsibility to organize riders to fight for motorcycle rights. As early as 1903, the Federation of American Motorcyclists recognized that the novelty of the "motor bicycle" left its status open to various legal definitions and that political action was necessary to ensure the legal legitimacy of this new form of transportation. In 1924, one of the primary goals of the newly founded American Motorcycle Association was to build a member base that would turn the AMA into "a live and active fighting organization" that would make law makers "think long and seriously before they attempt to put over anything on the motorcycle riders" (*Western Motorcyclist and Bicyclists,* 1924.) Organizing under the slogan "An organized minority can always defeat an unorganized majority," the AMA mobilized riders to promote the motorcycle as a form of transportation equal to the automobile. Their "fight" took a two pronged approach: one centered on protecting and preserving the public image of motorcycling, the other emphasizing the rights of the motorcyclist amidst the growing centrality of the automobile in American transportation. On the former, the AMA and its predecessors saw respectability as central to the legitimacy of motorcycling in the public eye, and worked to regulate standards of behavior, demeanor, dress and decorum in heritage motorcycle clubs and activities. The AMA promoted uniforms, club authority, and rider respectability in heritage motorcycle publications while simultaneously demonizing deviants like the "open pipe goofs" who violated community noise standards by removing the baffles from motorcycle mufflers. In 1948, the AMA launched its "Muffler Mike" campaign, which encouraged members to pledge to quiet riding by not modifying exhaust systems. On the latter, the AMA organized motorcycle enthusiasts to fight against restrictive motorcycle legislation, including speed and traffic rights, city motorcycle bans, and later, state mandatory helmet laws. (*American Motorcyclist*, 1984, p. 50).

Heritage motorcycling culture valorized other authority figures beyond the AMA, especially the military and police as they became increasingly reliant on the motorcycle. Beginning in 1916, both Indian and Harley Davidson began providing motorcycles to the US military for use in patrolling the US border with Mexico, and over the next five years, some 20,000 Harley Davidson and 50,000 Indian motorcycles were sold to the US military to be used in the War effort (Nichols, 2007, p. 77). Motorcycle enthusiasts and manufacturers celebrated the military use of the motorcycle. One early Harley Davidson advertisement praised the role of Harley Davidson in providing motorcycles to US military service with an image showing a fleet of service members riding their Harley Davidsons out of the opening hands of Uncle Sam (Uncle Sam's Choice, n.d.) Motorcycle enthusiasts saw the military use of the motorcycle as a validation of their own identity, praising military sales as "another strong boost for the motorcycle" (*Motorcycle Illustrated*, 1917, p. 7) and celebrating the motorcycle as a symbol of national strength and versatility.

Motorcycle enthusiasts of this era also saw the legitimacy of the motorcycle bolstered by its use in policing. Figure 31 depicts a graphic run in the August 3, 1922 issue of *Motorcycle and Bicycle Illustrated* under the caption "305 more Indians" celebrates the purchase of Indian Motorcycles for service in the New York City Mounted police by showing rows of jackbooted police officers standing at parade attention next to their motorcycles while the public looks on from metropolitan sidewalks. The image coincidently includes a caricatured Indian head-shot, the company logo of the 1920s which demonstrates a further level of in- out-group boundary maintenance within the industry.

In 1928, the public safety division of Harley Davidson produced and distributed a series of posters to motorcycle clubs promoting the use of the motorcycle for traffic policing. In one, a bumkin-looking cowboy cowers in his stopped car, arms raised in submission to a motorcycle traffic officer dressed as a member of the Canadian mounted police. Captions label the cowboy a "traffic outlaw run amuck" and the motorcycle as an "excellent steed" (The Only Force He Respects, 1928). In another, drivers in gangster attire speed cars morphed onto the bodies of grimacing lions down city streets while a uniformed motorcycle officer directs kittens across a suburban street. The caption reads "Have you noticed now those roaring lions of traffic become meek little kittens when the 'Lion Tamer' comes along?" (We need *more* Lion Tamers! 1928). Still another reads "Day after day the Mounted Officer rides his best—a

FIGURE 31   *305 More Indians, Indian Motorcycle Advertisement*
SOURCE: *MOTORCYCLE AND BICYCLE ILLUSTRATED,* 3 AUGUST 1922.

tireless warning to criminal and traffic law violators. Few are so foolhardy as to ignore his presence—his mere appearance on the street and highway compels obedience to the law" (Tireless Riders of the Law, 1928). The authoritarian optics of these posters is clear and suggests a coupling of aggression, submission, and rigid in and out-group boundaries. The officers always appear starched and stern, with chiseled bodies and facial features propped bolt upright on their motorcycles. Their military style haircuts and uniforms, coupled with references to "Mounties" or "Lion Tamers" give the image of authority and aggressiveness, and the message connotes strict in- and out- group boundaries: Automobile drivers are back country bumkins "run amuk" or gangster "roaring lions"; their *only cure* is the "adequate and constant patrol of our streets" by making "every policeman a traffic policeman" (The *Only Cure* for our Deplorable Traffic Conditions, 1928).

While heritage motorcycle culture focused verbal and visual contempt on these "outsiders," there were seldom situations of outright punishment or aggressive control. Altemeyer (1981, 1988) and Adorno, Frenkel-Brunswik, Levinson, and Sanford (1950) affirm that authoritarian aggression can be held in check by strong levels of conventionality and submission or strong social prohibitions (Altemeyer, 1988, p. 106). Thus we would expected to see less authoritarian aggression during periods of history where strong social conventions against outright aggression were in place. In the case of heritage motorcycling, the emphasis on conventionality outweighed potentially aggressive tendencies and channeled them into socially acceptable and organizationally sanctioned activities. The strong and vocal disapproval of anti-social behavior by policing bodies like the AFM, M&ATA or AMA limited the aggression displayed by motorcycle advocates in the pre-war era. As Adorno, Frenkel-Brunswik, Levinson, and Sanford suggest, it is not that aggressive tendencies have been outgrown but rather inhibited; the emphasis on conformity actually serving as a defense against an underlying hostility (1950, p. 162).

Adorno, Frenkel-Brunswik, Levinson, and Sanford (1950) and Altemeyer (1981, 1988) also note the role of ambivalence to conventional sexuality in expressions of authoritarianism, and this ambivalence is clearly notable within the culture of heritage motorcycling. In many ways, the concern over sexual mores mirrors that of society at large during this period, where the developing public life, greater independence, and new freedoms of expression for women increasingly challenged the Victorian gender sensibilities of the late-nineteenth century. This challenge was exacerbated by motorcycling in much the same way it was in equestrian culture of the Victorian era; focused quite literally on how a woman should "ride" and the sexual innuendo evident in that practice. In addition, concerns over the enhanced individualism and freedom that came with the motorcycle—like those of the bicycle that proceeded it—often questioned the greater potential for geographic independence the motorcycle allowed to women.

Heritage motorcycle culture, especially during the first decades of the twentieth century exhibits an almost obsessive concern the proper role of female motorcycle riders and their perceived challenge to conventional sexuality. The growing popularity of motorcycling during the early twentieth century drew increasing numbers of couples to this emerging leisure activity. This, in turn, fostered ongoing debate about the proper role of women in the sport. Did they belong? If so, what was their proper place? As a passenger or driver? Riding in a side-car, side saddle or astride the bike? And what should they wear? What stands out in this discussion is not a criticism of female riders *per se* but the criticism of women who choose to challenge conventional sexuality through their participation in motorcycling events. Magazines targeting motorcycle enthusiasts were filled with articles and editorials debating the respectability of female motorcyclists. A 1919 editorial about women riders at the Weirs Beach, NH rally is indicative of these gender politics. In an op-ed entitled "What's wrong with American Motorcycling," "Grandpa Grundy" complains about the attire and activities of female riders, arguing that women riding tandem in skirts and stockings, tight fitting jerseys or "clinging, form-fitting knitted sweaters" is "a crime against man's piece of mind" and, more importantly, gives the sport of motorcycling "another black eye" (Grundy, 1919, p. 23). Many readers agreed. Letters to the editor in the following issue, argued that "flappers in pants" left a blemish on the sport of motorcycling and should be prevented from participating either by city councils or an official ordinance of the Motorcycle and Allied Trades Association (The Viewpoint of the Reader, 1919).

The challenge of independent female drivers was also a source of concern among heritage motorcycle enthusiasts. "Are men necessary on a motorcycling trip?" asked an article in the July 5, 1917 issue of *Motorcycle and Bicycle Illustrated,* the debate centering on the propriety and safety of women touring unaccompanied by their husbands (The Manless Tour at Last! 1917). Other articles explored women driver's ability to effectively handle a heavy motorcycle in tight turns or unpaved terrain or their aptitude for making adjustments or repairs in the field when unaccompanied by male riders. In 1940, Linda Dugeau formed the Motor Maids of America, the first female motorcycle club, dedicated to proving that women could ride motorcycles and maintain their femininity without being "mannish," "man-haters" or lesbians. While it took Dugeau three years to organize enough willing female participants to seek an AMA charter, the organization quickly expanded into a hierarchically organized and multi-state motorcycle club (About Motor Maids, 2013; Motor Maids, n.d.; Yates 1999).

Finally, the names of motorcycle field games popular at heritage events provides further evidence of the ambivalence toward conventional sexuality. While games such as "ride the plank" (which involved piloting a motorcycle in a straight line atop a series of wooden planks), "bite the weenie" (where drivers maneuvered in order to allow their passenger to bite a hot dog suspended from overhead) or "whack the murphy" (where drivers tried to knock a potato off a short post with a stick while driving one handed) were in many ways playful demonstrations of motorcycle skill, their names suggest a double entendre that clearly exposes ambivalent attitudes toward conventional sexuality of the day. These names, coupled with the silence or invisibility of sexuality in the events themselves, mirrors the dual expression and repression central to authoritarian attitudes toward conventional sexuality (Altemeyer, 1981, pp. 155–156).

The culture of heritage motorcycling, either as spontaneous and local or formally organized under national governing bodies reflect tendencies toward conventionality, submission, aggression and rigid in/out group dichotomies often associated with authoritarianism. Although focused on a specific microcosm of social life, the activities and ethos of heritage motorcycling were rigid, mass-identified, submissive to authority structures and condemning of those who didn't follow the general conventions of the time. Cyclists of this era clearly felt threatened by the possibility that their sport would meet with public disapproval. The threat was both internal and external; it emanated from those cyclists who might offend the general sensibilities of the public at large as well as the increasingly popular and dominant use of the automobile as the primary form of transportation in American society. Motorcycle enthusiasts, sanctioning bodies, and the motorcycle industry itself reacted to this threat by developing an authoritarian culture and organizational structure to promote and protect their legitimacy.

Authoritarianism and the Economic Enclosure of Heritage Motorcycling

The authoritarian culture of heritage motorcycling was an important resources to the burgeoning motorcycle industry of the early twentieth century. Although the use of the motorcycle had a spontaneous, grassroots and relatively uncommodified birth, it did not take long for private enterprise to begin enclosing this arena of public life. Between 1903 and the beginning of World War II, nearly 300 motorcycle and scooter manufacturers went into business in the United States (Nichols, 2007, pp. 104–115). Coupled with the development of a market for subsidiary products (accessories, parts, tools, apparel, etc.) their competition fueled the need to expand consumption and solidify a consumer base. The economic enclosure of heritage motorcycling turned on the development of spectator and sponsorship markets. The industry needed to create an organized body of people who wanted to be seen within the experience of heritage motorcycling (spectators) and then connect this audience to markets of advertising and promotion (sponsorship). Enclosure was the outcome of developing networks of spectators as markets for sponsorship, and the rigid structure, conventional habitus, and authoritarian ethos of heritage motorcycling facilitated this process in several important ways.

While the earliest national motorcycle organization (the Federation of American Motorcyclists) was a civic organization, the organizations that replaced it (the M&ATA and AMA) were trade associations. Arguing that "no sport has ever amounted to anything without a strong controlling body, loyally supported by its membership" (Clayton & Despain, 1984, p. 31), these organizations worked to develop the membership networks that would serve as the initial spectator markets in American motorcycling. They published recruiting guides, sponsored membership campaigns, and held membership contests, complete with prizes, banquets, and public recognition to members and clubs who recruited the most new members each month.

The authority of the M&ATA and AMA and their rigid control over motorcycle clubs and activities was critical to tying motorcycle enthusiasts directly into a consumer network (History of the AMA, n.d.). As trade organizations, they served as the middle man between motorcycle enthusiasts and the motorcycle industry. Their regulation of membership and club status, their rigid sanctioning of racing and tours, and their "members only" approach to events made membership a necessity for anyone who wanted access to the motorcycling events of the day. As the sport grew, the ranks of the M&ATA and AMA swelled, fostering a network of consumers who could be more easily targeted for marketing and promotion. In many cases, industry leaders served in ranking positions of M&ATA or the AMA, further solidifying the relationship between national organizations, industry, and motorcycle enthusiasts. For example, a January 25, 1917 article in *Motorcycle Illustrated* identifies Lacy Crolius as both the advertising manager for Harley Davidson and the chairman of the Educational Committee of the M&ATA. In this dual roles, Crolius was responsible for organizing M&ATA events, including the 1917 National Gypsy Tour (Date for National Gipsy Tours, 1917). Crolius' booklet, "Suggestions for Conducting National Gypsy Holiday Tours," outlines M&ATA standards for national motorcycle events and provides direction on event promotion (Gypsy Tour Promotion Plans, 1917). Thus by 1917, motorcycle events were not simply local or spontaneous, but aligned with a clear strategy to reach out and organize a spectatorship market into a subculture of consumption.

Membership networks also provided an important communication conduit that connected the motorcycling public with the industry. Magazines including *Bicycling World & Motorcycle Review, Motorcycle Illustrated, American Motorcyclists & Bicyclists, The Motorcyclist, American Motorcycling* (renamed *American Motorcyclist* in 1977), *Motorcycle Enthusiast,* and *The Indian News* were published by national organizations or the motorcycle industry and made available to motorcyclists, often as part of their membership in the M&ATA or AMA. These publications were important to the development of early spectator markets. The M&ATA and AMA used these publications as their primary means of cultural dissemination. The articles, editorials and images published in these magazines tied motorcycle enthusiasts to a shared set of principles and behavioral expectations. This not only solidified the in-group boundaries of emerging spectator markets, it also reinforced the establishment ethos that was considered crucial to protecting the motorcycle market.

Finally, the spectator networks created by the M&ATA and AMA produced a body of obedient consumers sympathetic to pro-motorcycle political advocacy. One of earliest AMA slogans ("an organized minority can always defeat a disorganized majority") is an important indicator of their goal to mobilize riders into an organized political body. Industry leaders were aware that political restrictions on motorcycle use threatened the growth of their industry, and used the networks and publications of the M&ATA and AMA to create loyal interest group whose social and political capital could be mobilized to promote the legitimacy of motorcycle culture and thus protect the economic interests of the motorcycle industry.

The spectator markets developed in heritage motorcycling were also important to the development of early sponsorship markets. Although is well before the time of "official sponsorship," where events were named or corporations had exclusive rights to market themselves at or in association with an event, the early networks of motorcycle enthusiasts provided a captive audience for marketing and promotion. Industry publications, newsletters, and trade journals were filled with the advertisements of motorcycle and subsidiary manufacturers. Early tours and events were arranged in order to bring riders, dealers, and subsidiary merchandizers together. The M&ATA and AMA were considered mechanisms by which industry marketing could be standardized. In a 1917 editorial in *Motorcycle and Bicycle Illustrated*, J.H. DoneKue argues that the M&ATA should produce and standardize window displays to be used by dealers in order for motorcycle dealers to represent the motorcycle in the best light possible (DonKue, 1917).

The economy of heritage motorcycling thus turned on the enclosure of a previously public and uncommodified social activity. This enclosure primarily involved the development of formalized spectatorship—networks of motorcycle enthusiasts organized into membership networks by the M&ATA and AMA. These organizations centralized spectatorship through a structure that exercised increasing control over motorcycle clubs and events and required membership for access. Membership networks facilitated the development of sponsorship markets by creating a captive audience for the motorcycle industry to target for advertising. The motorcycle industry used the membership structure and oversight of national motorcycle organizations to tap into a controlled and obedient consumer base—one that was submissive to national organizations, would cast the motorcycle in good light to the general public, and work together to promote the rights, respectability, and representation of the motorcycle as a legitimate form of automobility. The authoritarian habitus and structure of heritage motorcycling was thus a direct outcome of economic enclosure. In order to develop spectator and sponsorship markets, the M&ATA and AMA relied upon their rigid control of membership and access to activities, promoted submission to AMA rules and mandates, and advanced the conservative attitudes central to heritage motorcycle culture.

Outlaw Bikers and Rebel Authoritarianism

By the mid-1940s, the threat to conventionalism feared by heritage motorcycle enthusiasts was becoming a reality. Text from a speech given at the 1947 Harley Davidson dealer's conference is telling of the new in- and out- group boundaries being solidified in American motorcycling: "Well-dressed motorcycle riders on shiny, good-looking motorcycles are likely to stay out of trouble. Riders dressed in overalls, on motor-cycles that are stripped down and generally dilapidated, are all dressed up for trouble and likely to find it." (Harley Davidson Dealer's Conference, 1947).

While an extant literature explores the post-war transformation of American motorcycle culture, a brief discussion is warranted here (for a full exploration see Austin, Gagne & Orend, 2010; Nichols, 2007; Reynolds, 2000; Thompson, H.S., 1967; Wood, 2003; Yates, 1999). In the immediate post-War era, increasing numbers of veterans were attracted to the libertarian possibilities of the motorcycle—especially its emphasis on freedom, adventure, risk and homosocial bonding. As Nichols (2007) notes, "this same strain of rebel had just returned, victorious, from an epic struggle against a mighty enemy. He was ready to shake off the horrors of war and get on with unbridled enjoyment of life in a vast, free country" (2007, p. 80). The rebelliousness of many of these men was stirred by their disenfranchisement from an increasingly specialized labor market. Not expecting to win, they had nothing to lose, and responded with a "full time social vendetta" organized under the structure of the motorcycle club (Thompson, H.S., 1967, p. 54). Newly formed clubs remained outside the normative standards, rules, sanctioning and membership structure of the AMA; they were "outlaw" in both their rejection of the AMA as well as their reputation for disrupting sanctioned AMA events and challenging civil authority.

The emerging habitus of post-war motorcycling challenged the "orthodox" authoritarian emphases of heritage motorcycle culture, and marked a shift toward a type of authoritarianism best captured in Adorno, Frenkel-Brunswik, Levinson, and Sanford's (1950) concept of "the rebel." In language that bears a striking resemblance to outlaw motorcycle culture, they argue that a subspecies of the authoritarian personality has "emerged with the increased insecurity of the post-war existence"; one that reflects nihilism and chance with a "penchant for tolerated excesses," anti-social destructiveness, the sadistic persecution of all things weak, and the fortitude to tolerate risk and bodily injury (1950, p. 763). Unlike orthodox authoritarian, the rebel does not oppose the principles of rugged individualism but rather carries them out *ad absurdum* (1950, p. 171).

While the concept of rebel authoritarianism remains relatively undeveloped in their work, their discussion of its characteristics bears a striking resemblance to outlaw motorcycling. In what follows, we explore the evidence of rebel authoritarianism in post-war motorcycle culture. Crucial to this analysis is the tension between reality and rhetoric. While significant evidence of rebel authoritarianism is present within the culture of outlaw motorcycling, virtually every analyst is quick to point out that rebellion among post-war motorcycle enthusiasts was exaggerated by sensationalist media attention and the widespread public panic that ensued. This exaggeration was crucial to the creation of dark spectacle and the enclosure of post-War motorcycling. The rebel authoritarianism of post-war motorcycle culture became an important cultural commodity exploited by the newspaper, magazine and film industries and later capitalized on by the motorcycle industry itself. This new diegesis, is in large part responsible for the massive growth of the economy of motorcycle spectacles after 1980.

Perhaps the clearest divergence from the orthodox authoritarianism of heritage motorcycling was the strong anti-establishment sentiments of outlaw motorcycle culture. While heritage motorcycling was organized under a structure that celebrated middle-class decorum, post-War motorcycling turned on hostility and the flagrant violation of social conventions. Any behavior that raised the eyebrows of the establishment—commonly referred to as "showing class" in the outlaw vernacular—was considered appropriate. Stock bikes were "chopped" or "bobbed" with the addition of extended front forks, cut away fenders, and stripped down suspension and accessories. Muffler baffles were routinely "cut out" in order to make a motorcycle as socially disruptive as possible. Dress and deportment shifted from the clean and uniformed to the unkempt and disheveled; greasy hair, unshaven faces, dirty jeans and leather jackets or vests that were left purposely unwashed, all visible indicators of one's commitment to the post-War motorcycling lifestyle. Club names like the Pissed Off Bastards of Bloomington, The Boozefighters, Hell's Angels, Market Street Commandos, Vagos, Bandidos, and the Warlocks, Sons of Silence, and Outlaws violated establishment values and public sensibly. Anti-social behavior, most commonly excessive drinking and brawling, but also risky driving, crude humor, and brazen sexual practices (including open-mouthed kissing between club brothers), were all considered appropriate ways of "show-ing class" (Nichols, 2007). In his now classic work on the Hell's Angels, H.S. Thompson (1967) argues that outlaw motorcyclists had an almost instinc-tual anti-establishment orientation, their economic disenfranchisement pro-ducing a reaction formation against respectability (1967, p. 158). "Unlike the normal, middle-class, hardworking American, a motorcycle outlaw has no vested interest in the system ... The values of that system are completely irrel-evant to him... he doesn't give a damn" (Thompson, H.S., 1967, p. 176).

Outlaw motorcycle clubs mirrored the strict regimentation and military style organization of heritage clubs, yet the level of their militarism challenged conventional limits. Many outlaw club members were veterans who were used to military order and had no problem accepting the rank and hierarchy of club structures. At the same time, their support for order, loyalty, and discipline of-ten pushed the boundaries of traditional society. This can be seen in the pre-dominant use of Nazi symbolism among the outlaw biker clubs of the 1960s and 70s. Nichols (2007) notes that the reason some outlaw bikers wore German WW II iron crosses, swastikas, SS medallions and helmets was because they respected the "organization, might, and spirit of the Third Reich" (2007 p. 146). While most took issue with the anti-Semitism of the Nazi agenda, they had respect and admiration for the discipline, loyalty and dedication of the party. H.S. Thompson (1967) quotes Sonny Barger, then President of the Oakland chapter of the Hell's Angels response to local tourist queries about the Angels being Nazis: "... there's a lot about [Germany] that we admire... They had dis-cipline, There was nothin' chickenshit about 'em. They might not of had all the right ideas, but at least they respected their leaders and they could depend on each other" (1967, p. 148)

Strict in- and out-group boundaries were maintained by secrecy, suspicion and aggression. Club members used secret names that marked their in-group membership and frustrated local policing efforts. Outsiders were treated with the suspicion that they might be an informant, reporter or police investiga-tor, and new club members were subject to intense initiation rights to prove their allegiance and value as club members. "Prospects" were treated as a long-term challenge of trust, often requiring years of menial and degrading service in order to prove themselves worthy of full club membership. Once proven, the prospect would be "patched," or given the official insignia of the club, to be sewn onto a denim or leather jacket or vest. Called "originals," a member's patch and cut were seldom if ever replaced; their accumulated grease and grime a visible challenge to conventional middle-class styles of dress and de-corum (Nichols, 2007, p. 146). Originals were in many ways carryovers from the uniforms of heritage motorcycling—and were just as regimented. Patches, rockers and colors were strictly controlled by club leaders; they were to be displayed in specific locations and severe punishments were inflicted on those considered undeserving of their patch. Outlaw club insignia was also noticeably anti-establishment and, more importantly, anti-AMA. Early outlaw patches boasted "AOA" (American Outlaws Association) as a direct affront to the 1960 AMA "Put your best wheel forward" advertising campaign. These patches were the precursor to the diamond shaped "One Percenter" patches common in outlaw motorcycling today (Nichols, 2007, p. 161). When Harley Davidson began selling café style motorcycles in the 1970s some outlaw club members sewed the traditional winged Harley Davidson patch upside down in visible animosity to Harley Davidson for "selling out." Other patches were used to signify rebellion and anti-social behavior: having sex with a woman during her period, an interest in anal sex, sex with a black woman, or in some cases killing in defense of club honor (Nichol, 2007).

The strength of in-group boundaries in outlaw motorcycling bound men together in a rigid homo-social bond. Club members regularly referred to each other as "brothers," a reference that wove them together as a unified force against outside influences. H.S. Thompson (1967) notes that despite their intense patriotism and high praise of capitalism, outlaw club members were strangely communistic, sharing food, money, lodging, beer and in some cases women with their brothers in need. They acted with strict discipline in following the dictates of club leadership, and their uniformity in thought and action fueled their narcissism and aggression. Outlaw biker literature is rife with references that denote club members as "wolves," "Vikings," or "Knights" and conventional middle-class society as "sheep." The imagery is clear; outlaw bikers are the free souls, acting with purpose and honor in a noble (yet often misunderstood) way. Outside their ranks are the sheep—stupid, senseless followers "who will inherit the earth in a bleating, vacant-minded void of dreamless, meaningless sleep" (Hays and Quattlebaum, 2010, p. 13). Their group-think fueled extreme and unpredictable behavior, an "ethic of excess in all things" including drinking, violence, sex, and retribution far beyond the boundaries of conventional society (Thompson, H.S., 1967, pp. 71–73; 165).

Post-war motorcycle culture demonstrates much greater ambivalence to authority than heritage motorcycle culture. On the one hand, the aggression and anti-social behavior of outlaw club members made then naturally antagonistic toward authority figures. On the other, their military past and social regimentation gave them an odd affinity to the very sources of authority they despised. H.S. Thompson (1967) documents the remarkable similarities between the Hell's Angels and the California police, operating on "on the same emotional frequency" yet simultaneously vilified and valorized for their service to society

(1967, p. 39). This ambivalence also explains the strong patriotism and pro-American sentiment in outlaw biker culture. H.S. Thompson (1967) considers the Hell's Angels violent reaction to the anti-Vietnam protests—which were supported by the same Berkeley hippies they had partied with a year before—as evidence of a "retrograde patriotism," that aligned the Angels with the same status quo and law enforcement that had persecuted them during the previous years (1967, pp. 248–249). In October 1965 Sonny Barger went so far as to write a letter to President Eisenhower indicating that members of the Hells Angels were available to train and serve as a branch of Special Forces behind enemy lines in Vietnam (Thompson, H.S., 1967, p. 257).

Finally, outlaw motorcycle culture demonstrates the sexual ambivalence of heritage motorcycle culture pushed to the extreme. Despite the unconventional sexual mores and behavior that are legend in outlaw biker culture, sexual activity wasn't chaotic or unstructured. In fact, a rigid structure lay beneath the anti-establishment sexuality of outlaw motorcycle enthusiasts that was firmly upheld and violently protected. Sexual partnerships were distinguished though a system of gender roles that applied predominantly to women. Though they weren't necessarily steady girlfriends or wives, "old ladies" were considered in a monogamous relationship and thus off limits to sexual advances from other men. "Mammas" were women that were loosely affiliated with a motorcycle club but considered communal sexual property and open to all sexual advances. "Strange chicks" were women who were not previously associated with a motorcycle club but considered available for sexual exploitation. The boundaries between roles were transient; "old ladies" could risk becoming a "mamma" if they moved between committed partners too quickly or too often; men who made advances on another man's "old lady" were often subject to violent retribution for the offense (Thompson, H.S., 1967, pp. 170–172).

Rebel Authoritarianism in post-War Spectatorship and Sponsorship Markets

The post-War era was a crucial transition point in the culture of American motorcycling as the rebel authoritarianism of a new breed of motorcycle enthusiasts faced off against the conventional, submissive and establishment orientation of heritage motorcycling. The rise of rebel authoritarianism also had an important influence over the spectatorship and sponsorship markets of post-War American motorcycling. While initially limited, rebel authoritarianism captured the attention of police, newspapers, magazines, and the film industry, whose sensationalized accounts of outlaw activity were marketed widely to the public. In the process, media attention transformed the cultural narration, or *diegesis,* of American motorcycling from establishment to outlaw. Saturated with the characteristics of rebel authoritarianism, this new diegesis transformed post-War spectator markets. Although initially feared, the outlaw diegesis was eventually embraced by the motorcycle industry and tied to the sponsorship markets of the 1980s.

Outlaw motorcycling accounted for a relatively small proportion of all American motorcycle activity in the immediate post-War era. The number of outlaw clubs and club members was somewhat insignificant. Only a handful of clubs existed outside AMA sanctioning at that time, primarily located in southern California (Yates, 1999, p. 24). There were roughly 60 members of the Boozefighters in 1947, membership in the Hell's never exceeded 400 prior to 1965, when it reached an all-time low of 85 (Hays and Quattlebaum, 2010, pp. 35–36; Thompson, H.S., 1967, pp. 28–29). Evidence of rebel authoritarianism at this time was also limited. Hays and Quattlebaum (2010) argue that while members of the Boozefighters liked to drink to excess and had a hardened, tough exterior conditioned by combat, they had all the anti-social characteristics of "Spanky and Alfalfa with a pack of firecrackers" (2010, p. 53). H.S. Thompson (1967) refers to the Hell's Angels as "bush league hoods" involved in petty drinking and brawling prior to 1965; anti-social, but not posing the threat more commonly associated with their contemporary national reputation (1967, p. 37).

The transformation in both the reality and the representation of outlaw motorcycling was in large measure the result of sensationalistic media attention and the widespread moral panic (Cohen, 1980; DeYoung, 1988) that ensued. Gypsy tours and motorcycle races became the fodder of media spectacle as early as 1947, beginning with the Fourth of July Gypsy Tour in Hollister, California. While the majority of attendees camped peacefully on the outskirts of town, several "outlaw" clubs, including the Boozefighters and the Pissed Off Bastards of Bloomington partied in the bars and brawled on the main streets of Hollister. Although several arrests were made (mostly on drunk and disorderly charges), the rally ended without fanfare the next morning when the California State Patrol escorted the more unruly participations out of town. Despite the limited impact, the event took on historic significance when Barney Peterson of the *San Francisco Chronical* published a staged photograph of a drunk Boozefighter astride a parked Harley Davidson. The rider was recruited from the crowd (the motorcycle didn't actually belong to him), and Peterson littered the street and sidewalk with empty beer bottles for added effect (Nichols, 2007, p. 91; Yates, 1999, pp. 17–18). The photo was picked up by the Associated Press and later reprinted full page in *Life* magazine. *Life* reproduced the image with the sensationalistic headline "Cyclist's Holiday: He and Friends

Terrorize Town," and a 100 word description saturated with themes of rebel authoritarian. Similar reports were published throughout the 1950s and early 60. Gypsy tours and race events in Riverside and Porterville, and Monterey Beach, California, in Weirs Beach, North Carolina, and in other smaller communities across the United States were used as evidence of the growing threat of rebel authoritarianism in American motorcycling. Each time the media distorted facts, ignored countervailing information, sensationalized headlines and embellished stories in order to make good press (see Nichols, 2007; Reynolds, 2000; Shellow & Roemer, 1966; Thompson, H.S., 1967; Wood, 2003; Yates, 1999).

Media sensationalism of the 1950s fueled aggressive police attention that contributed to the further development of public panic over outlaw motorcycling. In 1965 Attorney General Thomas C. Lynch launched a six month investigation of outlaw motorcycle activities in the state of California. "Heavily biased and consistently alarming" (Thompson, H.S., 1967, p. 24), the Lynch report included "unsubstantiated absurdities" such as gang rape or the planned takeover of small townships by motorcycle rebels (Dulaney, 2005). Sensationalistic accounts of the Weir's Beach "riots" of 1965 led authorities in Prince George's County Maryland to engage in two months of riot preparations in advance of the Labor Day National Motorcycle Races in Upper Marlboro, Maryland (Shellow & Roemer, 1966). The fear of motorcycle rebels led to a self-fulfilling prophesy in police precincts across the country. Exaggerated reports led authorities to intensify their policing of motorcycle riders and activities (Reynolds, 2000) and fueled ongoing public concern over threat of outlaw motorcycling.

Most importantly, sensationalistic accounts of outlaw motorcycling became fodder for a genre of outlaw biker cinema during the 1960s and 70s. Film producers like Stanley Kramer, Samuel Z. Arkoff and Roger Corman quite literally capitalized on the moral panic sparked by sensationalistic accounts of Hollister, Riverside, Monterey, Laconia, and other notorious motorcycle events of the 1950s and 60s. *The Wild One* (1953), a cinematic interpretation of Frank Rooney's 1951 *Harper's* magazine account of the Hollister "riots," became the first in a series of often low budget motorcycle films that targeted post-War youth culture (Nichols, 2007). The films that followed, including *Motorpsychos* (1965), *The Wild Angels* (1966), *Hells Angels on Wheels* (1967), *Rebel Rousers* (1969), *Cycle Savages* (1969), *Satan's Sadists* (1969), and the iconic *Easy Rider* (1969) popularized the rebel authoritarianism of motorcycle culture. The plot lines and characters of this genre are remarkably similar—a destructive yet romanticized protagonist leads a group of motorcycle outlaws as they rampage some quiet community or terrorize law abiding citizens who run to the aid of rigid and unyielding police officers—yet are tied to every antisocial perversion of the day, including lesbianism and homosexuality, sadomasochism, devil worship, drug use, necrophilia, monsters, space aliens, Nazis, the mafia and virtually every aspect of the occult (Yates, 1999, p. 53)

Interestingly, the economic enclosure of post-War motorcycling turned more on the sale of newspapers, magazines and films than it did on the sale of motorcycles. The media found rebel authoritarianism a potent news theme and used it to enhance their sales. As a latent consequence, they transformed the diegesis of American motorcycling in popular culture. Rebel themes increasingly superseded the conventional, submissive, and middle-class optics of heritage motorcycling. As the atrocity tales of motorcycle mayhem spread, the public responded with fear and outrage. As H.S. Thompson (1967) notes, media attention situated the outlaw biker squarely in the public mind, firmly established as the all-American bogeyman (1967, p. 40). Relying upon rebel authoritarianism as a cultural commodity, the media produced and disseminated the outlaw biker diegesis as it worked to sell newspapers, magazines and films.

The moral panic generated by sensationalistic media accounts and the emerging outlaw diegesis was a critical catalyst to the emerging spectator and sponsorship markets of post-War motorcycling. The wide and exaggerated publicity turned outlaw clubs from unknown to well-known and inspired increasing numbers of young men to swell the ranks of outlaw clubs. New outlaw clubs like the Bandidos, Vagos and Warlocks sprung up to absorb the masses drawn to this new American counterculture (Nichols, 2007; Yates, 1999). The outlaw biker diegesis also created a self-fulfilling prophesy among existing club members, who began living up to the reputation that had been seeded through the media orgy. The emerging outlaw diegesis gave members a legend to live up to and a national reputation to uphold. H.S. Thompson (1967) argues that the Hell's Angels as they exist today were quite literally "created" by *Time, Newsweek,* and the *New York Times* (1967, p. 36). Media attention gave them a "prima donna complex" that turned them from a "gang of bums" to a social menace with a national reputation to uphold (1967, pp. 40–41).

The motorcycle industry initially shunned the outlaw biker diegesis of the post-War era and worked to disassociate itself from the newly emerging spectator markets. Clinging to the ethos of heritage motorcycling, industry leaders feared that the growing anti-establishment reputation of outlaw clubs would erode the marketplace. As early as 1947, Harley Davidson responded to events in Hollister, California with a public relations statement claiming that the vast majority of motorcycle riders were good, clean, God-fearing Americans with jobs and families, and that the "rough" element of motorcycling accounted for only "one percent" of all motorcycle riders. (Nichols, 2007, p. 135). Outlaw club members responded to this disparagement by popularizing the "one percenter" patch as an icon of outlaw motorcycling. By 1954, the collapse of the Indian Motorcycle Company had left Harley Davidson the only remaining motorcycle manufacturer in America. Even so, Harley Davidson continued to ignore the market potential of the emerging outlaw biker diegesis and see its market dominance championed by fighting outlaw motorcycling. The company refused to honor warranties and dealerships refused to service motorcycles that had been chopped or otherwise modified from stock standards (Yates, 1999, p. 33). Harley Davidson retooled its marketing and manufacturing strategies to reflect those of Japanese motorcycle manufactures that flooded the American marketplace in the 1950s and 60. They hoped the establishment advertising themes ("You meet the nicest people on a Honda") would rub off on their own brand, and began producing café style road bikes that emulated the styling of strong selling Asian motorcycles (Nichols, 2007).

Although Harley Davidson toyed with the outlaw diegesis in 1971 when it began production of the "Super Glide"—a stock motorcycle that roughly emulated a chopper—it was not until the early 1980s that it began to exploit the sponsorship potential of the outlaw diegesis. In the interim, the company was acquired by American Machine and Foundry (AMF), who's "cash cow" approach to ownership boosted production while eroding quality. AMF executives had little working knowledge of the motorcycle market and little desire to associate their brand with the outlaw biker diegesis (Yates, 1999). As a result, Harley Davidson's market share dwindled in comparison to their British and Japanese competition and the company approached bankruptcy (Austin, Gagne, & Orend, 2010; Reynolds, 2000; Schembri, 2009).

Harley Davidson stockholders staged a leveraged buyout from AMF in the early 1980s. The company's resurgence during the 1980s was a result a number of variables, including increased federal tariffs on imported motorcycles, the relaxation of admissions standards set during Clinton administration (Yates, 1999), and the development of their more reliable and powerful Porsche designed Evolution engine (Nichols, 2007). Crucial to the rebirth of Harley Davidson, however, was a marketing strategy that situated the company directly within the outlaw motorcycle diegesis. In 1980, Harley Davidson began production of the FXDB Sturgis model, which associated the company with the Sturgis Motorcycle Rally, the quintessential outlaw motorcycle gathering in the United States. In 1983, they launched the first Harley Owners Group (HOG). HOGs were critical to Harley Davidson's enclosure of outlaw motorcycling. They exploited the intense loyalty and pro-American outlook that outlaw clubs had demonstrated since the 1940s. Akin to earlier AMA membership networks, HOGs allowed Harley Davidson to stay in touch with their base, promote communication, and market itself as the sole remaining motorcycle manufacturer in the United States. As such, HOGs provided a crucial link between spectators, sponsors and the outlaw biker diegesis itself.

The success of Harley Davidson's enclosure of the outlaw motorcycling is remarkable. Though its market share had crashed from 60% to 23% by 1983, Harley boasted nearly 90,000 HOG members and its market share rebounded to 40% by the end of 1987 (Nichols, 2007; Yates, 1999, pp. 157; 165). That same year, Harley Davidson led a successful campaign to eliminate the same import tariffs that had lifted it back on its feet in 1981. The publicity stunt mirrored the aggressive, scrappy, against all odds qualities of rebel authoritarianism. As the final coup, Harley Davidson make its first public stock offering in July 1987. Harley executives and loyal HOG members paraded down Wall Street on bikes reflecting the legend of the outlaw biker, escorted by the New York Police Department, who also rode Harleys. The underdog resurgence of Harley Davidson—knocked down by Japanese and British motorcycle manufacturers, further offended by AMF mismanagement, yet struggling back on its feet—mirrored the rugged individualism of rebel authoritarianism and is good evidence that Harley Davidson had situated itself squarely within the outlaw biker diegesis.

The post-War era was an important point of transition in the authoritarian characteristics and economic circuitry of spectatorship and sponsorship in American otorcycling. Exaggerated media and police attention to clubs outside the sanctioning of the AMA produced a moral panic that was crucial to the development of spectator markets of this period. As the media exploited the rebel authoritarianism of outlaw motorcycle clubs and used it to sell newspapers, magazines and films, they developed a new diegesis in American motorcycling, one that substituted the characteristics of rebel authoritarianism for the orthodox authoritarian characteristics of the heritage era. Although initially feared by industry, this new diegesis became central to the sponsorship markets of the 1980s—especially that of Harley Davidson—as it sought to align its brand with a diegesis that had taken over American motorcycling culture.

Rebel Authoritarianism and the Outlaw Biker Diegesis in Contemporary Motorcycle Culture

Harley Davidson's pioneering work to enclose motorcycle spectatorship and develop its sponsorship markets had a significant impact on the expansion of the outlaw biker diegesis in American motorcycling. Their marketing strategies popularized outlaw biker culture at the same time they commodified it. Less feared than fabled, the outlaw biker diegesis became a legend resonating deeply with a growing proportion of the motorcycle community. Infused with the characteristics of rebel authoritarianism, this diegesis grew to become the leitmotif of contemporary American motorcycle culture, firmly established in the cultural narration of American motorcycling.

The ubiquity of the outlaw biker diegesis is perhaps most clearly apparent in contemporary motorcycle rallying. These events are literally filled with images and activities that celebrate hostility, aggression, in-group loyalty, and anti-intraception. Virtually all rally merchandize—from t-shirts to shot glasses to body art—is themed with images that connote aggression or destructiveness. Screaming eagles, growling wolves, charging bison, coiled rattlesnakes, skulls, stylized flames, iron crosses, Nazi helmets, barbed wire, and blazing firearms associate a kind of hard, aggressive attitude with motorcycle rallies. Place names like the Knuckle, Full Throttle, Broken Spoke, One-Eyed Jacks or Dirty Harry's suggest an atmosphere of rebellion, danger and riskiness. Activities that celebrate displays of aggression are commonplace, from public cage fighting and bare knuckle boxing matches to roller derby to the "Guns of Freedom" weapons ranges, where spectators "pull the trigger and feel the power" as they shoot military grade weapons at effigies of Sadaam Hussein, Osama bin Laden, or other caricatured terrorist figures (Guns of Freedom, 2014). Posted placards openly display widespread NRA sloganeering that vilifies firearm regulations and the Obama administration. "One-percenter" motorcycle clubs typically make their presence public during motorcycle rallies by occupying official club houses in the public areas of rally sites and displaying their insignia and patches on leather jackets and cuts throughout town. Public accounts of past gang fights are common, and local and national news agencies contribute to their legend by highlighting the gang presence and reminding spectators to take care around gang members visible in public.

Motorcycle rallying also exudes elements of rebel authoritarian submission. Rally organizers regularly stage events that promote an uncritical attitude toward idealized moral authorities. One clear example is the staunch pro-Americanism and the passionate and uncritical celebration of the U.S. military at motorcycle rallies. Aircraft flyovers and military appreciation days are common at the larger rallies in Sturgis, Daytona Beach, and Laconia, and veteran's rides are annual events at most of the smaller rallies. The "American Veterans Traveling Tribute," a scale model replica of the Vietnam Memorial Wall makes an annual stop at the rallies in Sturgis and Daytona Beach. Sturgis' Buffalo Chip Campground's owner proudly earmarks one day of the Rally for its annual "Freedom Celebration," during which past and present members of the military are honored with concerts, public speeches, book signings, and meet and greet opportunities with veterans, pro-military journalists and activists, and government experts on global terror. The event is co-sponsored with the Patriot Guard Riders Motorcycle Club, who travel the country to veteran's funerals in order to "shield the mourning [families] from protest or groups of protestors" (American Veterans Traveling Tribute Memorial Wall, 2013). America flags are sacralized at the Rally and appear within virtually every sightline; on t-shirts, leathers, bandanas and other wearable merchandise, motorcycle saddle bags and gas tanks. A massive American flag flies at the entrance of the Buffalo Chip Campground, beneath which a battlefield cross marks the entrance to their veteran's memorial. Hyper-nationalist slogans including "these colors don't run," "try burn'in this one, asshole," and "America! Love it or leave it" appear throughout the rally. Fanatically conservative musical groups including Ted Nugent, Toby Keith, Lynrd Skynyrd, Madison Rising (who opened the Buffalo Chip's 2014 "Stand Behind our Heroes" concert with their heavily advertised performance of the Star Spangled Banner) and other lesser known bands are regular performers at rallies across the country.

Many of the activities at contemporary motorcycle rallies reinforce binary group boundaries—especially political boundaries—by celebrating insiders and vilifying outsiders. This is perhaps most obvious in the acclaim given to conservative politicians and policies and the blatant denigration their "liberal" counterparts. To date, no Democratic politician or candidate has made an appearance at a motorcycle rally, though Republican and Tea Party politicians make regular stops. Most famously, John McCain gave a stump speech at the Sturgis Rally prior to the 2008 Presidential election during which he paused for a veterans salute before criticizing Barrack Obama for his plans to withdraw US troops from Iraq and his refusal to exploit US oil reserves. To the roar of the crowd, he also implied his wife could serve as both First Lady and Miss Buffalo Chip (the featured winner of the campground's notorious wet t-shirt contest). In 2010, the Tea Party hosted its first annual Freedom Rally in conjunction with Daytona Bike Week. The event celebrated the anniversary of the first Tea Party protests in Washington DC, and was organized in an effort to "recharge the movement" against President Obama's bailout plan and other "massive spending measures" (Schilling, 2010). In 2011, Ted Nugent vilified "Japs," "Canadians," and the "French" for being "weak" and got a near sold-out audience at the Full Throttle Saloon to give President Obama the finger. The pop band "Liquid Blue" decided to remove the "Obama 2012" decals from its tour bus after receiving verbal insults and physical threats prior to their 2012 Sturgis debut (Sanford, 2012). The Young Obama Haters regularly set up vendor stands at motorcycle rallies and other motorsports venues, where they draw crowds by shouting "Obama Sucks!" through megaphones and hock "Deport Barrack *Hussein* Obama" and "My country, my future" t-shirts that proudly display the

United States superimposed by two crossed flint-lock rifles. Members of numerous conservative and evangelical Christian motorcycle clubs work the rally circuit converting lost souls and encouraging appropriate behavior.

Finally, the diegesis of contemporary motorcycle rallies exhibit evidence of authoritarian anti-intraception. First defined by Henry Alexander Murray as the avoidance of "an imaginative, subjective human outlook or Romantic action" (Murray, 2008 [1938], p. 148) anti-intraception involves inability or unwillingness to be intersubjective or empathetic. The outlaw biker diegesis includes an egocentric tenor that celebrates individualism and limits responsiveness to others. T-shirts that read "I can't hear you over the roar of my freedom," "my other toy has tits," "I'd rather see my sister in a whorehouse than my brother on a Honda," or "if you can read this, the bitch fell off" suggest a distaste or at least skewed perspective on intersubjectivity and empathy. Motorsports spectacles condense the sensations of noise and vibration into a diegesis that blocks opportunities for shared experience. Multiple city block lines of tandem V-twin motorcycles roar their way through town, a visual and auditory mass-ornament (Kracauer, 1975) that reduces all to a coagulated mass. Concert spectators roar their engines in "throttle applause" as a sign of approval and appreciation. Spectators find themselves amidst amorphous sexualized pulsations: greased midget bowling, jello-wrestling, pickle-licking contests, burnout pits, automatic-weapons trials, mechanical bull-riding and the ceaseless, disoriented milling of carnivalesque bodies as an indistinct conglomerate of oppressive, grotesque yet enticing sensations.

The Outlaw Biker Diegesis and the Economy of Dark Spectacle

The rapid evolution of the outlaw biker diegesis has been critical to the growth of spectator, sponsorship and trophy markets in American motorcycling. By the 1990s, motorcycle event coordinators and many American motorcycle manufacturers had come to rely on the outlaw diegesis for marketing and promotion. Unlike heritage or even early rebel cyclists, the spectators of the 1980s and 90s were less bonded by crosscutting social ties or a deeply-shared sense of community. Increasingly, they shared little more than a desire to purchase access to a spectacular diegesis awash in images of rebel authoritarianism. Event coordinators monetized this desire by cross-marketing rebel authoritarianism with increasingly diverse settings, experiences, and products (Krier & Swart, 2014a, 2014b).

We conceptualize events organized around this kind of authoritarian diegesis as "dark spectacle"; a hybrid form of "dark tourism" (Lennon & Foley, 2000) in which spectators immerse themselves in a commodified environment themed with authoritarian and destructive motifs. Much of the literature on dark tourism lacks a specific authoritarian framing. For example, all of the conceptualizations of dark tourism in Seaton's (1996) typology focus on travel to specific sites or memorials/museums that allow for "actual or symbolic encounters with death" (1996, p. 15) rather than the actual immersion in a dark diegesis. While Stone's (2006) "dark tourism spectrum" theorizes that "lighter" forms of dark tourism may have a contrived, commercialized quality (see also Seaton, 1999), and the emphasis on suffering, death rituals, morbid products, and thanatotic imagery (Stone, 2006) closely aligns with Erich Fromm's (1973) theorization of malignant aggression, the dark tourism literature is generally devoid of references to the more general authoritarian characteristics discussed above or the diegetic and memetic qualities of motorsports spectacles and spectators.

Dark spectacle, especially as evidenced within contemporary motorcycle events, serve as a form of form of performative tourism (McCannell, 1976; Edensor, 2001), where spectators come to play, perform, see and be seen within an authoritarian themed environment. As they load authoritarian images onto products and infuse authoritarian themes into experiences, dark spectacles turn authoritarianism into a cultural commodity to be bought and sold within the spectator markets of the economy of spectacle. The diegeses of dark spectacles and memeses through which spectators organize their activities at these events are thus the result of an economic circuit that provides an opportunity for participation without the necessity of real authoritarian personality characteristics.

Echoing our discussion in Chapter 3, the work of Erving Goffman (1967) helps explain the centrality of dark spectacle to the growth of spectator markets in contemporary American motorcycling. Goffman argues that "action" occurs when a person voluntarily assumes risk in a chancy situation, especially one that is critical to an individual's social reputation. Often this occurs through *"ephemeral ennoblement"*—temporarily occupying settings above our normal boundaries of prestige and status. Yet our study of dark spectacle demonstrates the opposite—that action may also be found in occupying settings below ones station. This *ephemeral debasement* attracts new markets of spectators as performative tourists who find action in the diegesis of dark spectacle. As Goffman (1967) notes, action requires social recognition. Ephemeral ennoblement or debasement done in secret does nothing to prove character beyond the individual ego, thus the value of action resides in its display. As sites of dark spectacle, contemporary motorcycle rallies provide popular locations for such display to occur. They serve as stages where riders risk character by performing in scenes steeped in rebel authoritarianism.

Motorcycle industry and event coordinators have successfully exploited the outlaw biker diegesis and the dark spectacle of motorcycle rallies to expand contemporary spectator markets. Rally attendance across the country grew dramatically with the exploitation of the outlaw biker diegesis. As discussed in Chapter 3, Sturgis Rally attendance between 1965 and 1985 grew at an annualized rate of 295%, and by 2000 boasted an attendance of 633,000 spectators. Much of this growth is due to the successful branding and promotion of the outlaw biker diegesis and opportunities to participate in dark spectacle. Recognizing the profit potential of growing spectatorship, the Daytona Beach Convention and Visitors Bureau created a second motorcycle rally in 1991. Since then, "Biketoberfest" has served as an off-season supplement the spectatorship markets realized during the long standing Daytona Bike Week.

Spectator markets have seen an especially dramatic growth in upper-middle class riders and event participants, who increasingly turn to dark spectacle for leisure. Since 1983, the annual income of the average Harley Davidson owner has increased from $37,000 to $67,000 (Yates, 1999; see also Thompson, 2009, 2012; Austin, Gagne, & Orend, 2010). Upper-middle class suburban outlaws have also become the primary demographic at motorcycle rallies across the country (Galahan, 2010). Thus, while the habitus of the lower and working classes may best fit the outlaw biker diegesis, it is the well-off, white collar professional who now figures most prominently in the spectator markets of American motorcycling. RUB's ("Rich Urban Bikers")—whose desk jobs, air-bag equipped mini-vans, and banal family activities generally lack opportunities for "action" yet whose incomes afford opportunities for high cost equipment, apparel, and leisure time—have turned to the dark spectacles of motorcycle riding and rallying as a way to consume prepackaged action that simultaneously tests and displays character. As Freud (1955) argued, the purpose of festivals is to recapture that which has been given up in pursuit of the ego ideal. In this sense, upper-middle class spectators use dark spectacle and their memesis of the outlaw within it to replace their first life prohibitions. Freed from the constraints and impositions of everyday life, consumers of dark spectacle experience a "magnificent festival of the ego" (Freud, 2010 [1921], p. 8401; see also Bakhtin, 1968; Krier & Swart, 2012; Langman and Ryan, 2009).

Sponsorship markets exploded as the motorcycle industry and event coordinators capitalized on increasing levels of spectatorship. The Sturgis Motorcycle Rally, which had relatively small scale economy through the 1970s, experienced massive economic growth as city officials and Rally organizers capitalized on the growing crowds of Rally participants. As discussed in Chapter 3, the City of Sturgis began developing its sponsorship markets in 1979. Although initial growth was small (less than 120 vendor licenses were requested in 1985), sponsorship markets swelled to nearly 1000 over the next fifteen years. "Paying to be seen," temporary vendors, official sponsors, and motorcycle manufacturers themselves associated their products with the outlaw diegesis of American motorcycle rallying. A host of cross marketing licensing agreements among companies such as Ford, Jack Daniels, Sony, Budweiser, Coca-Cola link their brands to the outlaw biker diegesis, and in some cases one another. In an attempt to commodify anti-intraception, Harley Davidson has worked since the early 1990s to trademark its exclusive exhaust sound, and in 2013, Harley-Davidson cross-marketed country-rock artist Kid Rock's famous lyric "I can't hear you over the rumble of my freedom" and used it to market the company's 110th anniversary. The integration of vendors and corporate sponsorship with the outlaw biker diegesis has had a significant impact on the profitability of the Sturgis Rally. Taxable revenues grew from $150,000 in 1965 to over $3,000,000 in 1985, and in the fifteen years that followed, Rally annual profits exceeded $14,000,000, increasing at an annualized rate of over 26% (Krier & Swart, 2014a).

In recent years, the drive to expand spectator and sponsor markets has also stretched the boundaries or in some cases directly negated the outlaw biker diegesis of motorcycle rallies. Much outlaw club activity has become legal and commercial rather than rebellious and violent. Clubs like the Hells Angels make millions of dollars selling trademarked apparel, and violence is intentionally avoided in settings like Sturgis and Daytona in order to protect profit streams (Kovaleski, 2013). Soft and adult rock bands like Boston, Loverboy, and Journey play alongside groups that express more fanatical right-wing lyrics; Train, a band whose lyrics can hardly be interpreted as fascist or authoritarian, headlined the 2014 Buffalo Chip concert series. Local church and community pancake breakfasts, chili suppers, and other folksy "pop odom" events gather the same groups annually for camping or reunions and mirror the "rotary club" ethos of heritage motorcycling. An increasing diversity of "off brand" products (Bayer Aspirin, Geico Insurance, Lakota Foods, South Dakota Pork) comingle with those that play upon themes more central to the outlaw/rebel diegesis (Jack Daniels, Harley Davidson, Old Smokey Moonshine, Sons of Anarchy). Angieland Exotic Dancers (a regular feature at the Full Throttle Saloon) donates a portion of their annual Sturgis proceeds to an animal rescue aimed at reducing the number of rescue kill facilities in the US. Charity rides that raise money for organizations including Toys for Tots, Muscular Dystrophy, or the Boys and Girls Clubs have become important events for local motorcycle clubs. While these sponsors, products and promotions expand spectatorship to more conventional people, their progressive decontextualization of spectator and sponsorship markets threatens dark spectacle and its rebel diegesis. Hell's Angels food stands, Gieco insurance stalls, and twelve foot high inflatable Bayer aspirin advertisements stretch thin or in some cases openly negate outlaw themes. They appear absurd and contradictory as they circulate within the diegesis of dark spectacle, and threaten the profit potential that has to this point been realized by the sponsorship markets of American motorcycling.

Finally, while there is evidence of very limited trophy markets in heritage motorcycling (motorcycle manufacturers and the AMA often provided souvenir items such as pins, watch fobs or belt buckles to gypsy tour participants), trophy markets have become one of the most profitable circuits in contemporary economies of spectacle. Trophies are crucial to the social recognition of action and ephemeral debasement. The psychic life of consumers of dark spectacle is energized by the imagined or realized envy of others. As discussed in Chapter 4, this invidiousness takes three forms. "Status trophies" generate envy by signaling superior status and prestige to others. "Action trophies" generate envy by revealing ones willingness to risk character or immerse oneself in ephemeral debasement. "Trophies of *jouissance*" generate envy by displaying ones participation in scenes of enjoyment or debauchery not available to others (see also Krier & Swart, 2014b). The trophy markets of American motorcycling provide opportunities for spectators to gather evidence of their participation in dark spectacle and display it to others for the purpose of status, action, and *jouissance*. Apparel emblazoned with the trademarked logos of motorcycle companies or events imply superior levels of wealth and leisure time. T-shirts suggesting the dark diegetic themes of motorcycle culture prove action and ephemeral debasement to those outside the immediate temporal or geographic setting. Digital photography—enhanced in the past decade by the personalization of mobile technologies and their connection to social media outlets—allow evidence of status, action and *jouissance* to be instantaneously transferred to those not *in situ*.

Although relatively limited in heritage motorcycling and virtually non-existent during the post-War era, trophy markets have exploded in contemporary motorcycling as one of the more important sources of industry revenue. Rally cities have optimized their built environments to support the trophy industry. Parking lots are cordoned off to accommodate vendor stalls, pushing parking to city streets and local access roads. City sidewalks have been built with wide setbacks in order to make space for temporary vendor stalls and still leave room for pedestrian traffic. Leases for commercial property in downtown Sturgis require that they be vacated for the month of August so that they can be converted into more valuable retail space. Major clubs, restaurants and bars sublease merchandising stalls in front of and inside of their buildings, stacking vendor upon vendor in order to maximize retail space. As a result, trophy markets appear to upstage the rally itself; the vast sea of vendor stalls and crowds of milling shoppers suggest that hunt for trophies has become the primary activity at motorcycle rallies (Krier & Swart, 2014b).

The active and rather obvious "stage-managing" of opportunities for photographic trophy collection has also become critical to the trophy markets of contemporary motorcycling. Event coordinators cover over the all-too-apparent lack of rebel authoritarianism with staged events that maintain the fantasy of dark spectacle. Scantily-dressed, tattooed, or body painted waitresses and barmaids double as subjects for trophy-photography. Cage-fighting matches, motorcycle "burn outs," and pickle-licking contests are meticulously scheduled and publicized so as not to interfere with other events and draw the largest crowds of spectators possible. Manufacturer exhibits encourage attendees to photograph themselves astride heavily modified and outrageously expensive designer motorcycles. In one instance, body guards escorted women to and from an open-air bar, where they rode a mechanical bull modified into a penis as a contrived photo-op for gathering crowds. Such events preserved the fantasy of dark spectacle the value of the trophies associated with them. The fact that many of these events were staged demonstrates the importance of the outlaw biker diegesis to the profitability of dark spectacle. Trophies not only preserve the outlaw diegesis, but in doing so, fuel the growth of spectatorship markets. When missing in reality, contrived opportunities to display action and ephemeral debasement and extract the envy of others are crucial to spectator's desire for immersion in dark spectacle.

In sum, the outlaw biker diegesis has become central to the cultural narration of American motorcycling since the 1980s; its' dark spectacle a crucial resource to the development of modern spectator, sponsor, and trophy markets. The diegesis and its profitability expanded as sponsors tied increasingly diverse events, products and services to the rebellious and authoritarian themes of outlaw motorcycling. Spectators flocked to engage in performative tourism centered in action and ephemeral debasement, as well as collect trophies that could be consumed for invidious social recognition. Authoritarian images and narratives thus remain central to the economic circuitry of American motorcycling and its ongoing enclosure by the motorcycle industry.

Conclusion

This chapter has explored the role of authoritarianism in the economic enclosure of American motorcycling. Our first order reading provided evidence of the orthodox authoritarian ethos and structure of heritage motorcycling and the transition to rebel authoritarianism in post-War motorcycle culture.

Our second order analysis examined the role of this authoritarian culture and structure in the economic enclosure of American motorcycling. Authoritarian structures of submission and control allowed the AMA to build networks of riders during the early and mid-twentieth century. These networks fueled early spectator and sponsorship markets by tying motorcycle enthusiasts, clubs, and their spontaneous events to the motorcycle industry. Although the rise of rebel authoritarianism in post-War motorcycling was initially feared, the motorcycle industry, especially Harley Davidson, eventually embraced rebel themes and coopted them into a marketing strategy centered on an outlaw biker diegesis. This diegesis provides the framework for dark spectacle—economic markets and performative tourism centered in the tropes of rebel authoritarianism of outlaw motorcycling. By 1990, the spectator, sponsorship, and trophy markets built upon this diegesis became the dominant circuits of the American motorcycle economy.

Debordian (1988) readings of spectacle suggest that they serve a dangerous ideological function—one that ingests all opportunities for democratic participation while reinforcing conservative and authoritarian mindsets. Similarly, much of the literature on authoritarianism would imply that those who would be drawn to situations of dark spectacle possess "real" authoritarian character structures. Our research shows that the authoritarian diegesis of dark spectacle serves an equally important economic function. This diegesis certainly *may* play a role in bringing out nascent authoritarianism or attracting spectators with already developed authoritarian personalities, but that argument lies beyond this book. What our data suggest is that the authoritarian ethos and organizational structures of American motorcycling were crucial to its economic enclosure and the continued profitability of its spectator, sponsorship and trophy markets.

Our study also suggests that while any megaspectacle has the potential for massing and the development of authoritarianism, economic circuits of spectatorship and sponsorship may serve to diffuse this potential. In late capitalism—a period of the near-total commodification of spectacle—this negating quality is even more pronounced. Markets erode *real* authoritarian tendencies by focusing psychic energy on the consumption of products rather than a conscious connection to a leader or ego-ideal. Like the Freudian father, economic structures (taxes, fees, licenses, permits, trade-marking, charging for bathrooms, channeling bodies through or between vendor stalls, restaurants, bars, concerts or other attractions) impose an order that disrupts pure massing and thus the potential for fascism to emerge. This is particularly evident at contemporary motorcycle events. Sponsorship circuits have expanded to include a diversity of products and services that are antithetical to authoritarianism.

As motorcycle spectatorship circuits erupted, myriad regulations and structures were put in place that eroded the potential for massing (see Hall, 2002 for similar evidence in the history of NASCAR). City regulations for traffic control, camping, alcohol consumption, and parking; the regulations against public nudity; the permitting and licensing of temporary vendors, increased policing and even admission fees (which limit spectatorship to those who can afford to pay) reduce the potential for the mass psychology of fascism to emerge.

As a result, dark spectacle becomes a "rally without rallying"; an event whose purpose is not to assemble people to reconstitute and realign them with an overarching authoritarian identity but to consume a diegesis that is themed in ways that support the ongoing revenue generated from spectators, sponsors and trophy markets. In fact, much of the real authoritarianism at motorcycle events has been pushed to the fringes; marginalized from the commodified event and pushed out to locations exempt from the economic circuits of dark spectacle. For those who remain, dark spectacle serves as deep play that allows them a temporary escape from the Protestant ethic and the extraction of envy from those without the resources to attend. In this sense, authoritarianism is central to the economy of American motorsports.

CHAPTER 8

The Future of Economic Spectacles: Virtual Augmentation and the Dialectics of Aura

In the previous chapters we explored the three circuits critical to economies of spectatorship—spectator markets, sponsorship markets, and trophy markets. Each market corresponded to a unique form of visual pleasure: (1) spectator markets profited from *desire to see,* (2) sponsorship markets profited from *desire to be seen*, and (3) trophy markets profited from *desire to be seen enjoying*. Our conclusion points to an emerging transformation in these markets—that of "virtually augmented spectatorship." Over the past half-decade, the economic circuits of spectatorship were augmented with digital technology. This does not simply mean broadcasting the televised spectacle digitally, but enhancing the spectator's view with deeply complex and rich data streams (camera angles, telemetry data, replay action, spectator control, individualized data, metadata tracking, etc.). Virtually augmented spectacles are rooted in visual pleasure where spectator, sponsor, and trophy markets generate profit from the *desire for Lacanian omnivoyance,* or the impossible ability to see like a god. The dynamics of scopophilia are central to virtually augmented spectacles, which represent a new breed of spectacle with newly emerging mechanisms for focusing social energy and extracting value.

Drivers of Virtually Augmented Spectatorship

The rise of virtually augmented spectatorship was tied to the recent crises of in-venue and broadcast spectatorship, as well as the emerging context of virtually augmented reality in postmodern culture. Economies of spectacle were inherently self-negating. As discussed in previous chapters, the very mechanisms used to grow spectator, sponsor, and trophy markets inevitably led to progressive decontextualization and diegetic banality, incoherence and undesirability. As progressive decontextualization stretched spectacular diegeses, their influence in drawing spectators declined. The resulting decline of in-venue spectatorship fundamentally threatened the very profitability of spectatorship, sponsorship, and trophy markets that progressive decontextualization sought to enhance.

Broadcast spectacles were an early virtual augmentation that projected the event beyond the temporal and geographic limitations of in-venue spectatorship in order to draw more spectators into their diegeses and expand sponsorship markets. Although saturated with advertising, the increasingly rich experience of broadcast spectacles (multiple camera angles, replays, insider and professional commentary) overshadowed in-venue spectatorship. But the expansion of broadcast markets was also self-negating—although the broadcast enhanced spectatorship and increased the revenue possibilities from sponsorship contracts, broadcasts also created free access to spectators who had previously paid for in-venue spectatorship. One solution imposed by many professional sporting associations (including NASCAR) was to "black out" the broadcast to those within commuting distance to the venue. While this served well in the short term, the rise of ESPN and other cable sports packages (e.g. Speed Channel) overcame the geographic blackout opportunities of network television. Over time, new digital technologies further negated the economic vitality of television broadcasts. Digital Video Recording systems allowed spectators to fast-forward past commercials, forcing professional sports associations to creatively engage in new forms of product placement that turned the stadium itself into a sponsorship market. The ubiquity of internet access further challenged the profitability of broadcast spectacles. As the limited selection of cable TV channels who carry sporting events struggled to compete with the unlimited availability of the individualized, always-available content of the internet (Netflix, HULU, Amazon Prime, YouTube, etc.,) the value of CMLN's marketing and advertising in the broadcast arena declined. The proliferation of micro-spectacle delivery devices (smartphones, ipods, tablet computers), their penetration into younger generations, and the resultant distractibility and interpassivity of these generations put other forms of spectatorship, both in-venue and broadcast, on life support. Younger audiences relied upon the distraction of multiple screens to maintain focus on anything—their consciousness ill-suited to traditional in-venue experiences. The consequences for motorsports spectatorship are clear: in both NASCAR and large-displacement motorcycle events, the primary demographic increasingly greyed out and was not replaced in kind by younger spectators. These phenomena created a crisis of spectatorship in both the in-venue and broadcast experience that challenged long-term profit stability. The negative consequences for the economy of spectacle led spectacle developers to seek other mechanisms to boost profits, and ushered in new forms of spectacle that relied on augmented reality, virtual experiences, and new forms of marketing and product placement.

The rise in virtually augmented spectatorship was coupled with a general rise in virtual reality and "augmented reality" (AR) in postmodern culture. Whereas virtual reality refers to a computer generated simulation of reality or the "rendering" of symbolic data in digital form (most notable in computer gaming), AR denotes the overlay of virtual enhancements upon experiences in the real world. Google and Innovega, Inc., became leaders in the development of AR technologies. Google Glass, for example, coupled an optical head-mounted display with voice activated internet commands in order to overlay digital information onto lived experience. Innovega, Inc. produced similar AR capable contact lenses (iOptic AR) that provided a 120 degree 3D virtual overlay onto normal viewing (Dillow, 2012). In February, 2012 Innovega contracted with the Defense Advanced Research Projects Agency (DARPA) to develop the "Soldier Centric Imaging via Computational Cameras (SCENICC)" program (Kaiser, 2012); in April, 2012 the U.S. Pentagon placed an order for iOptic AR lenses to be beta tested for combat situations (Sanford, 2012; See Coker, 2013, pp. 127–132 for additional discussion of the role of augmented reality to military training). This technology superimposed camera angles from drone aircraft, including night vision and infrared vision to soldiers on the ground. Like a video game, the lenses allowed soldiers to "see through" structures ahead and use these augmented views to pinpoint the location of targets – human and otherwise. AR also infiltrated the advertising arena. In one of the newest forms of "shoppertainment," Net-a-Porter allowed consumers to take digital images of products, which were then instantly animated or modeled in three dimensions on one's mobile phone or tablet. Consumers ordered the clothes they liked by simply clicking on their screen. Absolut Vodka's "Absolute truths" AR advertising campaign used a tag on the bottle as an AR marker that scrolled the viewer through a host of high end cocktail recipes on their smart phone. Clearwater, Florida used an AR virtual tour to guide people through important tourist sites of the city (11 Amazing Augmented Reality Ads, 2012).

Both virtual reality and augmented reality were crucial to the virtual augmentation of motorsports spectatorship. NASCAR produced a wealth of digital information during races; data ripe for virtual rendering in a host of ways, from replay and rebroadcast, to the doubling of races in virtual reality, to the virtual augmentation of real-world spectatorship. One of the earliest virtual augmentations to NASCAR was its incorporation of FanVision technologies. FanVision got its start in the Formula 1 racing market in 2003 as "Kangaroo TV," a handheld audio and video device that allowed in-venue spectators to tune-in to camera feeds from around the circuit and radio communications between drivers and their race crews. In 2005 Kangaroo TV signed with NASCAR under the name FanVision, and became a staple in-venue virtual augmentation.[1] Like

---

1 FanVision entered the NFL market in 2009 when it contracted with the Miami Dolphins. Later that year, Dolphins owner Stephen Ross purchased Kangaroo Media and began marketing the controller to other professional sporting companies (Sandomir, 2010).

Formula 1, FanVision allowed NASCAR spectators to monitor the race leader-board, in-car audio and video feeds, and real time telemetry data including average speed, lap times, and throttle and brake use for up to three drivers at a time. Broadcasts ran twelve hours per race day and included pre- and post-race news, video games and movies to hold spectator attention to this dynamic and intensively penetrated advertising space beyond the actual race. Systems were purchased or rented at the track, and required additional broadcast subscriptions for each race or season. The unit sold for up to $370, including a one year subscription to race broadcasts.

NASCAR, Formula 1, and professional football associations secured Fan-Vision profitability by broadcasting on an encrypted UHF signal, thus making it impossible for spectators to tune-in with personal electronic devices. The only exception was Daytona International Speedway, whose 2016 remodel was the first to incorporate enough cellular bandwidth to allow personally owned mobile devices to mirror FanVision. In 2016, NASCAR will market iphone and android apps that allow spectators to follow the newly integrated digital dashboards of NASCAR drivers, as well as share posts and photos on social media feeds that were not accessible through FanVision. At this time, Daytona International Speedway is the only track to include these network upgrades—all others continue to rely on FanVision technology to virtually augment their in-venue spectatorship experience.

NASCAR virtually augments its broadcast spectacles through its partnership with SportVision, Inc. SportVision was the Google or Innovega of the sports word, possibly most known for its 1998 development of the "1st and 10" computer system which generated the (now famous) virtual 1st down line during professional football broadcasts. Since then SportVision has won ten Emmy Awards for its digital enhancements to a wide array of sport broadcasts, including NFL, MLB, NASCAR, The Olympic Games, NHL, PGA TOUR, LPGA Tour, NBA, NCAA, WTA, MLS, IRL, X Games, and the America's Cup (SportVision Company Profile, 2014). In 2000, NASCAR revolutionized its broadcast spectacle by part-nering with SportVision and launching the "Racef/x" system. Racef/x used a GPS locater within every vehicle to record the speed, acceleration/deceleration, time behind leader, exact car position (within 4cm), RPM, brake indicator, and throttle percentage five times per second to create a complete digital re-cord of each race. NASCAR used SportVision's data to thicken their broadcast by overlaying telemetry data within a virtual banner over each car, making it easier for fans to identify drivers, positions, and race statistics during the broadcast. SportVision's virtual augmentations gave broadcast spectators an experience not available to in-venue spectators, and gave NASCAR a number of new revenue opportunities that extend beyond in-venue spectatorship.

The digital record produced by SportVision also revolutionized NASCAR's presence in the video gaming market, which represents a third virtual augmentation to its economy of spectatorship. Gaming became an important way for NASCAR to monetize its vast accumulation of telemetry data and reach millennials. There were at least 46 NASCAR video games in production and multiple others (such as Mario Kart) that, while not marketed by NASCAR, utilized NASCAR telemetry data to render the driving and track dynamics of a virtual race car. NASCAR's premier online gaming platform, iRacing, is a subscription based racing simulation rendered from track specifications (to millimeter precision) and car telemetry data. Originally, iRacing allowed gamers to compete with other gamers and virtually doubled NASCAR drivers in a simulated reproduction of previously real NASCAR races. In 2010, iRacing and NASCAR launched their first officially-sanctioned online racing series, complete with sponsorship contracts and virtual advertising. Gamers could compete on multiple levels, from amateur series open to qualifying subscription holders to Pro-series where the top iRacer compete for a spot in the iRacing World Championships. iRacing currently provides a training platform for rising drivers and a practice field for current drivers. Overall, NASCAR's gaming license agreements became one its top five revenue streams and a recognized mechanism for attracting younger generations: "For a sport that doesn't have pickup games and can't be played in the backyard, gaming also offers a way to reach young people at a time that TV ratings are declining in the 18- to 34-year-old demographic" (Mickle, 2010).

Finally, NASCAR partnered with SportVision to repackage its digital data into two "second screen" virtual enhancements to NASCAR broadcasts: RaceBuddy, and RaceView. Second screen spectatorship enhanced the broadcast spectacle in much the same way that FanVision enhanced in-venue spectatorship—by providing spectators with additional data, virtual renderings, and individualized control, typically on a second electronic device that supplements the broadcast of the race. RaceBuddy is a free service that streams off of NASCAR. com during each race. It provided spectators with a live leaderboard, live Twitter feed (NASCAR was the first major sports company to partner with Twitter), and 10 high-definition camera feeds, including a selection of in-car and bumper-mounted cameras on a pre-selected rotation of cars. Weekly corporate sponsorship kept the site free, though its page design and functionality were saturated with advertising—the site contained a number of AdChoice windows and spectators must endure commercials that interrupt the video stream at regular intervals. RaceView is an animated reproduction (using skin from iRacing) of the race rendered in real time by repackaging and selling telemetry data from SportVision. This enhancement is subscription based and advertised as "commercial free," yet ironically, the widespread commercial degradation of the in-venue event makes a truly commercial free option impossible. NASCAR offers RaceView in three formats: RaceView Audio, an audio only feed that mimics the in-venue audio scanners used by NASCAR prior to its partnership with FanVision, RaceView Premium, which streams to computers and tablets via internet access to NASCAR.com, and RaceView Mobile, an iPhone and Android app that gives spectators mobile access to the RaceView animated overlay and race data in a mobile platform that also includes a virtual time-trial game allowing fans to race a virtual car against the previous year's pole winner at each track. RaceView Premium and RaceView Mobile are touted as "fully customizable"—users can customize their viewing angle of the race and have complete freedom to choose the audio feeds and telemetry data they wish to monitor. Prior to 2013, RaceView also allowed subscribers to replay races at their convenience; this service was discontinued for the 2013 season.

These virtual augmentations provided an important mechanism for motorsports spectacles, especially NASCAR, to forestall crises of in-venue spectatorship and bolster the flagging profit streams of spectator, sponsor and trophy markets. Virtual augmentations like gaming, SportVision and RaceView targeted spectators outside NASCAR core. The enhanced broadcast spectacle and gaming options made the sport appealing to millennials and other spectators who might not be attracted to the high-cost, low-action in-venue spectatorship of a field of cars turning perpetually left. Virtual augmentation also advanced sponsorship markets by allowing NASCAR to sell advertising space in virtual reality. Peak AntiFreeze, for example, was title sponsor of the 2014 iRacing season, and sponsored three drivers in the 2015 virtual race season (KevinB, 2015). Other sponsors paid NASCAR to display their advertising on the RaceBuddy web-page and in the animated virtual environments of RaceView and iRacing. Overall, NASCAR's internet enhancements became a significant revenue stream. In April 2014 International Speedway Corporation (ISC) added the position of "chief digital officer" to manage the expansion of digital sponsorship contracts. A 2014 ISC study indicated that its digital media consumption on mobile devices increased twenty percent in the previous 4 years, digital viewing time had doubled since 2012, and 52 percent of online retail traffic originated from mobile devices. Overall, the growth of NASCAR's online presence represents an important site for targeting sponsorship. ISC's 2014 corporate report verified the increasing importance of virtual spectatorship and sponsorship:

> NASCAR experienced significant growth, exceeding one billion aggregate
> page views across NASCAR.com, NASCAR mobile web and the NASCAR

Mobile app in 2014. The billion page view milestone marks a 45 percent year-over-year increase in engagement on the platform.... In the 2014 NASCAR season, NASCAR.com averaged 1.4 million unique visitors on NASCAR Sprint Cup race days; and the NASCAR Mobile applications were downloaded 4.5 million times.

    2014 ISCA Annual Report, 2014

Visually-discernable enhancements also served as in-venue envy-inducing trophies of surplus enjoyment. In-venue, FanVision systems stuck out: bright, almost neon, yellow full-coverage headphones the size of inverted coffee cups tethered to an equally neon yellow controller marked their users as virtuoso spectators. FanVision systems were designed to mirror the equipment used by "official" NASCAR track staff—the only identifying difference was the color of the headset (red instead of yellow) and the lack of a microphone on FanVision systems. Similarly, FanVision's sub-logo, "Welcome to the inside!" was indicative of its role as a trophy of surplus enjoyment. Like skybox seating or infield-passes, FanVision subscribers were insiders, their premium spectatorship made clearly visible by their brightly colored virtual augmentation devices. The social media connectivity of NASCAR's newly emerging in-venue mobile phone apps will only further expand the trophy possibilities of virtual augmentation.

While virtual augmentation did not transform the interrelated markets of economies of spectatorship, it demonstrated their dialectical development. The decline of in-venue and broadcast spectatorship necessitated their virtual enhancement. Some of these enhancements sustained and attracted in-venue spectators, some sustained and attracted new broadcast spectators, and others built new "virtual spectators" mobilized through the variety of digital devices now connected to spectacular events. But these developments robbed Peter to pay Paul. Augmentation in one area negated the development of other areas. For example, the rewiring of Daytona International Speedway to boost cellular bandwidth makes new forms of virtual augmentation possible, yet limits investment in other arenas. Here again, micro-primitive accumulation, especially in the form of accelerated asset depreciation that coincided with the longstanding "NASCAR Tax Credit" was a central force in stalling the internal limits to growing new forms of spectatorship.

The Consequences of Virtually Augmented Spectatorship

Virtually augmented spectatorship is a uniquely postmodern mode of spectatorship—simultaneously integrated and disintegrated—united by all

manner of digital enhancements and data streams, yet incredibly heteroge-
neous and interfused with multiple streams of action, information, and symbols that are impossible within a non-technological/non-virtual experience.
While "looking" at the race in-venue, on-television, or on-digital device, one
sees an array of virtually rendered data streams, digital augmentations, and
impossible camera angles. This heterogeneity has a transformative influence
on postmodern modes of spectatorship—transforming social spectatorship to
interpassivity. Virtually augmented spectatorship is diverse, individuated, and
personalized; spectators have the possibility of tapping into widely atomized
spectator experiences that alienate them from the others in their immediate
presence. Thus the virtually augmented spectacle is socially disintegrating; the
plethora of information streams and the multiplicity of ways that spectators
customize them devolves their experiences. In essence, each spectator attends
to a unique "event"—a non-reproducible series of interlaced, layered images,
sensations, and data streams. Drivers, racers, "stories" that are not of interest
to the particular spectator are suppressed and disregarded while drivers,
racers and stories that are of interest are elongated, thickened, and opened to
intimate access. This is fundamentally different from modern spectatorship,
where an entire crowd shares its reaction to a jointly-observed event: evident
in the introjections at touchdowns, injuries, or crashes. Virtual augmentation allows action to be regarded visually, auditorily and symbolically through
rendered data—organized to uniquely suit each viewer and diffusing rather
than focusing the highs and lows of spectatorship. The Durkheimian collective
effervescence of virtually augmented spectacle is thus significantly dissipated.
Postmodern spectatorship is not "interaction" so much as "intra"-action or
interpassive in the Žižekian sense (Žižek, 2008 [1989]).

Finally, virtually augmented spectatorship renders impossible views
possible. The digital ability to monitor multiple in-car or bumper cameras simultaneously or follow the commentary of other spectators on social
media allows spectators to occupy multiple subject positions at the same
time. Virtual augmentation allows spectators to see from individualized
viewpoints—not only to see, but to control what they see through customizable views and pause/replay options. Virtual augmentation allows spectators
to see both the real and symbolic; SportVision's "draft track" allowed viewers
to "see the air" as it flowed over cars in real time, "stromotion" freeze-framed
action into moment-by-moment snap-shots, "Pitchf/x tracked the live trajec-
tory of a baseball from the pitcher's hand to the catcher's mitt, "LiveLine"
overlaid wind, current, and course data onto America's Cup race broadcasts.
The virtually enhanced spectator is thus no longer psychologically situated
within the diegetic reality, but free to move above and outside the diegesis at

will—an omnivoyant or 'god's eye" view that puts the spectator in a position of sublime spectatorship. A classic example of these changes to spectatorship is captured in the 2009 Superbowl GoDaddy.com commercial featuring then sponsored driver Danica Patrick. After accessing his new domain name through godaddy.com, a young college student announces to his friends "now that I'm online, I can make anything happen." The three are immediately presented with camera feed of Danica Patrick, the *femme fatale* of NASCAR legend, stepping into the shower. To their delight, the men find themselves capable of augmenting their fantasy by inserting "Miss Schmitt," the attractive German secretary in the Dean's office into the shower with Patrick. In an odd twist, the tables turn so that Patrick and her new German friend—laying in bed together clad only in towels—begin spectating on the young men, enthusiastically celebrating their newly discovered control over their fantasies. The commercial's final caption "GoDaddy.com puts me in control," captures all elements of sublime spectatorship embedded in the virtually augmented spectacle. Spectators delight in their *omnivoyance* as they spectate from multiple subject positions and multiple time-frames in an infinitely manipulable spectator experience.

Early critical theorists of film such as Sigfried Kracauer and Erwin Panofsky argued that the cinema creates a "dynamization of space" where the spectator, though in a fixed seat, was in permanent aesthetic motion (Kracauer, 1947). Virtually augmented spectatorship deepens and expands this dynamization. Sublime spectatorship includes levels of perception impossible within traditional forms of spectatorship: Views from the bumpers of cars moving at 200+mph, the ability to see the movement of wind and air, to see ephemeral "doubles" of racers from previous laps superimposed over the current race. The virtually augmented spectacle represents a new genre of spectatorship that pushes *paying to see, paying to be seen, and paying to be seen enjoying* beyond their corporeal limits. It creates new opportunities to map both the psychodynamic implications as well as the institutional pillars that support its development and expansion into arenas of social life beyond motorsports spectatorship.

Conclusion: The Dialectics of Aura

Being a dialectician means having the wind of history in one's sails. The sails are the concepts. It is not enough, however, to have sails at one's disposal. What is decisive is knowing the art of setting them.

WALTER BENJAMIN, 1999, p. 473.

> The development of the productive forces of a society is determined not
> only by the raw materials and instruments at that society's disposal, but
> also by its milieu and the experiences it has there.
>
> BENJAMIN, 1999, p. 911

In the *Arcades Project,* Walter Benjamin (1999)famously designated Paris the
"Capital of the 19th century," the location of capitalism's most pronounced
dialectical development. It was in the iron-traced, glass-roofed passageways
of the arcades, part department store, part commercialized public square, and
part red-light district that the antinomies of bourgeois society were especially
concentrated. A century old at the time of his writing, the arcades were chosen by Benjamin as the focal point of his investigation precisely because their
moment on the Parisian urban stage had already past. The arcades flowered in
the Second Republic as a frenetic scene of trade, vibrant milling and dense
crowds. By the *fin-de-siècle*, the leading edges of urban development had by-
passed the arcades, retail trade had vanished and the crowds were gone. The
physical carcass of the arcades remained as an archaeological "ruins of the
bourgeoisie." The arcades filled Benjamin's sails with the "wind of history"
precisely because they were a patinaed Simmelian ruin whose very decay was
steeped with aura.

Following Benjamin, we dub NASCAR and the Sturgis Motorcycle Rally as
the "Capital of the late 20th century." Could Benjamin attend the Daytona 500
or ride into the Sturgis Motorcycle Rally, he would recognize them as concentrated sites of *fin-de-siècle* modernity that exhibit neoliberal global capitalism's
most pronounced dialectical development, already etched with traces of decay.

Like everything else in post-Fordist capitalism, the process of "ruin" has
accelerated; the post-Fordist reduction in "turnover time" creates "ruins" with
great rapidity. We argue that motorsports is one such ruin: an economy of spectacle whose steady development throughout the Fordist mid-twentieth century accelerated in explosive growth at the *fin-de-siècle* before abruptly wilting.
Motorsports spectacles were once remarkably diverse: competitive sporting
events ranged from go-carts, sprint-cars (World of Outlaws), dirt-track modi-
fieds, sports cars (SCCA), to elite open-wheel racing (IRL, Grand Prix Racing,
Formula 1). Crowds flocked to shock-and-awe monster truck rallies, demolition
derbies, tractor-pulls and the carnivalesque displays of large-displacement
motorcycle rallies. What remained of the aura in these spectacles, heavily degraded by decades of progressive decontextualization, nearly vanished with
the financial crisis of 2007. Open-wheel racing in the U.S. split into the competing Indy Racing League (IRL) and Championship Auto Racing Teams (CART),
viewers, sponsors and profits evaporated: CART went bankrupt while the INDY

league stagnated as a weak, anemic alternative to NASCAR racing. NASCAR's rapid expansion of viewership, sponsorships and profits stalled after 2007 and it now exists as a shadow of its former self. Outlaw-biker themed motorcycle rallies ride their own fading aura; diminished spectacles attended by an aging remnant who have outlived their legend.

Spectacular economies are actively managed, heavily financed, and capable of immense capital outlay to reconstruct their content and find new ways to attract eyeballs, bodies and profits. Yet the spectacular life cycle has shortened dramatically. Sports management and sports marketing professionals have progressed to the point of anticipating crises as they are happening and divining solutions as soon as the fading of aura is detected. Long-running spectator events like NASCAR are living ruins—they contain in their present functioning the negated remains of their already-dead past. If it were once possible for critical theorists to take the measure of history's fair and steady breezes, hoist the appropriate canvas and "set it and forget it," the winds of history are now blowing with greater force and variability, requiring near constant sail management and active helmsmanship.

References

11 Amazing Augmented Reality Ads. (2012, 28 January). *Business Insider*. Retrieved 25 April 2012 from http://www.businessinsider.com/11-amazing-augmented-reality-ads-2012-1#net-a-porter-makes-storefronts-interactive-1.

2014 ISCA Annual Report. (2014). Retrieved 5 January 2015 from http://ir.internationals peedwaycorporation.com/phoenix.zhtml?c=113983&p=irol-reportsannual.

2015 Rally Expenses. (2015). Retrieved 5 January 2016 from http://www.sturgis-sd.gov/index.aspx?nid=752.

2015 Rally Reports. (2015). Retrieved 5 January 2016 from http://www.sturgis-sd.gov/index.aspx?nid=752.

Abere, A., Bronsteen, P., & Elzinga, K.G. (2012). The economics of NASCAR. *The Oxford Handbook of Sports Economics Volume 1: The Economics of Sports*, 1, 318.

About Motor Maids. (2013). Motor Maids Incorporated. Retrieved 12 April 2015 from http://www.motormaids.org/AboutUs/AboutMotorMaids.aspx.

Adorno, T.W. (1991). *The culture industry: Selected essays on mass culture*. Bernstein J.M. (ed.). London and New York: Routledge.

Adorno, T.W., & Horkheimer, M. (1972). *Dialectic of enlightenment*. New York, NY: Herder and Herder, Inc.

Adorno, T.W., Frenkel-Brunswik, E., Levinson, D.J. & Sanford, R.N. (1950). *The authoritarian personality*. New York, NY: Norton.

Allen, J. (n.d.). Jay Allen's road show. Retrieved consulted 21 February 2013 from http://app.imcreator.com/static/7084B3F9A2C04CD79EA7041C50DFA84C/welcome.

Alt, J. (1982). Popular culture and mass consumption: the motorcycle as cultural commodity. *The Journal of Popular Culture*, 15(4), 129–141.

Altemeyer, B. (1981). *Right wing authoritarianism*. Winnipeg: The University of Manitoba Press.

Altemeyer, B. (1988). *Enemies of freedom: Understanding right wing authoritarianism*. San Francisco, CA: Jossey-Bass Publishers.

AMA Hall of Fame. (2012). American Motorcycle Association. Retrieved 15 January 2013 from http://www.motorcyclemuseum.org/halloffame/detail.aspx?racerid=344.

American Motorcyclist Association. (2002). *Heroes of Harley-Davidson: JC Hoel*. Retrieved 15 January 2013 from http://www.motorcyclemuseum.org/asp/museum/exhibits/heroesofharley/biopage1.asp?id=198.

American Veterans Traveling Tribute Memorial Wall at the Buffalo Chip was erected with the help of active duty service men and the Patriot Guard Riders. (2013). Retrieved 4 June 2013 from http://www.buffalochip.com/EVENTS/Military-Tributes/Veterans-Memorial-Wall.

Amidon, K.S., & Sanderson, Z.G. (2012). On subjectivity and the risk pool; or, Žižek's lacuna. *Telos,* 160, 121–138.

Andrews, D.L. (2006). Disneyization, Debord, and the integrated NBA spectacle. *Social Semiotics,* 6(1), 89–102.

Antonio, R.J. (2000). After postmodernism: reactionary tribalism. *American Journal of Sociology,* 106(1), 40–87.

Arnould, E.J., & Thompson, C.J. (2005). Consumer Culture Theory (CCT): Twenty years of research. *Journal of Consumer Research,* 31(4), 868–882.

Austin, D.M., Gagne, P., & Orend, A. (2010). Commodification and popular imagery of the biker in American culture. *Journal of Popular Culture,* 45(5), 942–963.

Bakhtin M.M. (1968) *Rabelais and his world.* Bloomington, IN: Indiana University Press.

Bakhtin, M. (1973). *Problems of Dostoevsky's poetics.* (R.W. Rotsel, Trans.). New York: Ardis Publishers.

Bakhtin, M. (1981). *The dialogic imagination.* Austin: The University of Texas Press.

Barger, R., Zimmerman, K., & Zimmerman, K. (2000). *Hell's Angel: The life and times of Sonny Barger and the Hell's Angels Motorcycle Club.* New York: HarperCollins.

Barker, T. (2008). *Biker gangs and organized c rime.* Newark, NJ: Matthew Bender Publishing.

Barrett, R. (2013, 28 August). In quest to expand market, Harley-Davidson reaches out to women. *Milwaukee Journal Sentinel.* Retrieved 10 April 2015 from http://www.jsonline.com/business/in-quest-to-expand-market-harley-davidson-reaches-out-to-women-b99845731-221524671.html.

Baudrillard, J. (1983a). *Simulations.* New York: Semiotext(e), Inc.

Baudrillard, J. (1983b). *In the Shadow of the Silent Majorities or, The End of the Social and Other Essays.* New York: Semiotext(e), Inc.

Baudrillard, J. (1988). Simulacra and simulations. In M. Poster (ed.), *Jean Baudrillard: Selected Writings.* Stanford: Stanford University Press.

Baudrillard, J. (1996 [1968]). *System of objects.* London: Verso.

Beckychr007. (2008). *McCain at Sturgis Motorcycle Rally.* Retrieved 24 January 2009 from http://www.youtube.com/watch?v=sK-LEyyf7d4.

Belk, R.W., & Costa, J.A. (1998). The mountain man myth: a contemporary consuming fantasy. *Journal of Consumer Research,* 25(3), 218–240.

Benjamin, W. (1936). *The work of art in the age of mechanical reproduction.* Retrieved May 30, 2015 from https://www.marxists.org/reference/subject/philosophy/works/ge/benjamin.htm.

Benjamin, W. (1999). *The arcades project.* (H. Eiland & K. McLaughlin, Trans.). Cambridge, MA: Harvard University Press.

Benjamin, W. (2002 [1936]). The work of art in the age of its technological reproducibility, second version. In E. Jephcott, H. Eiland, & M.W. Jennings (eds.) *Walter Benjamin: Selected Writings, Volume 3, 1935–1938* (pp. 101–133). London: Belknap Press.

Berman, M. (1983). *All that is solid melts into air: The experience of modernity.* London: Verso.

Best, S., & Kellner, D. (1997). *The postmodern turn.* New York, NY: The Guilford Press.

Best, S., & Kellner, D. (2001). *The postmodern adventure: Science, technology, and cultural studies at the third millennia.* New York, NY: Guilford Press.

Bikers for Christ: East Bay Chapter. (n.d.) *Biker's prayer.* Retrieved 20 February 2013 from http://www.rideforhim.com/BikersPrayer.htm.

Bikers for Christ: Orange County Chapter. (n.d.) *Jesus a biker tract.* Retrieved 20 February 2013 from http://www.ocbikersforchrist.org/wp-content/uploads/2009/12/jesus-a-biker-tract.pdf.

Bonilla, C.F. (1988). A South Dakota rendezvous: the Sturgis Motorcycle Rally and Races. *South Dakota History,* 38(3), 123–144.

Bourdieu, P. (1984). *Distinction: A social critique of the judgement of taste.* Cambridge, MA: Harvard University Press.

Boyle, J. (2003). The second enclosure movement and the construction of the public domain. *Law and Contemporary Problems,* 66(1/2), 33–74.

Boyle, J. (2008). *The public domain: Enclosing the commons of the mind.* New Haven, CT: Yale University Press.

Brandist, C., & Tihanov, G. (2000). *Materializing Bakhtin: The Bakhtin circle and social theory.* New York, NY: St. Martin's Press.

Buffalo chip to begin collecting taxes. (2015, 3 December). KOTA Territory News. Retrieved 5 January 2016 from http://www.kotatv.com/news/south-dakota-news/Buffalo-Chip-to-begin-collecting-taxes/36765644.

Byford, S. (2012, 13 April). Pentagon places order for iOptik dual focus augmented reality contact lenses. *The Verge.* Retrieved 25 April 2013 from http://www.theverge.com/2012/4/13/2945498/pentagon-ioptik-dual-focus-augmented-reality-contact-lenses.

Camille, M. (1992). *Image on the edge: The margins of medieval art.* Cambridge, MA: Harvard University Press.

Camille, M. (1996). *Master of death: The lifeless art of Pierre Remiet, Illuminator.* New Haven & London: Yale.

Cassano, G. (2008). The acquisitive machine: Max Weber, Thorstein Veblen and the culture of consumptive individual. In D. Chalcraft, F. Howell, M.L. Menendez & H. Vera (eds.), *Max Weber matters: Interweaving past and present,* (pp. 177–190). Farnham: Ashgate.

Cassano, G. (2009). Symbolic exploitation and the social dialectic of desire. *Critical Sociology,* 35(3), 379–393.

Cassano, G. (2014). Working class self fashioning in 'Swing Time'. *Critical Sociology,* 40(3), 329–347.

Celsi, R., Rose, L.R., & Leigh, T.W. (1993). An exploration of high-risk leisure consumption through skydiving. *Journal of Consumer Research,* 20(1), 1–23.

Christian Index. (2009). *Bikers meet baptists in the Black Hills.* Retrieved 24 August 2013 from http://www.christianindex.org/5723.article.print.

City of Sturgis Rally and Events Department. (2009). *Meet the sponsors.* Retrieved 21 January 2009 from http://www.sturgismotorcyclerally.com/sponsorship/spon sorship-info.php.

City of Sturgis Rally and Events Department. (2013). *Sponsors of the Rally.* Retrieved 20 February 2013 from http://www.sturgismotorcyclerally.com/sponsorship/#2.

Clark, J.M., Cornwell, T.B., & Pruitt, S.W. (2009). The impact of title event sponsorship announcements on shareholder wealth. *Marketing Letters*, 20(2), 169–182.

Clayton, S., & Dispain, D. (1984). The first 60 years: An illustrated history of the American Motorcyclist Association. *American Motorcyclist.* Retrieved 15 December 2013 from https://books.google.com/books?id=M_kDAAAAMBAJ&lpg=PA1&pg=PA 1#v=onepage&q&f=false.

Cluley, R. (2009). Engineering great moments: The production of live music. *Consumption Markets & Culture*, 12 (4), 373–388.

Cohen, S. (1980). *Folk devils and moral panics: the creation of the mods and the rockers* (2nd Ed.). New York, NY: St. Martin's Press.

Coker, C. (2013). Warrior *geeks: How 21st century technology is changing the way we fight and think about war.* Oxford: Oxford University Press.

Collins, R. (2004). *Interaction ritual chains.* Princeton, NJ: Princeton University Press.

Connell, J. (2012). Film tourism – evolution, progress and prospects. *Tourism Management, 33*(5), 1007–1029.

Cova, B., & Cova, V. (2002). Tribal marketing: the tribalisation of society and its impact on the conduct of marketing. *European Journal of Marketing, 36*(5/6), 595–620.

Cova, B., & Dalli, D. (2009). Working consumers: The next step in marketing theory? *Marketing Theory*, 9 (3), 315–339.

Cova, B., Kozinets, R., & Shankar, A. (2012). *Consumer Tribes.* New York, NY: Routledge.

Date for National Gipsy Tours. (1917, 25 January). *Motorcycle Illustrated.* Retrieved 17 December 2013 from https://books.google.com/books?id=46kAAAAAMAAJ&print sec=frontcover&authuser=0&source=gbs_ge_summary_r&cad=0#v=onepage&q= Gipsy&f=false.

DeAngelis, M. (2007). *The beginning of history: Value struggles and global capital.* London: Pluto Press.

Debord, G. (1988). *Comments on the Society of the Spectacle.* Retrieved January, 10, 2013 from Marxists.org http://www.notbored.org/commentaires.html.

Debord, G. (2006 [1967]a). *The society of the spectacle.* (K. Knabb. Trans.). Oakland, CA: AK Press.

Debord, G. (2006 [1967]b). *The society of the spectacle.* Retrieved 28 September 2013 from http://www.marxists.org/reference/archive/debord/society.htm.

Delaney, K.J., & Eckstein, R. (2003). *Public dollars, private stadiums: The battle over building sports stadiums.* New Brunswick, NJ: Rutgers University Press.

Delaney, K.J., & Eckstein, R. (2007). Urban power structures and publicly financed stadiums. *Sociological Forum*, 22, 331–353.

DeGaris, L., West, C., & Dodds, M. (2009). Leveraging and activating NASCAR sponsorships with NASCAR-linked sales promotions. Journal of Sponsorship, 3(1).

DeYoung, M. (1998). Another look at moral panics: the case of satanic day care centers. *Deviant Behavior*, 19(3), 257–278.

Dillow, C. (2012, 1 February). DARPA invests in megapixel augmented-reality contact lenses. *Popular Science*. Retrieved 25 April 2013 from (http://www.popsci.com/diy/article/2012-05/2012-invention-awards-augmented-reality-contact-lenses; http://www.popsci.com/technology/article/2012-02/video-nano-enhanced-contact-lens-makes-augmented-reality-more-realistic.)

DoneKue, J. (1917, 7 June). M&ATA Bureau of Window Displays needed. *Motorcycle and Bicycle Illustrated*.

Dulaney, W.L. (2005). A brief history of "outlaw" motorcycle clubs. *International Journal of Motorcycle Studies*. Retrieved 7 April 2015 from http://ijms.nova.edu/November2005/IJMS_Artcl.Dulaney.html.

Durkheim, E. (1951 [1897]). *Suicide: A Study in Sociology*. New York: Free Press.

Durkheim, E. (1965 [1915]). *The elementary Forms of the religious life*. New York, NY: Free Press.

Durkheim, E. (1984 [1893]). *Division of labor in society*. New York, NY: Free Press.

eBay. (n.d.) BIKER JESUS action figure Jesus riding motorcycle Harley new in box gift quality. Retrieved 20 February 2013 from http://www.ebay.com/itm/BIKER-JESUS-Action-Figure-Jesus-Riding-Motorcycle-Harley-New-in-Box-Gift-Quality-/151168964378?pt=LH_DefaultDomain_0&hash=item23325f571a.

Eco, U. (1984). The frames of comic freedom. In Sebeok, T.A., (ed.), *Carnival!* (pp. 1–10). Berlin: Mouton.

Edensor, T. (2001). Performing tourism, staging tourism: (re)producing tourist space and practice. *Tourist Studies*, 1(1), 59–81.

Edwards, M.B., Alderman, D.H., & Estes, S.G. (2010). An appraisal of stock car racing's economic and geographic development in North America: NASCAR as flexible accumulation. *International Journal of Sport Management and Marketing*, 8(1/2), 160–179.

Elias, N. (2006). *The court society*. (E. Jephcott, Trans.). Dublin: University College Dublin Press.

Endres, T.G. & Ferrar, A. (2002). *Sturgis stories: Celebrating the people of the world's largest motorcycle rally*. Edina, MN: Kirk House Publishing.

Featherstone, M. (1991). *Consumer culture and postmodernism*. London: Sage.

Fellrath, T. (2009). Literature review on economic development. Unpublished Mauscript. Retrieved 27 August 2012 from http://fellrath.wordpress.com.

Ferrell, J. (1999). Cultural Criminology. *Annual Review of Sociology*, 25, 395–418.

Fink, B. (1997). *A clinical introduction to Lacanian Psychoanalysis: Theory and technique*. Cambridge, MA and London: Harvard University Press.

Finn, J.S. (2014). Old Billingsgate. Retrieved 27 September 2011 from http://www.oldbillingsgate.co.uk/.

Firat, A.F. & Venkatesh, A. (1995). Liberatory Postmodernism and the Reenchantment of Consumption. *Journal of Consumer Research*, 22(3), 239–267.

Fischer, D.H. (1989). *Albion's seed: Four British folkways in America.* Oxford: Oxford University Press.

Flinn, J., & Frew, M. (2014). Glastonbury: managing the mystification of festivity. *Leisure Studies*, 33(4), 418–433.

Forbes 400. (2013). Retrieved 12 October 2013 from http://www.forbes.com/forbes-400/.

Frazer, J.G. (1900). *The golden bough: A study in magic and religion, Vol. II.* New York: MacMillan.

Freud, S. (1950 [1919]). *Totem and taboo.* London: Routledge Press.

Freud, S. (2010 [1921]). Group psychology and the analysis of the ego. In I. Smith (ed.) *Freud – Complete Works* (pp. 8280–8427). Retrieved from http://www.valas.fr/IMG/pdf/Freud_Complete_Works.pdf.

Fromm, E. (1955). The *sane society.* New York, NY: Reinhart.

Fromm, E. (1973). *The anatomy of human destructiveness.* New York, NY: Holt, Rinehart and Winston.

Fuchs, C. (2014). *Digital labour and Karl Marx.* New York, NY: Routledge.

Galahan, K. (2010, 10 August). 'oos: a new century. *Rapid City Journal.* Retrieved 6 January 2014 from http://rapidcityjournal.com/news/local/state-andregional/article_91958fcc-9d3f-11df-ab9d-001cc4c03286.html.

Ganje, F. (2013, 28 January). Sturgis prepares to announce selection of Rally sponsorship agent. Big 81: Ranch Radio News. Retrieved 1 February 2013 from http://www.newrushmoreradio.com/kbhb/news/sdr-kbhb-news-rally-sponsorship-agent-20130128,0,3435525.story.

Geertz, C. (1972). Deep play: notes on the Balinese cockfight. *Daedalus,* 101(1), 1–37.

Girard, R. (1965). *Deceit, desire, and the novel: Self and other in literary structure.* (Y. Freccero, Trans.). Baltimore, MD: Johns Hopkins University Press.

Girardi, A. (2013). Iowa tax increment financing tax credits program evaluation study. Iowa Department of Revenue. Retrieved 15 November 2015 from https://tax.iowa.gov/sites/files/idr/TIF%20Evaluation%20Study%202013.pdf.

Gladwell, M. (1997, 17 March). The Coolhunt. *The New Yorker.* Retrieved 31 January 2013 from http://www.gladwell.com/1997/1997_03_17_a_cool.htm.

Goffman, E. (1951). Symbols of class status. *The British Journal of Sociology,* 2(4), 294–304.

Goffman, E. (1961). *Encounters: Two studies in the sociology of interaction.* New York, NY: Bobbs Merrill.

Goffman, E. (1967). *Interaction ritual: Essays on face-to-face behavior.* New York, NY: Anchor Books.

Goffman, E. (1971). *Relations in public: Microstudies of the public order.* New York, NY: Basic Books.

Goffman, E. (1974). *Frame analysis.* New York, NY: Harper Colophon Books.

Goldsmith, A.L., & Walker, M. (2015). The NASCAR experience: Examining the influence of fantasy sport participation on 'non-fans'. *Sport Management Review,* 18(2), 231–243.

Goss, J. (2004). The souvenir: conceptualizing the object(s) of tourism consumption. In A.A. Lew, C.M. Hall, & A.M. Williams (eds.), *A Companion to Tourism,* (pp. 327–335). Malden, MA: Blackwell Publishing.

Gotham, K.F. (2002). Marketing Mardi Gras: commodification, spectacle and the political economy of tourism in New Orleans. *Urban Studies,* 39(10), 1735–1756.

Gotham, K.F. (2007). *Authentic New Orleans: Tourism, culture, and race in the Big Easy.* New York: New York University Press.

Gotham, K.F. (2011). Theorizing carnival: Mardi Gras as perceived, conceived and lived space. In J. Braun & L. Langman (eds.), *Alienation and the carnivalization of society,* (pp. 93–118). New York, NY: Routledge.

Gotham, K.F. (2012). Make it right? Brad Pitt, post-Katrina rebuilding, and the spectacularization of disaster. In S. Banet-Weiser & R. Mukherjee (eds.), *Commodity Activism: Cultural Resistance in Neoliberal Times* (pp. 97–113). New York, NY: New York University Press.

Gotham, K.F., & Krier, D. (2008). From the culture industry to the society of the spectacle: critical theory and the Situationist International. *Current Perspectives in Social Theory,* 25, 155–192.

Gottdiener, M. (Ed.). (2000), *New forms of consumption.* Lanham, MD: Rowman and Littlefield.

Gottdiener, M. (2001). *Theming of America: Dreams, visions, and commercial spaces* (2nd Ed.). Boulder, CO: Westview Press.

Gottdiener, M., Collins, C.C., & Dickens, D.R. (1999). *Las Vegas: The social production of an all-American city.* Malden, MA: Blackwell.

Grundy, G. (1919, 2 July). What's wrong with American motorcycling? *Motorcycling and Bicycling.* Retrieved 20 December 2013 from https://books.google.com/books?id=4gI9AAAAYAAJ&pg=RA1-PA25&lpg=RA1-PA25&dq=grandpa+grundy&source=bl&ots=v_qou-NNJX&sig=JkZhaMNAiIs8xymtU2r3o1PJhSk&hl=en&sa=X&ei=8xz5VLvmO4HsgwSyioC4AQ&ved=0CDwQ6AEwBw#v=onepage&q=grandpa%20grundy&f=false.

Guns of Freedom: The Ultimate 2nd Amendment Experience. (2014). Retrieved 5 June 2014 from http://gunsoffreedom.com/.

Gypsy Tour Promotion Plans. (1917, 15 March). *Motorcycle Illustrated.* Retrieved 17 December 2013 from https://books.google.com/books?id=46kAAAAAMAAJ&prin tsec=frontcover&authuser=0&source=gbs_ge_summary_r&cad=0#v=onepage&q= Gipsy&f=false.

Hale, G.E. (2011). *A nation of outsiders: How the white middle class fell in love with rebellion in postwar America.* New York, NY: Oxford University Press.

Hall, R.L. (2002). Before NASCAR: The corporate and civic promotion of automobile racing in the American South, 1903–1927. *The Journal of Southern History, 68*(3), 629–668.

Halnon, K.B. (2004). Inside shock music carnival: spectacle as contested terrain. *Critical Sociology, 30*(3), 743–779.

Hansen, M. (2005, 18 April). And now, the rest of the racetrack story. *Newton Daily News.* Retrieved 15 November 2015 from http://docmnts0010.tripod.com/news/ ndn/04182005b.jpg.

Hardt, M. & Negri, A. (2005). *Multitude.* Cambridge, MA: Harvard University Press.

Hardt, M. & Negri, A. (2009). *Commonwealth.* Cambridge, MA: Harvard.

Harley Davidson Dealers Conference. (1947). Harley Davidson Museum, Milwaukee, WI.

Harley-Davidson annual report. (2012). United States Securities and Exchange Commission. Retrieved 15 October 2013 from http://ar.harley-davidson.com/_files/pdf/ HD_10k_2012.pdf.

Harvey, D. (1989). *The condition of postmodernity: An enquiry into the origins of cultural change.* New York, NY: Wiley.

Hayes, B., & Quattlebaum, J. (2010). *The original Wild Ones: Tales of the Boozefighters Motorcycle Club.* Minneapolis, MN: Motorbooks.

Hegel, G.W.F. (1967 [1910]). *The phenomenology of mind.* (J.B. Bailie, Trans.). Retrieved 30 March 2013 from http://www.marxists.org/reference/archive/hegel/works/ph/ phba.htm.

Heidelberger, C.A. (2014, 20 December). Meade County plans giant TIF Disctrict to fund east Sturgis bypass. *Madville Times.* Retrieved 30 May 2015 from http://madvilletimes. com/2014/12/meade-county-plans-giant-tif-district-to-fund-east-sturgis-bypass/.

History of Laconia. (n.d.) Retrieved 14 January 2013 from http://www.weirsbeach.com/ Largejpgs/bikeweekguidecovers.html.

Holland, D. (2013, 29 January). Ex-Sturgis Rally agent accuses city of violating their contract. *Rapid City Journal.* Retrieved 1 February 2013 from http://rapidcityjournal. com/sturgisrallydaily/news/ex-sturgis-rally-agent-accuses-city-of-violating-their -contract/article_f6eec602-8002-5200-85a0-ef1c4d2e1f64.html.

Holland, D. (2013, 30 July). Sturgis throws support to rally trademark group. *Rapid City Journal.* Retrieved 5 January 2015 from http://rapidcityjournal.com/sturgis-throws -support-to-rally-trademark-group/article_019520a0-0f58-51d3-be4d-55988ad1adf9. html.

Holland, D. (2015, 20 February). Sturgis, Buffalo Chip, keep trying to outmaneuver the other. *Rapid City Journal.* Retrieved 13 July 2015 from http://rapidcityjournal. com/news/local/sturgis-buffalo-chip-keep-trying-to-outmaneuver-the-other/ article_89e42060-ab48-5799-a810-acdf15e26cc9.html.

Holland, D. (2015, 3 May). Sturgis' try at stopping Buffalo Chip incorporation election rebuffed again. *Rapid City Journal.* Retrieved 13 July 2015 from http://rapidcity-journal.com/news/local/sturgis-try-at-stopping-buffalo-chip-incorporation -election-rebuffed-again/article_57d53a94-5ba3-511f-bdd9-a13cf5e1dafb.html.

Holland, D. (2015, 14 May). Buffalo Chip is State's newest town. *Rapid City Journal.* Retrieved 30 May 2015 from http://rapidcityjournal.com/news/local/buffalo-chip -is-state-s-newest-town/article_e6489953-3c34-5332-a13c-087662465e29.html.

Holland, D. (2015, 12 May). Sturgis to break with tradition and open park to vendors during 75th rally. *Rapid City Journal.* Retrieved 15 December 2015 from http:// rapidcityjournal.com/sturgisrallydaily/news/sturgis-to-break-with-tradition-and -open-park-to-vendors/article_7ddbecd8-6f9d-5341-92e1-76ef4b7c4dbe.html.

Holland, D. (2016, 20 January). SD Municipal League joins in Buffalo Chip lawsuit. *Rapid City Journal.* Retrieved 20 January 2016 from http://rapidcityjournal.com/ news/local/sd-municipal-league-joins-in-buffalo-chip-lawsuit/article_978096d2 -bf10-536b-8c4d-60744338002b.html?utm_medium=social&utm_source=facebook &utm_campaign=user-share.

Holquist, M. (1990). *Dialogism: Bakhtin and his world.* London and New York: Routledge.

Holt, D.B. (1995). How consumers consume: a typology of consumption practices. *Journal of Consumer Research, 22*(1), 1–16.

Holt, D.B. (1997). Poststructuralist lifestyle analysis: conceptualizing the social pattern-ing of consumption in postmodernity. *Journal of Consumer Research, 24*, 326–350.

Holt, D.B. (2004). *How brands become icons.* Boston, Ma: Harvard University Press.

Holt, D.B., & Thompson, C.J. (2004). Man-of-action heroes: the pursuit of heroic mas-culinity in everyday consumption. *Journal of Consumer Research, 31*(2), 425–444.

Horkheimer, M. & Adorno, T.W. (1972 [1944]). *Dialectic of enlightenment.* (J. Cumming, Trans.). New York: Herder and Herder.

Horsey, D. (2002, 25 August). Biker's raunchy rally is closer to the mainstream than you think. *Seattle Post-Intelligencer.* Retrieved 12 March 2009 http://seattlepi .nwsource. com/opinion/83476_focus25.shtml.

Hubert, H., & Mauss, M. (1964). *Sacrifice: Its nature and function.* Chicago, IL: University of Chicago Press.

Humphrey, C. (2001). *The politics of carnival: festive misrule in medieval England.* Manchester and New York, NY: Manchester University Press.

Huntington, S. (2015, 13 May). New town of Buffalo Chip holds first meeting. KOTA Territory News. Retrieved 13 July 2015 from http://www.kotatv.com/news/ south-dakota-news/New-town-of-Buffalo-Chip-holds-first-meeting/33011726.

Husband, T. (1980). *The wild man: Medieval myth and symbolism*. New York, NY: Metropolitan Museum of Art.

Hussmann, P. (2005, 11 March). Rumors of demise might be overstated. *Newton Daily News*. Retrieved 15 November 2015 from http://docmntsoo10.tripod.com/news/ndn/03112005.jpg.

Hyde, L. (2005). *Frames from the framers: How America's revolutionaries imagined intellectual property*. Berkman Research Publication No. 2005–08. Cambridge, MA: Harvard University—Berkman Center for Internet and Society. Retrieved from http://papers.ssrn.com/sol3/Papers.cfm?abstract_id=870073.

Hyman, T., & Malbert, R. (2000). *Carnivalesque*. London: Hayward.

If you build it they will come. (2003, 21 April). *Newton Daily Informer*. Retrieved 15 November 2015 from http://docmntsoo9.tripod.com/news/informer/04212003a.jpg.

Ivanov, V.V. (1984). The semiotic theory of carnival as the inversion of bipolar opposites. In T.A. Seboeok (Ed.). *Carnival!* (pp. 11–36). Berlin: Mouton.

Jameson, F. (1991). *Postmodernism, or the cultural logic of late capitalism*. London: Verso.

Jameson, F. (1997). Culture and finance capital. *Critical Inquiry*, 24 (1), 246–265.

Jappe, A. (1999). *Guy Debord*. Berkeley, CA: University of California Press.

Jay, M. (1993). *Downcast eyes: The denigration of vision in twentieth century French thought*. Berkeley, CA: University of California Press.

Jennings, J. (2006, 24 March). Hotel and waterpark planned near racetrack. *Newton Daily News*. Retrieved 15 November 2015 from http://docmntsoo12.tripod.com/news/ndn/03242006.jpg.

Jesus the Biker (n.d.). James Russell Publishing. Retrieved 20 February 2013 from http://www.jamesrussellpublishing.biz/jesusbiker.html.

Johnson, C.L., & Man, J.Y. (2001). *Tax increment financing and economic development: Uses structures and impact*. Albany, NY: State University of New York Press.

Jones, M. (1990). *Dostoyevsky after Bakhtin: Readings in Dostoyevsky's fantastic realism*. Cambridge: Cambridge.

Justice, S. (1994). *Writing and rebellion: England in 1381*. Berkeley, CA: University of California Press.

Kaiser, T. (2012, 2 February). New augmented reality contact lenses/eyeglasses offer entertainment, help soldiers. *Daily Tech*. Retrieved 25 April 2013 from http://www.dailytech.com/New+Augmented+Reality+Contact+LensesEyeglasses+Offer+Entertainment+Help+Soldiers/article23919.htm.

Karr, A. (2005, 17 May). Speedway created cash cow for Kansas City. *Newton Daily News*. Retrieved 15 November 2015 from http://docmntsoo10.tripod.com/news/ndn/05172005b.jpg.

Karr, A. (2005, 6 June). City funding to aces still unknown. *Newton Daily News*. Retrieved 15 November 2015 from http://docmntsoo10.tripod.com/news/ndn/06072005.jpg.

Karr, A. (2005, 24 June). Iowa Speedway to be built for success. *Newton Daily News.* Retrieved 15 November 2015 from http://docmnts0010.tripod.com/news/ndn/06242005a.jpg.

Karr, A. (2006, 2 September). Newton race city, or how I learned to stop worrying and love Iowa Speedway. *Newton Daily News.* Retrieved 15 November from http://docmnts0013.tripod.com/news/ndn/09202006.jpg.

Karr, A., & Hussmann, P. (2005, 28 February). Five years coming, track news welcomed. *Newton Daily News.* Retrieved 15 November 2015 from http://docmnts0010.tripod.com/news/ndn/02282005.jpg.

Kellner, D. (1995). *Media culture: Cultural studies, identity and politics between the modern and the postmodern.* London: Routledge.

Kennedy, D. (2009). *The spectator and the spectacle: Audiences in modernity and postmodernity.* Cambridge: Cambridge University Press.

Kevin, B. (2015, 23 April). Peak sponsors top sim racers. Retrieved 22 October 2015 from http://www.iracing.com/peak-sponsors-top-sim-racers/.

Kim, H., & Richardson, S.L. (2003). Motion picture impacts on destination images. *Annals of Tourism Research, 30*(1), 216–237.

Kimmel, M.S. (1994). Consuming Manhood: The Feminization of American Culture and the Recreation of the American Man Body, 1832–1920. *Michigan Quarterly Review, 33,* 7–36.

Klein, M. (1963 [1932]). *The psychoanalysis of children.* London: Hogarth Press.

Klein, M. (1975 [1957]). *Envy and gratitude and other works, 1946–1963.* New York, NY: Free Press.

Klinger, B. (1997). The road to dystopia: landscaping the nation in Easy Rider. In S. Cohan & I.R. Hark (Eds.), *The Road Movie Book,* (pp. 170–203). New York, NY: Routledge.

Kojeve, A. (1969). *Introduction to the reading of Hegel: Lectures on the Phenomenology of Spirit.* (J.H. Nichols, Trans.). Ithaca, NY: Cornell University Press.

König, W. (2004). Adolf Hitler vs. Henry Ford: The Volkswagen, the role of America as a model, and the failure of a Nazi consumer society. *German Studies Review, 27*(2), 249–268.

Kovaleski, S.F. (2013, 29 November). Law and regulation: despite outlaw image, hells angels sues often. *New York Times.* Retrieved December 10, 2013 from http://www.cnbc.com/id/101235239.

Kozinets, R.V. (2002). Can consumers escape the market? Emancipatory illuminations from Burning Man. *Journal of Consumer Research, 29*(1), 20–38.

Kozinets, R.V., Sherry, J.F., Storm, D., Duhachek, A., Nuttavuthisit, K., & DeBerry-Spence, B. (2004). Ludic agency and retail spectacle. *Journal of Consumer Research, 31*(3), 658–672.

Kracauer, S. (1947). *From Caligari to Hitler: A psychological history of the German film.* Princeton, NJ: Princeton University Press.

Kracauer, S. (1975). The Mass Ornament. *New German Critique, 5*, 67–76.

Krier, D. (2005). *Speculative management: stock market power and corporate change.* Albany, NY: SUNY Press.

Krier, D. (2008). Critical institutionalism and financial globalization: a comparative analysis of American and continental finance. *New York Journal of Sociology, 1*, 130–186.

Krier, D. (2009a) Finance capital, neo-liberalism and critical institutionalism. *Critical Sociology*, 35(3), 395–416.

Krier, D. (2009b). Speculative finance capital, corporate earnings and profit fetishism. *Critical Sociology,* 35(5), 657–675.

Krier, D., & Swart, W.J. (2012). The dialectics of carnival: from Bakhtin to Baudrillard. In J. Braun & L. Langman (Eds.). *Alienation and the Carnivalization of Society* (pp. 133–165). New York, NY: Routledge.

Krier, D., & Swart, W.J. (2014a). The commodification of spectacle: spectators, sponsors and the outlaw biker diegesis at Sturgis. *Critical Sociology.* doi: 0896920514524605.

Krier D, and Swart WJ (2014b) Trophies of Surplus Enjoyment. *Critical Sociology,* doi: 0896920514528819.

Krier, D., & Swart, W.J. (2015). How legends become brands: The culture industry in the Second Enclosure Movement. In H.J. Dahms (Ed.), *Globalization, Critique and Social Theory: Diagnoses and Challenges,* (pp. 234–266). Bingley: Emerald Group Publishing Limited.

Lacan, J. (1997). *The seminar of Jacques Lacan, VII: The ethics of Psychoanalysis.* New York, NY and London: Norton.

Lacan, J. (2006 [1966]). *Ecrits: The first complete edition in English.* New York, NY and London: Norton.

Lacan, J. (2007 [1969]). *The seminar of Jacques Lacan: The other side of Psychoanalysis, Book XVII.* New York, NY and London: Norton.

Langman, L. (2005). *Carnivalization of the world.* Thousand Oaks, CA: Sage.

Langman, L. (2008). Punk, porn and resistance: carnivalization and the body in popular culture. *Current Sociology,* 54(4), 657–677.

Langman, L. (2012). Cycles of contention: the rise and fall of the Tea Party. *Critical Sociology,* 38(4), 469–494.

Langman, L., & Lundskow, G. (2012). Down the rabid hole to a Tea Party. *Critical Sociology,* 38(4), 589–597.

Langman, L., & Ryan, M. (2009). Capitalism and the carnival character: the escape from reality. *Critical Sociology,* 35(4), 471–492.

Lefebvre, H. (1991). *Critique of everyday life, Volume 1.* (J. Moore, Trans.) London: Verso.

Lennon, J., & Foley, M. (2000). *Dark tourism: The attraction of death and disaster.* London: Continuum.

Levin, A.M., Beasley, F., & Gilson, R.L. (2008). NASCAR fans' responses to current and former NASCAR sponsors: The effect of perceived group norms and fan identification. *International Journal of Sports Marketing & Sponsorship*, 9(3), 193.

Levi-Strauss, C. (1963). *Structural anthropology, Volume 1*. New York, NY: Basic Books.

Levi-Strauss, C. (1976). *Structural anthropology, Volume 2*. New York, NY: Basic Books.

Luedicke, M.K., Thompson, C.J., & Giesler, M. (2010). Consumer identity work as moral protagonism: how myth and ideology animate a brand-mediated moral conflict. *Journal of Consumer Research*, 36 (6), 1016–1032.

Lukacs, G. ([1923]1967). *History and class consciousness*. Retrieved 15 May 2015 from https://www.marxists.org/archive/lukacs/works/history/.

Lundskow, G. (2012). Authoritarianism and destructiveness in the tea party movement. *Critical Sociology*, 38(4), 529–547.

Lyng, S.G. (1990). Edgework: a social psychological analysis of voluntary risk taking. *American Journal of Sociology*, 95(1), 851–886.

MacCannell, D. (1973). Staged authenticity: arrangements of social space in tourist settings. *American Journal of Sociology*, 79(3), 589–603.

MacCannell, D. (1976). *The tourist: A new theory of the leisure class*. New York, NY: Schoken Books.

Marcuse, H. (1964). *One dimensional man: studies in the ideology of advanced industrial society*. Boston, MA: Beacon Press.

Marshall, D.A. (2002). Behavior, belonging, and belief: a theory of ritual practice. *Sociological Theory*, 20(3), 360–380.

Marshall, D.A. (2010). Temptation, tradition, and taboo: a theory of sacralization. *Sociological Theory*, 28(1), 64–90.

Martin, D.M., Schouten J.W. & McAlexander, J.J. (2006). Claiming the throttle: multiple femininities in a hyper-masculine subculture. *Consumption Markets & Culture*, 9(3), 171–205.

Marx, K. (1991 [1894]). *Capital, Volume 3*. New York, NY: Penguin.

Marx, K. (2010 [1867]). *Capital: A critique of political economy, Volume 1*. Retrieved 30 March 2013 from https://www.marxists.org/archive/marx/works/1867-c1/.

Marx, K. (2010 [1894]). *Capital, Volume 2: The process of capitalist production as a whole*. Retrieved 30 March 2013 from http://www.marxists.org/archive/marx/works/1894-c3/ch08.htm.

Matthews, G. (2015, 25 November). Low bid means no contractual obligation for Buffalo Chip owner. Big 81: Ranch Radio News. Retrieved 7 December 2015 from http://www.kbhbradio.com/news/low-bid-means-no-contractual-obligation-for-buffalo-chip-owner/article_7533ac12-9391-11e5-aa7c-53c64284cbe1.html#.VlZWwlKKrUF.facebook.

Mauss, M. (1967). *The gift: Forms and functions of exchange in archaic societies*. London: Cohen and West.

Maverick. (2007, 23 October). Presidential bike on exhibit at Sturgis motorcycle museum. *Cycle Matters*. Retrieved 29 January 2009 from http://www.cyclematters.com/motorcycle-blog/industry-news/president-bush-desperado-motorcycle-sturgis-halloffame.cfm.

McAlexander, J.H., Schouten, J.W., & Koening, H.F. (2002). Building brand community. *Journal of Marketing*, 66(1), 38–54.

McCracken, G. (1986). Culture and consumption: a theoretical account of the structure and movement of the cultural meaning of consumer goods. *Journal of Consumer Research*, 13(1), 71–84.

Mead, G.H. (1934). *Mind, self and society: From the standpoint of a social behaviorist.* Chicago, IL: University of Chicago Press.

Meade County Taxpayers for Responsible Government. (2015). In Facebook [Community page]. Retrieved 5 January 2016 from https://www.facebook.com/Meade-County-Taxpayers-for-Responsible-Government-390681471098508/.

Meade Country lowers vendor fees during Sturgis Motorcycle Rally; Buffalo Chip expands vendor opportunities. (2013, 4 October). *Buffalo Chip News*. Retrieved 5 January 2016 from http://www.buffalochip.com/NEWS-INFO/News/Buffalo-Chip-Announcements/articleType/ArticleView/articleId/267/Meade-Country-Lowers-Vendor-Fees-During-Sturgis-Motorcycle-Rally-Buffalo-Chip-Expands-Vendor-Opportunities.

Mellström, U. (2004). Machines and masculine subjectivity: Technology as an integral part of men's life experiences. *Men and Masculinities*, 6(4), 368–382.

Mickle, T. (2010, 2 November). Nascar changes gaming strategy. *Sporting News*. Retrieved 2 November 2012 from http://www.sportingnews.com/nascar-news/171138-nascar-changes-gaming-strategy.

Morris, F. (2015, 28 April). A look back at the day that saved KCK, a look forward at the windfall to come. KCUR. Retrieved 11-15-2015 from http://kcur.org/post/look-back-day-saved-kck-look-forward-windfall-come#stream/0.

Mort, F. (1996). *Cultures of consumption: Masculinity and social space in late twentieth century Britain*. London: Routledge.

Morton, J. (1999). Biker movies. In J. Sargeant & S. Watson (Eds.), *Lost Highways: An Illustrated History of Road Movies* (pp. 55–66). New York, NY: Creation Books.

Motor Maids. (n.d.). Wikipedia. Retrieved 12 April 2015 from http://en.wikipedia.org/wiki/Motor_Maids.

Motorcycle Illustrated. (1917). Retrieved 17 December 2013 from https://books.google.com/books?id=46kAAAAAMAAJ&printsec=frontcover&authuser=0&source=gbs_ge_summary_r&cad=0#v=onepage&q=Gipsy&f=false.

Mundt, J. (2002). The branding of myths and the myths of branding: Some critical remarks on the branding of destinations. *Tourism*, 50, 339–348.

Muniz, A.M., & O'Guinn, T.C. (2001). Brand community. *Journal of Consumer Research*, 27(4), 412–432.

Murray, H.A. (2008 [1938]). *Explorations in personality*. New York, NY: Oxford University Press.

Nalbandian, J. (2005). Professionals and the conflicting forces of administrative modernization and civic engagement. *The American Review of Public Administration*, 35: 311–326.

Naming Rights. (2015). Retrieved 15 November 2015 from http://www.iowaspeedway .com/aspx/RacePage.aspx?pid=115.

NASCAR official sponsors. (2015). Retrieved 15 November 2015 from http://www.jayski .com/news/pages/story/_/page/NASCAR-Sponsors.

Newman, J.I., & Giardina, M.D. (2008). NASCAR and the "southernization" of America: spectatorship, subjectivity, and the confederation of identity. *Cultural Studies↔ Critical Methodologies, 8*(4), 479–506.

Newman, J.I., & Giardina, M.D. (2010) Neoliberalism's last lap? NASCAR nation and the cultural politics of sport. *American Behavioral Scientist, 53*(10), 1511–1529.

Newman, J.I., & Giardina, M.D. (2011). *Sport, spectacle, and NASCAR Nation: Consumption and the cultural politics of Neoliberalism*. New York, NY: Palgrave Macmillan.

Nichols, D. (2007). *One percenter: The legend of the outlaw biker*. Minneapolis, MN: MotorBooks International.

Nichols, D., & Peterson, K. (2010). *One percenter: The legend of the outlaw biker*. Minneapolis, MN: MotorBooks International.

Partners. (2015). Retrieved 15 November 2015 from HendrickMotorsports.com.

Peters, A., & Fisher, P. (2004). The failures of economic development incentives. *Journal of the American Planning Association, 70*(1), 27–37.

Prescott, A.L. (1998). *Imagining Rabelais in renaissance England*. Cambridge: Yale University Press.

Pruitt, S.W., Cornwell, T.B., & Clark, J.M. (2004). The NASCAR phenomenon: auto racing sponsorships and shareholder wealth. *Journal of Advertising Research*, 44(03), 281–296.

Quinn, J.F. & Forsyth C.J.. (2009). Leathers and rolexes: the symbolism and values of the motorcycle club. *Deviant Behavior*, 30(3), 235–265.

Rabelais, F. (1873). *The works of Rabelais. Faithfully translated from the French with variorum notes and numerous illustrations by Gustav Dore*. London: Chatto & Windus.

Reynolds, T. (2000). *Wild ride: How outlaw motorcycle myth conquered America*. New York, NY: TV Books, Inc.

Rickly-Boyd, J.M. (2012). Authenticity & Aura: A Benjaminian Approach to Tourism. *Annals of Tourism*, 39 (1), 269–289.

Riley, R., Baker, D., & Van Doren, C. (1998). Movie-induced Tourism. *Annals of Tourism Research*, 25 (4), 919–935.

Ritzer, G. (2005). *Enchanting a disenchanted world: Revolutionizing the means of consumption* (2nd Ed.). New York, NY: Pine Forge Press.

Ritzer, G. (2007). *The globalization of nothing 2*. Los Angeles, CA: Sage Publications.

Ritzer, G. (2008). *The Blackwell Companion to Globalization*. New York, NY: John Wiley and Sons.

Ritzer, G. (2013). *The McDonaldization of society* (20th Ed.). Los Angeles, CA: Sage Publications.

Ritzer, G. (2014). Automating prosumption: The decline of the prosumer and the rise of the prosuming machines. *Journal of Consumer Culture*, doi: 1469540514553717.

Ritzer, G., & Jurgenson, N. (2010). Production, consumption, prosumption: The nature of capitalism in the age of the digital 'prosumer'. *Journal of consumer culture*, 10(1), 13–36.

Roche, M. (2000). *Mega-events and modernity: Olympics and expos in the growth of global culture*. London: Routledge.

Sales Tax History. (2015). Retrieved 5 August 2015 from http://www.sturgis-sd.gov/index.aspx?nid=752.

Sandomir, R. (2010, 21 September). FanVision gadget makes debut in some N.F.L. stadiums. *The New York Times*. Retrieved 25 April 2012 from http://www.nytimes.com/2010/09/22/sports/football/22sandomir.html?_r=2.

Sanford, J.A. (2012, 15 August). Liquid Blue battles bikers at Sturgis, Playing Democratic Nat'l Convention. *San Diego Reader*. Retrieved 10 June 2014 from http://www.sandiegoreader.com/weblogs/jam-session/2012/aug/15/liquid-blue-battles-bikers-at-sturgis-playing-demo/#.

Schembri, S. (2009). Reframing brand experience: the experiential meaning of Harley-Davidson. *Journal of Business Research*, 62(12), 1299–1310.

Schilling, C. (2010, 26 February). Tea Party weekend: Daytona Bike Week Freedom Rally ready to rock. *The Other McCain*. Retrieved 9 April 2015 from http://theothermccain.com/2010/02/26/tea-party-daytona-bike-week-freedom-rally/.

Schouten, J.W., & McAlexander, J.H. (1993). Market impact of a consumption subculture: the Harley-Davidson mystique. *European Advances in Consumer Research*, 1(1), 389–393.

Schouten, J.W., & McAlexander, J.H. (1995). Subcultures of consumption: an ethnography of the new bikers. *Journal of Consumer Research*, 1(1), 43–61.

Schouten, J.W., Martin, D.M., & McAlexander, J.H. (2007). The evolution of a subculture of consumption. In B. Cova, R. Kozinets & A. Shankar (eds.), *Consumer Tribes* (pp. 67–75). New York, NY: Routledge.

Schroeder, J. (2004). Visual consumption in the image economy. In A. Ekström & H. Brembeck (Eds.), *Elusive consumption* (pp. 229–244). Berg: Oxford, UK.

Schumpeter, J. (1975). *Capitalism, Socialism, Democracy.* New York, NY: Harper.

Seaton, A.V. (1996). Guided by the dark: From thanatopsis to thanatourism. *International Journal of Heritage Studies, 2*(4), 234–244.

Seaton, A.V. (1999). War and thantourism: Waterloo 1815–1914. *Annals of Tourism Research, 26,* 130–158.

Shellow, R., & Roemer, D.V. (1966). The Riot that Didn't Happen. *Social Problems,* 14 (2), 221–233.

Simmel, G. (1950). *The sociology of Georg Simmel.* K. Wolff (Ed.). New York, NY: Free Press.

Smith, D.N. (1998). The ambivalent worker. *Social Thought and Research,* 21(1/2), 35–83.

Smythe, D. (1981). On the audience commodity and its work. In Durham M.G., & Kellner, D. (Eds.), *Media and cultural studies, keywords* (pp. 230–256). Malden, MA: Blackwell Publishing.

Spinda, J.S., Earnheardt, A.C., & Hugenberg, L.W. (2009). Checkered flags and mediated friendships: Parasocial interaction among NASCAR fans. *Journal of Sports Media,* 4(2), 31–55.

Sponsorship Open House. (2015, 23 March). Retrieved 5 August 2015 from http://www.sturgis-sd.gov/Search/Results?searchPhrase=Sponsorship%20Open%20House%202015&page=1&perPage=10.

SportVision Company Profile. (2014). Retrieved 26 August 2014 from https://www.sportvision.com/about.

Stemp, M. (2015, 26 October.) Bikers Scenic Byway. *Motorcycle and Powersports News.* Retrieved 5 December 2015 from http://www.motorcyclepowersportsnews.com/bikers-scenic-byway/.

Stone, P. (2006). A dark tourism spectrum: Towards a typology of death and macabre related tourist sites, attractions and exhibitions. *Tourism: An Interdisciplinary International Journal,* 54(2), 145–160.

Sturgis Biker's Scenic Byway. (2015, 22 October). *Hot Bike.* Retrieved 5 December 2015 from http://www.hotbikeweb.com/sturgis-bikers-scenic-byway.

Swart, W.J. & Krier, D. (2009). Sturgis and the Integrated Spectacle. Presented at the Annual Meeting of the Midwest Sociological Society, Des Moines, IA.

Swart, W.J., & Krier, D. (2016). Dark Spectacle: Authoritarianism and the Economic Enclosure of American Motorcycling. In D. Krier & M.P. Worrell (Eds.), *Capitalism's Future* (pp. 240-276). Brill.

Swenson, D. (2010). *An evaluation of the economic impact of the Iowa Speedway to the Jasper County regional economy.* Iowa State University. Retrieved 27 August 2012 from http://www.icip.iastate.edu/sites/default/files/uploads/IRI/An%20Evaluation%20of%20the%20Economic%20Value%20of%20the%20Iowa%20Speedway%20to%20the%20Jasper%20County%20Regional%20Economy%20SWENSON.pdf.

The Enthusiast. (1939). Harley-Davidson Corporation.

The History of the AMA. (2013). Retrieved 18 January 2015 from http://www.american motorcyclist.com/about/history.

The Manless Tour at Last! (1917). *Motorcycle and Bicycle Illustrated.* New York, NY: Trade Journal Corporation. Retrieved 5 February 2015 from https://books.google.com/books?id=magAAAAAMAAJ&printsec=frontcover&authuser=1#v=onepage&q&f=false.

The *Only Cure* for our Deplorable Traffic Conditions [Poster]. (1924). Milwaukee, WI: Harley Davidson Museum.

The Only Force He Respects [Poster]. (1924). Milwaukee, WI: Harley Davidson Museum.

The Viewpoint of the Reader. (1919, 16 July). *Motorcycling and Bicycling.* Retrieved 20 December 2013 from https://books.google.com/books?id=4gI9AAAAYAAJ&pg=RA1-PA25&lpg=RA1-PA25&dq=grandpa+grundy&source=bl&ots=v_qou-NNJX&sig=JkZhaMNAiIs8xymtU2r3o1PJhSk&hl=en&sa=X&ei=8xz5VLvmO4HsgwSyioC4AQ&ved=oCDwQ6AEwBw#v=onepage&q=grandpa%20grundy&f=false.

Thompson, E.P. (1967). Time, work-discipline, and industrial capitalism. *Past & Present, 38,* 56–97.

Thompson, H.S. (1967). *Hell's Angels: A strange and terrible saga.* New York, NY: Ballentine.

Thompson, W.E. (2008). Pseudo-deviance and the "new biker" subculture: hogs, blogs, leathers, and lattes. *Deviant Behavior, 30*(1), 98–114.

Thompson, W.E. (2012a). Don't call me "biker chick": women motorcyclists redefining deviant identity. *Deviant Behavior, 33*(1), 58–71.

Thompson, W.E. (2012b). *Hogs, blogs, leathers and lattes: The sociology of modern American motorcycling.* Jefferson, NC: McFarland.

Thornton, D.D. (2012). Tax increment financing: magical tool or moral hazard? *Policy Study, 12*(4), 1–18.

Tireless Riders of the Law [Poster]. (1924). Milwaukee, WI: Harley Davidson Museum.

Turner, V. (1969). *The ritual process: Structure and anti-structure.* Chicago, IL: Aldine Press.

Turner, R.H., & Killian, L.M. (1987). *Collective behavior.* Englewood Cliffs, NJ: Prentice-Hall.

Urry, J. (2004). The 'system' of automobility. *Theory, Culture & Society, 21,* 25–39.

US District Court: District of South Dakota. (2000). *Sturgis Chamber of Commerce vs. Sturgis Rally and Races, Inc. 2000 SD 26.* Retrieved 1 February 2013 from http://www.sdbar.org/Federal/2000/2000dsd026.htm.

US Patent and Trademark Office. (1982). *Sturgis: Serial number 73358530, Registration Number 1260886.* Retrieved 8 October 2013 from http://tess2.uspto.gov/bin/showfield?f=doc&state=4804:3zgdxt.3.537.

VanOstrand, M. (2015, 14 October). Meade County Commissioners set the 1st reading on proposed bypass. KOTA Territory News. Retrieved 30 November 2015 from http://www.kotatv.com/news/south-dakota-news/meade-county-commissioners-set-the-1st-reading-on-proposed-bypass/35841290.

Veblen, T.B. (1906). The socialist economics of Karl Marx and his followers. *Quarterly Journal of Economics, 20.* Retrieved 30 March 2013 from http://www.marxists.org/subject/economy/authors/veblen/soc-econ.htm#1.

Veblen, T.B. (1915 [1904]). *Theory of business enterprise.* New York, NY: Charles Scribner and Sons.

Veblen, T.B. (1934 [1899]). *The theory of the leisure class: An economic study of institutions.* New York, NY: Modern Library Press.

Von Saldern, A. (1992). Cultural conflicts, popular mass culture, and the question of Nazi success: The Eilenrieder Motorcycle Races, 1924–1939. *German Studies Review,* 15(2), 317–228.

Wagner, H. (2013, 10 January). Sturgis approves contract with rally trademark holder, despite objections. Dealernews.com. Retrieved January 10, 2014 from http://www.dealernews.com/dealernews/article/sturgis-approves-contract-rally-trademark-holder-despite-objections.

Walker, M. (2006). *Hitchcock's motifs.* Amsterdam: Amsterdam University Press.

Walker, C. (2016, 23 January). How many commercials did you watch during the 2015 NASCAR Spring Cup season? Retrieved 25 January 2016 from http://www.cawsnjaws.com/author/Cheryl+Walker/.

Wallerstein, I. (1980). *The modern world-system II. Mercantilism and the consolidation of the European world economy, 1600–1750.* New York, NY: Academic Press.

Wang, N. (1999). Rethinking authenticity in tourism experience. *Annals of Tourism Research,* 26(2), 349–370.

We need *more* Lion Tamers! [Poster]. (1924). Milwaukee, WI: Harley Davidson Museum.

Weber, M. (1949). *The methodology of the social sciences.* Glencoe, IL: The Free Press.

Williams, T. (2009, 29 September). The fives: from Pappy Hoel to the 50th to today, the arc of the Sturgis Rally. *The Rapid City Journal.* Retrieved 31 January 2013 from http://rapidcityjournal.com/news/2009_sturgis_rally/news/the-fives-from-pappy-hoel-to-the-th-to-today/article_30a8b205-f977-539e-82f5-d4526556e022.html.

Willmott, H. (2010). Creating 'value' beyond the point of production: branding, financialization and market capitalization. *Organization,* 17, 517–542.

Wood, J. (2003). Hell's Angels and the illusion of the counterculture. *The Journal of Popular Culture,* 37, 336–351.

Woodruff, R. (2015). The 7 most influential players in the Sturgis Rally. Retrieved 22 December 2015 from http://www.buffalochip.com/NEWS-INFO/News/Sturgis-Rider-News-Blog/ArtMID/2002/ArticleID/469/The-7-Most-Influential-Players-in-Sturgis-Rally-History.

Wooster, K. (2010, 10 August). '40s: 'heck of a good time'. *Rapid City Journal*. Retrieved 17 January 2013 from http://rapidcityjournal.com/news/local/state-and-regional/article_91958fcc-9d3f-11df-ab9d-001cc4c03286.html.

Wooster, K. (2015, 14 May). Buffalo Chip Campground wins city incorporation. KELO-LAND TV. Retrieved 13 July 2015 from http://www.keloland.com/newsdetail.cfm/buffalo-chip-campground-wins-city-incorporation/?id=180029.

Worrell, M.P. (2005). Surplus, excess, waste, leftovers and remainders: the dialectic of anti-Semitism and the vicissitudes of social forces. In G. Lundskow (ed.) *Religious Innovation in a Global Age* (pp. 7–36). Jefferson, NC: McFarland Press.

Worrell, M.P. (2008a) *Dialectic of solidarity: Labor, Antisemitism, and the Frankfurt School*. Chicago, IL: Haymarket Press.

Worrell, M.P. (2008b) Gods and devils. In G. Lundskow (ed.) *The sociology of religion: A substantive and transdisciplinary approach,* (pp. 269–272). Thousand Oaks, CA: Pine Forge Press.

Worrell, M.P. (2009). The cult of exchange value and the critical theory of spectacle. *Fast Capitalism,* 5(2). Retrieved from http://www.uta.edu/huma/agger/fastcapitalism/5_2/Worrell5_2.html.

Worrell, M.P., & Krier, D. (2012). The imperial eye. *Fast Capitalism*, 9.1. Retrieved 30 March 2013 from http://www.uta.edu/huma/agger/fastcapitalism/9_1/worrellkrier9_1.html.

Yates, B. (1999). *Outlaw machine: Harley-Davidson and the search for the American soul*. New York, NY: Little, Brown and Company.

Žižek, S. (1992) *Looking awry: An introduction to Jacques Lacan through popular culture*. Cambridge, MA: October/MIT Press.

Žižek, S. (1997). *The abyss of freedom*. Ann Arbor, MI: University of Michigan Press.

Žižek, S. (2007). *How to read Lacan*. New York, NY: Norton.

Žižek, S. (2008 [1989]). *The sublime object of ideology. New Edition*. London: Verso.

Žižek, S. (2009). *Sublime object of ideology* (2nd Ed.). London: Verso.

Žižek, S. (2010 [1992]). Alfred Hitchcock, or, the form and its historical mediation. In S. Žižek (ed.) *Everything you always wanted to know about Lacan (But were afraid to ask Hitchcock)* (pp. 1–14). London: Verso.

Index

CPSIA information can be obtained
at www.ICGtesting.com
Printed in the USA
LVOW11s1110190218
566799LV00007B/2/P